BIBLIOGRAPHY OF
RUSSIAN LITERATURE
IN ENGLISH TRANSLATION
TO 1945

BIBLIOGRAPHY OF
RUSSIAN LITERATURE
IN ENGLISH TRANSLATION
TO 1945

BRINGING TOGETHER:

A BIBLIOGRAPHY OF RUSSIAN LITERATURE
IN ENGLISH TRANSLATION TO 1900

By MAURICE B. LINE

AND

RUSSIAN LITERATURE, THEATRE AND
ART; A BIBLIOGRAPHY OF WORKS IN
ENGLISH, PUBLISHED BETWEEN 1900-1945

By AMREI ETTLINGER
AND
JOAN M. GLADSTONE

ROWMAN AND LITTLEFIELD
TOTOWA, NEW JERSEY

METHUEN & CO. Ltd.
LONDON

128261

LINE, M. B.   Bibliography of Russian Literature in Translation to 1900, First published in 1963.

Copyright © B. LINE, 1963

ETTLINGER, A. and GLADSTONE, J. M.   Russian Literature, Theatre and Art. First published in 1947.

This Edition Published in 1972 by

ROWMAN AND LITTLEFIELD

AND

METHUEN & CO. LTD.

Rowman and Littlefield ISBN—0-87471-094-4

Methuen ISBN—416-76050-3/32

PRINTED IN THE UNITED STATES OF AMERICA

CONTENTS

3

INTRODUCTION

Scope. This bibliography is an attempt at a complete list of translations from Russian literature into English in book form up to and including 1900. (The years after 1900 are already catered for to some extent by A. Ettlinger & J. M. Gladstone's *Russian literature, theatre, and art: a bibliography of works in English published 1900–1945 (London, 1945)* and Unesco's *Index Translationum*). It does not attempt to cover translations in periodicals, nor early translations from non-literary works such as Lomonosov's *Chronological abridgment of the Russian history (London, 1767)* or Tatishchev's *Testament (Paris, 1860)*; non-literary works by writers who are also literary figures, such as Tolstoï, are however included. There are also a few books which, though not wholly or primarily devoted to translations from Russian, contain substantial translations. All known editions of a translation are included. There are 426 items in all, of which 271 are main entries. Forty-eight authors are represented, and 131 translators are involved.

Method of Compilation and Use of Authorities. A fairly comprehensive list of Russian authors was checked against the printed catalogue of the Library of Congress and the British Museum catalogue, and a more selective list against the catalogues of the Bodleian Library, Cambridge University Library, and the London Library. These checks were supplemented by the use of numerous bibliographies, the most relevant of which are listed at the end of this Introduction. I tried to see as many items as possible, and in fact examined 248 (roughly three-fifths) out of the total of 426 books listed, nearly all of them in the British libraries whose catalogues I checked; these are the entries that have no asterisk or dagger against them. A dagger against an entry indicates that, while I did not see the book, the authority for it (generally the Library of Congress catalogue) is thoroughly reliable; there are 85 of these entries. Entries marked with an asterisk (78) were found in sources of lesser authority or accuracy, such as the English Catalogue and the American Catalogue, and bibliographies contained in critical works; full details are usually lacking in these sources and it is often difficult to distinguish editions. Some of the marked items are important, and I made special efforts to see them in provincial libraries or obtain them on inter-library loan; it is fairly safe to assume that copies, if they exist in England at all, are very rare, and even an extended bibliographical tour of the United States might not have yielded much result. All items, whether main or subsidiary entries, or merely mentioned in notes, are appropriately marked (or unmarked).

5

Arrangement. Anthologies and collections containing works by more than one author, and exclusively or mainly devoted to Russian works, are grouped at the beginning, numbered A1–23. (Borrow's *Targum*, which contains only a small proportion of Russian works, is included because it is of exceptional interest and was later reprinted with *The talisman*, which is entirely Russian in contents).

Anthologies are followed by individual authors in alphabetical order. The arrangement of entries under each author is alphabetical by the most used or best-known English title, with appropriate references from alternative English forms of the title. (Individual works by Gogol', Pushkin and Tolstoĭ are preceded by collections of two or more of their works). For each work, translations are arranged chronologically by date of publication, translations of the same year being in order of month of publication where ascertainable. Each author has his own sequence of numbering, one number being allocated to each translation; the original edition is followed by other editions, impressions and reprints. Some numbers are probably 'ghosts', that is to say the book in question may be a new impression or a reprint of a translation already listed; to have identified these translations would have involved a great deal of work on the part of several libraries (mostly American), even if copies could have been traced in all cases. Where I suspect an entry of being a 'ghost', the number is enclosed in square brackets.

Analytical entries are made for substantial works (e.g. Pushkin's *Dubrovsky*) contained in general collections, and, with Dostoevskiĭ, Tolstoĭ and Turgenev, for items contained in collections of their own works; in these latter cases, the numbers referred to belong, of course, to the sequence for that particular author.

Form of Entry. Owing to my inadequate knowledge of the entries marked with an asterisk, consistency in form of entry was unattainable. Wherever possible I have observed the following practice:

Title. Transcribed exactly, with the omission of the author's name, unless it occurs in an unrecognisable form, and of any mention of illustrations, and the abbreviation of "translated" and "translation" to "tr."; the punctuation is standardized. The title, in transliteration, of the original Russian work, with the date of its first appearance in print, follows the title (preceding indications of translator, etc.); where there is a considerable interval between completion of the ms. and publication, I have added the date when the work was written. Some of Tolstoĭ's works were first published outside Russia; in these instances I have given the place of imprint.

Imprint. Publisher's initials are given where full forenames are used on the title-page; "and co." is omitted (but not "and bros." or "and son"); and "New York" is abbreviated to "N.Y.".

Date. "&c." following a date indicates that further impressions under the same imprint appeared in subsequent years. Where a later impression described itself as "2nd ed.", "new ed.", etc., details are given in a note.

Collation. Preliminary pages are not indicated where they are unnumbered and consist only of half-title and title-page. The English Catalogue was in the habit of using an inclusive pagination, e.g. pp. vii, 266, appears as 273, so that the collation of asterisked entries must be regarded with caution.

My use of bibliographical terms for reprints, etc., demands some explanation. I am aware that the terms used are by no means wholly satisfactory: if an established terminology for nineteenth-century books suited to a bibliography of this nature existed, I would of course have used it. I have at any rate aimed at complete consistency in my usage, which is as follows:

"*American issue*" (or "*English issue*"): a book appearing in America (or England) simultaneously with, or fairly soon after, an English (or American) book with identical typesetting. Such a book may have been printed from the same plates (or stereotypes of them) in America, or been bound up in America from sheets printed in England; even if it had been possible always to say which method was used, such information would have been irrelevant for the purposes of this bibliography.

"*another impression*": a publication of a later date than the original edition and issued by a different publisher, but with identical (or virtually identical) typesetting.

"*further impression*" (a term used only in notes): another impression by the same publisher as the original; details are only given where the title-page describes the book as "2nd ed.", "new ed." etc. (see above, under **Date**).

"*reprint*": the same text, with reset type.

"*edition*": a text substantially changed.

With some asterisked entries, I do not know for certain whether the book is a new impression or a reprint, and I have therefore made no attempt at an indication.

Translations via Languages Other than Russian. Many translations, especially the earlier ones, were made from existing versions in French, German, or other languages, probably considerably more than are stated on the book to have been so made; where I have been able to identify with tolerable certainty the versions used, I have done so. It is dangerous to assume that "translated from the Russian" on the title-page of a work indicates that it was directly translated from the Russian; there are some instances where this is definitely not so.

Transliteration. The scheme used is that of British Standard 2979: 1958 ("British" system), which is based on the joint recommendations of the Royal Society and the British Academy in 1953.

Notes. These have been kept to a minimum, and are mainly bibliographical. No attempt is made at critical evaluation.

Chronological List of Translations. To indicate the spread of Russian literature in England and the U.S.A. during the nineteenth century,

8 INTRODUCTION

and thence the growth of possible influence on English writers, a
chronological list of first appearances of translations in both England
and America (and other countries where occasion arises) has been
appended.

Translator Index. Since those responsible for introducing Russian
literature to us may themselves be of some interest, I have given
references to common sources of biographical information, and, for
the benefit of fellow-librarians, headings appear in as full a form as
possible.

The most obviously striking thing about nineteenth-century translations from Russian is the extraordinary predominance of two
authors: Turgenev between 1867 and 1886, and Tolstoï between
1886 and 1900. Tolstoï's numerical superiority is to some extent
deceptive, as many of the items are quite short non-literary works or
collections of translations previously published separately. It is
curious that some great works, such as Dostoevskiï's *The brothers
Karamazov*, were untranslated until well after 1900, while compar-
atively obscure works by Golovin, Karazin and Markevich are
represented in the bibliography. It will be noted that many works of
the first importance appeared in translation in America before they
appeared in Britain, the interval in some cases (such as Turgenev's
Fathers and sons) being several years. An instructive comparison
with translations into French in the same period may be made by
consulting V. Boutchik's *Bibliographie des oeuvres littéraires russes
traduites en français (Paris, 1935–36, 2 vols., and Suppléments 1938,
1941 and 1943)*; most, but by no means all, Russian works which
were translated into English had already appeared in French.

The Chronological List shows how some periods were much more
prolific than others in Russian translations. The articles by E. A.
Osborne in *The Bookman* (details of which are given in the list of
sources at the end of the Introduction), and two articles by Gilbert
Phelps in *The Slavonic and East European Review* entitled *The early
phases of British interest in Russian literature (vol. 36, 1957/8, pp.
418–433, and vol. 38, 1959/60, pp. 415–430)* describe some of the
early translations and the manner of their reception in Britain, and
help to relate the periods of activity in translation to phases of
British interest in Russia generally, which was of course partly
conditioned by historical events.

Many nineteenth-century translations were published in popular
or cheap series; most of them were reprints, but some made their
first appearance in these series. Information about these series,
which are of considerable relevance and intrinsic interest, may be
found, for English publications, in Michael Sadleir's *19th century
fiction: a bibliographical record (London, 1951, 2 vols.)*, and for
American publications, in M. B. Stern's *Imprints on history (Indiana*

Univ. Press, 1956) and R. H. Shove's *Cheap book production in the United States, 1870 to 1891 (Univ. of Illinois Library, 1937).*

Limitations. Even within my stated limits, the bibliography cannot claim to be absolutely complete. While I believe that few translations can have entirely escaped my net, many appeared in numerous editions and reprints, and some of these are bound to be missing.

The bibliography of Tolstoĭ in translation, *Khudozhestvennȳe proizvedeniya L. N. Tolstogo v perevodikh na inostrannȳe yazȳki (Moscow, 1961)* was published when my work was nearly completed. In some cases where I was able to check its accuracy I found it unreliable, and consequently I have not included entries from it.

The story of Russian translations into English in the nineteenth century is not, of course, complete without translations appearing in periodicals. I have a considerable amount of material relating to such translations, but it is likely to be in a very incomplete state for some time. Meanwhile, I should be glad to hear of any additions or corrections to the present list.

Acknowledgments. I would like to make acknowledgment to the following: to Mr. J. W. Thirsk, Borough Librarian of Acton, for additions and corrections; to Mr. John Dean, Librarian of Ghana University, Mr. Piers Tyrrell, Cambridge University Library, Mr. John L. Mish, New York Public Library and Mr. I. Yu. Bagrov, Lenin State Library, Moscow, for help and information; to Mr. Alexander Anderson, my colleague at Southampton University Library, for advice and criticism; to my wife for much practical assistance; and to Mrs. M. Christmas for her very intelligent execution of an exacting piece of typing. To Mr. Thirsk I feel I owe an apology as well as a debt, as when my bibliography was nearly completed I discovered that he had done a great deal of work in the same field; he hopes, however, to issue a sequel to this Bibliography for post-1900 translations.

Sources. The following are the principal sources used:

General Catalogues:
> British Museum Catalogue of printed books.
> Library of Congress Catalog, and Supplements.
> English catalogue of books, 1801–1900.
> Roorbach's Bibliotheca Americana, 1820–1860.
> Kelly's American catalogue of books, 1861–1871.
> American catalogue of books, 1876–1900.

Russian Literature in General:
> Griswold (W. MacC.) A descriptive list of novels and tales dealing with life in Russia. Cambridge, Mass., Griswold, 1892. (Part 9 of his Descriptive lists).

Morse (A. L.) Reading list on Russia. Albany, N.Y. State
   Library, 1899. (in Bull. of the New York State Library
   (Bibliography) no. 15; also issued separately).
Osborne (E. A.) Early translations from the Russian. (7 articles
   in The Bookman, v. 82–84, 1932–33; the last two are entitled
   "Russian literature and translations". A very useful survey,
   chiefly from the collector's standpoint).
Wiener (L.) Anthology of Russian literature. 2 vols. N.Y. &
   London, Putnam, 1902–03. (Contains a great deal of bib-
   liographical material, often inaccurate).

Individual Authors:
Gettman (R. A.) Turgenev in England and America. Urbana,
   Univ. of Illinois Press, 1941. (Illinois Studies in Language
   and Literature, v. 27, no. 2).
Heifetz (*Mrs.* A.) Lermontov in English: a list of works by and
   about the poet. N.Y., N.Y. Public Library, 1942. (in Bull. of
   the New York Public Library, v. 46, no. 9; also issued
   separately).
Muchnic (H. L.) Dostoyevsky's English reputation (1881–
   1936). Northampton, Mass., Smith College, 1939. (Smith
   College Studies in Modern Languages, v. 20, no. 3/4).
Yarmolinsky (A.) *ed.* Pushkin in English: a list of works by
   and about Pushkin. N.Y., N.Y. Public Library, 1937. (in
   Bull. of the New York Public Library, v. 41; also issued
   separately).
Yassukovitch (*Mrs.* A) Tolstoi in English 1878–1929: a list of
   works by and about Tolstoi available in the New York
   Public Library. N.Y., New York Public Library, 1929. (in
   Bull. of the New York Public Library, v. 33; also issued
   separately).

Symbols. †: indicates that the item has not been examined, but has
          been found in a reliable authority.
        *: indicates that the item has been found in a less reliable
          authority. (see paragraph on p. ii on Method of Com-
          pilation and Use of Authorities).

COLLECTIONS & ANTHOLOGIES

BARATYNSKAYA (Anna Davydovna) *knyazhna* Abamelik.

A1.* Translations from Russian and German poets by a Russian lady. Baden-Baden, pr. by A. von Hagen, 1878.

BLUMENTHAL (Verra Xenophontovna de) *née* Kalamatiano, *comp. & tr.*

A2.* Stories from the folklore of Russia. Paris, 1897. (Studies in European Storiology.)

BORROW (George) *comp. & tr.*

A3. The talisman, from the Russian of Alexander Pushkin, with other pieces. St. Petersburg, pr. by Schulz & Beneze, 1835. pp. 14.

   100 copies only printed.
   Contains also: The mermaid, *by* Pushkin; 3 "ancient Russian songs";
   and 2 other poems.

A4. Targum, or, Metrical translations from thirty languages and dialects. St. Petersburg, pr. by Schulz & Beneze, 1835. pp. viii, 106.

   100 copies only printed.
   The following Russian poems are included: The glory of the Cossacks,
   by Boris Fedorov; The black shawl, *and* Song [*from The gipsies*]
   (Hoary man, hateful man!) *by* Pushkin; *and* The Cossack, an ancient
   ballad, from the Malo-Russian.

A5.† Targum, or Metrical translations from thirty languages and dialects; and, The talisman, from the Russian of Alexander Pushkin, with other pieces. London, Jarrold & Sons, 1892. pp. viii, 106, 14, [2].

   A page-for-page reprint in one vol. of the two previous items.

BOWRING (*Sir* John) *comp. & tr.*

A6. Россійская антологія: Specimens of the Russian poets, with preliminary remarks and biographical notices. London, pr. for the author, sold by R. Hunter, 1821. pp. xxii, 240.

   Contains 46 complete poems and 5 excerpts, as well as a translation of a
   Dutch poem on Ossian. Copy in Whitechapel Public Library.

————. 2nd ed., with additions. London, pr. for the author, sold by R. Hunter, and A. Constable, Edinburgh, 1821. pp. xxxv, 239.

   Contains 47 complete poems and 5 excerpts; 3 of the poems in the 1st
   ed. are omitted, and 4 new ones included.

*————. Boston, Cummings, Hilliard, 1822.

A7.   Россійская антологія: Specimens of the Russian poets, with introductory remarks. Part the second. London, pr. by G. & W. B. Whittaker, 1823.   pp. xxi, 271.

Contains 54 poems, one of which had already appeared in the first part.

——. 2nd ed.   London, pr. for G. & W. B. Whittaker, 1823. pp. xxi, 271.

Contains 56 poems.

CURTIN (Jeremiah) *comp. & tr.*

A8.†   Myths and folk-tales of the Russians, Western Slavs, and Magyars.   Boston, Little, Brown, 1890.   pp. xxv, 555.

Contains 20 Russian pieces (pp. 1–270).

——. *[English issue].*   London, S. Low, Marston, Searle & Rivington, 1890, &c.

DIETRICH (Anton) *comp.*

A9.   Russian popular tales; tr. from the German version [1831] of Anton Dietrich.   With an introduction by Jacob Grimm. London, Chapman & Hall, 1857.   pp. xiii, 225, front.

HAPGOOD (Isabel Florence) *comp. & tr.*

A10.† The epic songs of Russia.   With an introductory note by Francis J. Child.   N.Y., C. Scribner's sons, 1886.   pp. xiii, 358.

Contains 30 byliny.

——. *[another impression].*   N.Y., C. Scribner's sons; London, B. Quaritch, [1895?].

HODGETTS (Edith M. S.) *comp. & tr.*

A11.   Tales and legends from the land of the Tsar: a collection of Russian stories; tr. from the original Russian.   London, Griffith, Farran, Okeden, & Welsh, (& at Sydney), 1890. pp. x, 324.

LEWIS (William David) *comp. & tr.*

A12.† The Bakchesarian fountain, by Alexander Pooshkeen, and other poems by various authors; tr. from the original Russian. Dedicated to my Russian friends.   Philadelphia, C. Sherman, printer, 1849.   pp. 72.

Contains 20 poems (incl. The Bakchesarian fountain).

LINEVA (Evgeniya Eduardovna) *née* Paprits, *comp. & tr.*

A13.† Russian folk-songs as sung by the people, and peasant wedding ceremonies customary in northern and central Russia, from authentic material; collected and tr. by mme. Eugenie Lineff, with a preface on Russian folk-songs by H. E. Krehbiel. Chicago, C. F. Summy, [1893].   pp. 63, front., illus.

NAAKÉ (John Theophilus) *comp. & tr.*
A14. Slavonic fairy tales, collected and tr. from the Russian, Polish, Servian, and Bohemian. London, H. S. King, 1874. pp. viii, 272, front., plt.
Contains 40 tales, of which 8 are Russian.
*——. N.Y., G. Routledge & sons, 1876.

POLEVOĬ (Petr Nikolaevich)
Russian fairy tales, *see under* Polevoĭ *in* **Individual Authors** sequence.

POLLEN (John) *comp. & tr.*
A15. Rhymes from the Russian; being faithful translations of selections from the best Russian poets, Pushkin, Lermontof, Nadson, Nekrasof, count A. Tolstoi, Tyoutchef, Maikof, Lebedef, Fet, K. R., etc. London, K. Paul, Trench, Trübner, 1891. pp. xiv, 118.
Contains 81 poems.

RALSTON (William Ralston Shedden) *comp. & tr.*
A16. Russian folk-tales. London, Smith, Elder, 1873. pp. xvi, 382.
51 stories from the collections of Afanas'ev, Khudyakov, Erlenvein, and Chudinskiĭ.
*——. N.Y., Lovell, Adam, Wesson, 1877.
†——. N.Y., R. Worthington, 1879, &c. pp. 388.

RUSSIAN STORIES
A17. Russian stories, vol. I. Makár's dream, and other stories. London, T. F. Unwin, 1892. pp. 182. (The Pseudonym Library, no. 13.)
Numbered "14" in the Pseudonym Library in a list in another vol. in the series.
Contains: Makár's dream, *and* Bad company, *by* V. Korolenko; The "New Life": a Siberian story, *by* F. Volkhovskiĭ.

A18. Russian stories, vol. II. The Saghalien convict, and other stories. London, T. F. Unwin, 1892. pp. 217. (The Pseudonym Library, no. 18.)
Contains: The Saghalien convict, *and* Easter Eve, *by* V. Korolenko [tr. by William Gaussen]; Vae victis: a sketch of Siberian life, *by* G. Machtet; Wounded in battle, *by* V. Garshin.

SAUNDERS (W. H.) *comp. & tr.*
A19.* Poetical translations from the Russian language. London, 1826.

STORIES BY FOREIGN AUTHORS: RUSSIAN

A20*. Stories by foreign authors: Russian. N.Y., C. Scribner's sons, 1898.

> *One of a set of 10 vols. of* Stories by foreign authors.
> *Contains:* Mumu, *by* Turgenev; The shot, *by* Pushkin [tr. by T. Keane]; St. John's Eve, *by* Gogol'; An old acquaintance, *by* L. N. Tolstoï.

TALES FROM THE RUSSIAN

A21. Tales from the Russian. I. Dubrovsky, by Pushkin; II. New Year's Eve, by Gregorovitch; III. Taman [*from A hero of our times*], by Lermontoff. London, The Railway and General Automatic Library, [1891]. pp. 251.

> *Possibly translated by Mrs. Henry Sutherland Edwards.*

VOYNICH (*Mrs.* Ethel Lilian) *née* Boole, *comp. & tr.*

A22. The humour of Russia. With an introduction by Stepniak. London, W. Scott; N.Y., C. Scribner's sons, 1895. pp. xvi, 349, front., illus. ([International] Humour Series, ed. by W. H. Dircks).

> *Contains 5 plays:* Marriage, *by* Gogol'; At the police inspector's, *and* Before the justice of the peace, *by* Gorbunov; A domestic picture, *and* Incompatibility of temper, *by* Ostrovskiï; *and 14 stories:* The crocodile, *by* Dostoevskiï; A madman's diary, *by* Gogol'; "La traviata", *and* A seventeenth century letter from Ems, *by* Gorbunov; The eagle as Mecaenas, The recollections of Onésime Chenapan, *and* The self-sacrificing rabbit, *by* Shchedrin [*i.e.* Saltykov]; Choir practice, *by* Sleptsov; The story of a kopeck, *by* Stepnyak [*i.e.* Kravchinskiï]; The steam chicken, *and* A trifling defect in the mechanism, *by* G. I. Uspenskiï; Porridge, *and* The village schoolmaster, *by* N. V. Uspenskiï; The dog's passport (told by a peasant).

WILSON (Charles Thomas) *comp. & tr.*

A23. Russian lyrics in English verse. London, Trübner, 1887. pp. xvi, 244.

> *Contains 108 poems, including fables and epigrams as well as "lyrics".*

Translations from Russian literature, both complete works and extracts, can also be found in the following works:

GENERAL ANTHOLOGIES

> Garnett (Richard) *ed.* The universal anthology: a collection, of the best literature. 33 vols. London, Clarke; N.Y., Merrill & Baker, 1899–1902.
> Warner (Charles Dudley) *ed.* The library of the world's best literature. 30 vols. N.Y., R. S. Peale & J. A. Hill, [1896–97].

CRITICAL & HISTORICAL WORKS

> Edwards (Henry Sutherland). The Russians at home. London, W. H. Allen, 1861.
> ——. The Russians at home and the Russians abroad. 2 vols. London, W. H. Allen, 1879.

Grahame (F. R.) (*pseud. for* Catherine Laura Johnstone). The progress of science, art and literature in Russia. London, J. Blackwood, [1865].

Morfill (William Richard). Russia. London, T. F. Unwin; N.Y., G. P. Putnam's sons, 1890. (The Story of the Nations, 23.)

——. Slavonic literature. London, S.P.C.K., 1883.

Ralston (William Ralston Sheddon). The songs of the Russian people as illustrative of Slavonic mythology and Russian social life. London, Ellis & Green, 1872.

Talvj (*pseud. for* Therese Albertine Luise von Jacob, *afterw.* Robinson). Historical view of the languages and literatures of the Slavic nations; with a sketch of their popular poetry. N.Y., G. P. Putnam, 1850.

Turner (Charles Edward). The modern novelists of Russia. London, Trübner, 1890.

——. Studies in Russian literature. London, S. Low, 1882.

INDIVIDUAL AUTHORS

AKSAKOV (Sergeĭ Timofeevich) 1791–1859.
1. Memoirs of the Aksakof family [*A family chronicle, part 1*] (*Semeĭnaya khronika, 1856: parts published anon. 1846*): a sketch of Russian rural life, 70 years ago; tr. into English by a Russian lady. Calcutta, pr. at the "Englishman" Press, 1871. pp. 287.

BESTUZHEV (Aleksandr Aleksandrovich) 1797–1837 (A. Marlinskiĭ, *pseud.*).
1. The snow of Shah-Dagh (*Mulla-Nur, 1826*), and Ammalat Bey (*Ammalat-Bek, 1832*): posthumous romances by Alexandre Dumas père; tr. [from the French] by Home Gordon. London, Simpkin, Marshall, Hamilton, Kent, [1899].   pp. xiii, 480, facsim. front., illus.
   Translations of Dumas' French versions of Bestuzhev.
2. *The Tartar chief, or, A Russian colonel's head for a dowry; from the Russian of Marlinsky by G. C. Hebbe. N.Y., 1846.

BULGARIN (Faddeĭ Venediktovich) 1789–1859.
1. Ivan Vejeeghen (*Ivan Vȳzhigin, 1829*), or, Life in Russia; [tr. by George Ross]. London, Whittaker, Treacher; Edinburgh, H. Constable, 1831. 2 vols.
*——. Philadelphia, Carey & Lea, 1832. 2 vols.
   The first translation of Russian fiction published in the U.S.A.

CATHERINE II, 1729–96, *Empress of Russia.*
1. Ivan Czarowitz (*Skazka o tsareviche Khlore, c.1782*), or, The rose without prickles that stings not: a tale written by her Imperial Majesty; tr. from the Russian language. London, pr. for Robinson & sons, G. Edwards, T. Kay, and T. Chapman, 1793. pp. 29.
   The first translation into English of imaginative Russian literature; it had previously appeared in The Bee (Edinburgh).

CHERNYSHEVSKIĬ (Nikolaĭ Gavrilovich) 1828–89.
1. A vital question (*Chto delat'? 1863*), or, What's to be done? tr. from the Russian by Nathan Haskell Dole and S. S. Skidelsky. N.Y., T. Y. Crowell, [1886]. pp. ix, 462.
†——. [*another impression*]. N.Y., J. W. Lovell, 1888. (Lovell's Library, no. 1017).
2. *What's to be done? (*Chto delat'? 1863*): a romance; tr. by B. R. Tucker. Boston, B. R. Tucker, 1886.

DANILEVSKIĬ (Grigoriĭ Petrovich) 1829–90.

1. The Princess Tarakanova (*Khyazhna Tarakanova, 1883*): a dark
chapter of Russian history; tr. from the Russian by Ida de
Mouchanoff. London, S. Sonnenschein, 1891. pp. xxviii,
252, port. front., ports.
†——. [*American issue*]. N.Y., Macmillan [etc., etc.], [1891].

DERZHAVIN (Gavriil Romanovich) 1743–1816.

1. Ode to the Deity (*Oda Bog, 1784*) (tr. from the Russian).
London, pr. for Wm. Stokes, for the use of his pupils, [1861].
broadsheet.
Bowring's translation (see A6) with minor alterations.

Ode to God; [tr. by Sir John Bowring]. Aurora, Ill., Anti-
Vivisection Print, [c. 1880]. ff. [14].

*Ode to Deity. Boston, D. Lothrop, [1887]. (Stream of Life
Series).

DOSTOEVSKIĬ (Fedor Mikhaĭlovich) 1821–81.

Buried alive, *see* The house of the dead.

1. *Crime and punishment (*Prestuplenie i nakazanie, 1866*): a
Russian realistic novel [tr. from the French of Victor Derély
(1884)]. London, Vizetelly, 1886 (April). pp. 456. (Vizetelly's
One-Volume Novels, no. 13).
*Translation erroneously ascribed to Frederick Whishaw in the Every-
man's Library edition of 1911. Further impressions: 1886 ("2nd ed");
1889 ("new ed.").
*——. [*American issue*]. N.Y., T. Y. Crowell, [1886] (Oct.).
pp. 456, port. front.
——. [*another impression*]. London, W. Scott, [1893].
The eternal husband, *see* The permanent husband.

2. The friend of the family (*Selo Stepanchikovo, 1859*), and The
gambler (*Igrok, 1866*); tr. from the Russian by Frederick
Whishaw. London, Vizetelly, 1887. pp. 317. (Vizetelly's
One-Volume Novels, no. 22).
*Further impression: *1889 ("new ed.").*

3. [*The house of the dead*] (*Zapiski iz mertvogo doma, 1860–62*)
Buried alive, or, Ten years of penal servitude in Siberia; tr.
from the Russian by Marie van Thilo. London, Longmans,
Green, 1881 (Jan.). pp. 361.
*Further impressions: *1881 (March) ("2nd ed."); 1881 (May) ("4th
ed.").*
*——. N.Y., H. Holt, 1881 (April). (Leisure Moment Series).
†——. [*reprint*]. N.Y., G. Munro, 1881. pp. 44. (Seaside
Library, vol. 5, no. 1056).

4. [*The house of the dead*] Prison life in Siberia; sole and authorised translation [from the French of Charles Neyroud (1884)] by H. Sutherland Edwards. London, J. & R. Maxwell, [1887] (May). pp. xviii, 368.
   †——. [*reprint*]. N.Y., Harper & brothers, [1887] (Aug.). pp. 64. (Franklin Square Library, no. 594).

5. The idiot (*Idiot, 1868–69*); tr. from the Russian by Frederick Whishaw. London, Vizetelly; N.Y. [etc.], Brentanos, 1887. pp. 480. (Vizetelly's Russian Novels).

   Dole says this is translated from the French (*presumably of Victor Derély (1887)*). Further impression: *1888 (cheaper ed.).

6. Injury and insult (*Unizhennȳe i oskorblennȳe, 1861*); tr. from the Russian by Frederick Whishaw. London, Vizetelly, 1886. pp. xii, 332, port. front. (Vizetelly's One-Volume Novels, no. 17).

   Further impression: 1887 ("2nd ed.").

   The permanent husband (*Vechnȳĭ muzh, 1870*), *in* 8 (1888 &c.).

7. Poor folk (*Bednȳe lyudi, 1846*); tr. from the Russian by Lena Milman; with an introduction by George Moore. London, E. Mathews & J. Lane; Boston, Roberts brothers, 1894. pp. xx, 191. (Keynote Series, no. 3).

   Published in the U.K. in June, in the U.S.A. in July.

   Prison life in Siberia, *see* The house of the dead.

8. Uncle's dream (*Dyadyushkin son, 1859*), and The permanent husband (*Vechnȳĭ muzh, 1870*); tr. from the Russian by Frederick Whishaw. London, Vizetelly, 1888. pp. 298. (Vizetelly's Russian Novels).
   *——. [*another impression*]. 2nd ed. London, Vizetelly, 1889. (Celebrated Russian Novels).

   The village of Stepanchikovo, *see* The friend of the family.

GARSHIN (Vsevolod Mikhaĭlovich) 1855–88.

1. Mad love (*Nadezhda Nikolaevna, 1885*), or, An artist's dream; tr. from the Russian. London, S. Blackett & Hallam, 1889 &c. pp. 160. (Select Shilling Novels).

2. Stories from Garshin; tr. by E. L. Voynich; introduction by S. Stepniak. London, T. F. Unwin, 1893. pp. 230. (Independent Novel Series).

   Contains: The scarlet flower (in memory of I. S. Turgenev) (*Krasnȳĭ tsvetok, 1883*); From the memoirs of private Ivanov, concerning the campaign of 1877 (*Iz vospominaniĭ ryadovogo Ivanova, 1883*); A coward (*Trus, 1879*); An occurrence (*Proisshestvie, 1878*).

   Wounded in battle (*Chetȳre dnya, 1877*), *in* A18 (Russian Stories, vol. II. 1892).

GOGOL' (Nikolaĭ Vasil'evich) 1809–52.

Collections

1. Cossack tales; tr. from the original Russian by George Tolstoy. London, J. Blackwood, [1860]. pp. xv, 245.

   Contains: The night of Christmas Eve: a legend of Little Russia (*Noch' pered rozhdestvom, 1832*); Tarass Boolba (*Taras Bul'ba, 1835*).

2. St. John's Eve, and other stories from "Evenings at the farm" and "St. Petersburg stories"; tr. from the Russian by Isabel F. Hapgood. N.Y., T. Y. Crowell, [1886]. pp. 383, tables.

   Contains: St. John's Eve (*Vecher nakanune Ivana Kupala, 1831*); Old-fashioned farmers (*Starosvetskie pomeshchiki, 1835*); The tale of how Ivan Ivanovitch quarrelled with Ivan Nikiforovich (*Povest' o tam kak possorilsya Ivan Ivanovich s Ivanom Nikiforovich, 1835*); The portrait (*Portret, 2nd version, 1842*); The cloak (*Shinel', 1842*).

   ——. [*English issue, with title* "St. John's Eve"]. London, J. & R. Maxwell, [1887].

3. Taras Bulba; also St. John's Eve, and other stories. London, Vizetelly, 1887 &c. pp. 308. (Vizetelly's Russian Novels).

   Contains: Taras Bulba (*Taras Bul'ba, 1835*); St. John's Eve (*see 2 above*); Akakiy Akakievitch's new cloak (*Shinel', 1842*); How the two Ivans quarrelled (*see 2 above*); The mysterious portrait (*see 2 above*); The king of the gnomes (*Viĭ, 1835*); The calash (*Kolyaska, 1836*); Old-fashioned folks (*see 2 above*). *All but* The king of the gnomes *and* The calash *are Hapgood's translations with some alterations.*

Individual Works

4. [*Dead souls*] (*Mertvы̆e dushi, 1842–46*) Home life in Russia, by a Russian noble; revised by the author of "Revelations of Siberia" [Col. Krystyn Lach-Szyrma]. London, Hurst & Blackett, 1854. 2 vols.

   An adaptation of part 1 only, with an altered ending.

5. [*Dead souls*] Tchitchikoff's journeys, or, Dead souls; tr. from the Russian by Isabel F. Hapgood. N.Y., T. Y. Crowell, 1886. 2 vols.

   Contains the spurious conclusion by A. E. Zakharchenko, translated from Charrière's French version.

   ——. [*English issue, with title* "Dead souls"]. London, J. & R. Maxwell, [1887] (April). 2 vols.

   Dead souls. London, Vizetelly, 1887 (May) &c. pp. x, 11–372. (Vizetelly's Russian Novels).

   Hapgood's translation with minor alterations.

6. The inspector (*Revizor, 1836*): a comedy; tr. from the Russian by T. Hart-Davies. Calcutta, Thacker, Spink, [1890]. pp. iii, 104.

   *——. [*another impression*]. London, Thacker, [1892].

7. The inspector-general (or "Revizór"): a Russian comedy; tr. from the original, with introduction and notes, by Arthur A. Sykes. London, W. Scott, 1892. pp. xix, 185, port. front., table.

†——. [*another impression*]. London, W. Scott, [1892]. (Camelot Series).
Lacks port. front.

*——. N.Y., A. Lovell, 1892.

——. [*another impression*]. London, W. Scott, [1893] &c. (Scott Library, no. 87).
Lacks port. front.

A madman's diary (*Zapiski sumasshedshogo, 1835*), *in* A22 (Voynich: The humour of Russia, 1895).

Marriage (*Zhenit'ba, 1842*), *in* A22 (Voynich: The humour of Russia, 1895).

St. John's Eve (*Vecher nakanune Ivana Kupala, 1831*), *in* A20 (Stories by Foreign Authors: Russian, 1898).

8. †Taras Bulba (*Taras Bul'ba, 1835*); tr. from the Russian by Isabel F. Hapgood. N.Y., T. Y. Crowell, [1886]. pp. 295, port. front.

——. [*English issue*]. London, J. & R. Maxwell, [1887].

——. [*another impression*]. N.Y., J. W. Lovell, 1888. (Lovell's Library, no. 1016).
Lacks port. front.

9. †Taras Bulba: a historical novel of Russia and Poland; tr. from the Russian by Jeremiah Curtin; with a preface by the translator. N.Y., J. B. Alden, 1888. pp. xxv, 21–208, port. front.

GOLOVIN (Konstantin Fedorovich) 1843–1913 (K. Orlovskiĭ, *pseud.*).

1. Nadia (*Vne kolei, 1882*), or, Out of the beaten track; tr. from the Russian of R. Orloffsky [*sic*] by the Baroness Langenau. London, S. Sonnenschein, 1888. 3 vols.

GONCHAROV (Ivan Aleksandrovich) 1812–91.

1. A common story (*Obyknovennaya istoriya, 1847*): a novel; tr. from the Russian by Constance Garnett. London, W. Heinemann, 1894. pp. xii, 283. (Heinemann's International Library, no. 17).

†——. [*American issue*]. [N.Y., P. F. Collier, 1894]. 2 vols. in 1, paged continuously. (Once-a-Week Library).

GORBUNOV (Ivan Fedorovich) 1831–95.

At the police inspector's [*play*] (*Kvartal'nyĭ nadziratel', 1870*), Before the justice of the peace [*play*] (*Y mirovogo sud'i, 1874*), "La traviata" [*story*] (*Traviata, 1874*) *and* A seventeenth century letter from Ems [*story*] (*Pis'mo iz Èmsa, 1874*), *in* A22 (Voynich: The humour of Russia, 1895).

GRIBOEDOV (Aleksandr Sergeevich) 1795–1829.

1. Gore ot ouma (*Gore ot uma, 1833; written 1822–23, fragments publ. 1825*): a comedy; tr. from the Russian by Nicholas Benardaky. London, Simpkin, Marshall; Edinburgh, M. MacPhail; Dublin, M'Glashan & Gill, 1857. pp. x, 134.

GRIGOROVICH (Dmitriĭ Vasil'evich) 1822–99.

1. The cruel city (*Stolichnye rodstvenniki, 1857*); after the Russian, with a sketch of the author, by Ernest De Lancey Pierson. N.Y., Cassell, 1891. pp. vii, 290. (Sunshine Series, no. 84).
   Also issued in London by Cassell.

   New Year's Eve (*Zimniĭ vecher, 1854*), in A21 (Tales from the Russian, [1891]).

KARAMZIN (Nikolaĭ Mikhaĭlovich) 1766–1826.

1. *Julia (*Yuliya, 1794*); tr. from the Russian into French by M. du Boullier [*i.e.* de Boulliers (1797)], and from the French by Ann P. H[awkins]. St. Petersburg, 1803.

2. Russian tales; tr. into English by John Battersby Elrington. London, pr. by G. Sidney, 1803. pp. [viii], 262, port. front., plt.
   Contains: Lisa (*Bednaya Liza, 1792*); Flor Silin (*Flor Silin, 1791*); Natalia (*Natal'ya, 1792*); Julia (*Yuliya, 1794*). The note "To my friends" states that the translator is writing from prison. Translation attributed to A. A. Feldborg by Erslew's Almindeligt Forfatter-Lexicon. See next entry.

   ——. [*with title* "Tales from the Russian."] London, pr. for J. Johnson by G. Sidney, 1804. pp. xii, 262.
   Identical with the above apart from preliminary matter and plates; translation attributed to A. A. Feldborg by British Museum, Library of Congress, and Bodleian Library. The preface states that the translator, "a native of Denmark", had "already had the honor of introducing my author to the British public by the translation of his Travels." Feldborg was in England 1802–9, and wrote several works in English.

3. Travels from Moscow, through Prussia, Germany, Switzerland, France, and England (*Pis'ma russkogo puteshestvennika, 1797–1801*); tr. from the German [of J. Richter by A. A. Feldborg]. London, pr. for J. Badcock by G. Sidney, 1803. 3 vols.
   Translation attributed to Feldborg by British Museum and Erslew (see notes to 2 above).

KARAZIN (Nikolaĭ Nikolaevich) 1842–1908.

1. The two-legged wolf (*Dvunogiĭ volk, 1876*): a romance; tr. from the Russian by Boris Lanin. Chicago & N.Y., Rand, McNally, 1894. pp. 322, front., plts. (Rialto Series, no. 61).

KOKHANOVSKAYA (N.) *pseud., see* **SOKHANSKAYA** (Nadezhda Stepanovna).

KOROLENKO (Vladimir Galaktionovich) 1853–1921.
Bad company (*V durnom obshchestve, 1885*), *in* A17 (Russian Stories, vol. I. 1892).

1. The blind musician (*Slepoĭ musikant, 1886*); (from the Russian) by Sergius Stepniak and William Westall. London, Ward & Downey, 1890 (May). pp. viii, 187.

   There are slight omissions in this version. Further impression: *1893 ("new ed.").

   †The blind musician; from the Russian by William Westall and Sergius Stepniak. [*also,* A professional lady-killer, by Ethel Marryat]. N.Y., J. W. Lovell, [1890]. pp. [ii], 161, [iv], [163]–230. (Lovell's International Series, no. 100).
   *——. 2nd ed. N.Y., J. W. Lovell, 1893.
   *——. N.Y., G. Munro, 1890. (Seaside Library, Pocket Edition, no. 1515).

2. †The blind musician; tr. from the Russian by Aline Delano; with an introduction by George Kennan. Boston, Little, Brown, 1890 (July). pp. xv, 244, illus.

   Easter Eve (*V noch' pod svetlyĭ prazdnik, 1886*); tr. by W. Gaussen, *in* A18 (Russian Stories, vol. II. 1892).

3. †In two moods (*S dvukh storon, 1888*). [*also,* In bad society (*V durnom obshchestve, 1885*)]; [tr.] by Stepniak and Wm. Westall. N.Y., J. W. Lovell, [1891]. (Lovell's International Series, no. 178). pp. 288.
   ——. London, Ward & Downey, 1892. pp. vii. 280.
   *——. N.Y., G. Munro, 1892. (Seaside Library, no. 1943).

   Makar's dream (*Son Makara, 1885*), *in* A17 (Russian Stories, vol. I. 1892).

   The Saghalien convict (*Sokolinets, 1885*); tr. by W. Gaussen, *in* A18 (Russian Stories, vol. II. 1892).

4. †The vagrant and other tales; tr. from the Russian by Mrs. Aline Delano. N.Y., T. Y. Crowell, [1887], pp. iii, 285.

   Contains: The old bellringer (*Starȳi zvonar', 1886*); The forest soughs (*Les shumit, 1886*); Easter night (*V noch' pod svetlyĭ prazdnik, 1886*); A Saghalinian (*Sokolinets, 1885*); Sketches of a Siberian tourist (*Ocherki sibirskogo turista, 1885*).
   *——. 2nd ed. N.Y., T. Y. Crowell, 1896.

KOSTROMITIN
The last day of the carnival; tr. from the Russian [by J. Sosnin]. London, T. F. Unwin, 1893. pp. 190.

I have been unable to find out anything whatever about Kostromitin.

KOVALEVSKAYA (Sof'ya Vasil'evna) *née* Korvin-Krukovskaya, 1850–91.

1. Sonya Kovalevsky: a biography, by Anna Carlotta Leffler,

Duchess of Cajanello; and Sisters Rajevsky [*Recollections of childhood*] (*Vospominanya detstva, 1890*), being an account of her life by Sonya Kovalevsky. Tr. by A. de Furuhjelm and A. M. Clive Bayley; with a biographical note by Lily Wolff-sohn. Authorized ed. London, T. F. Unwin, 1895 (June). pp. vi, 377, port. front., port.

The sisters Rajevsky, *originally written in Russian, was translated from the Swedish version of Furuhjelm by Bayley.*

2. Sonia Kovalevsky: biography and autobiography. I: Memoir by A. C. Leffler (Edgren) duchessa di Cajanello. II: Reminiscences of childhood, written by herself. Tr. into English by Louise von Cossel. London, W. Scott, 1895 (June). pp. 317, port. front., ports.

3. †Sonya Kovalévsky: her recollections of childhood; tr. from the Russian by Isabel F. Hapgood, with a biography by Anna Carlotta Leffler, Duchess of Cajanello, tr. from the Swedish [of A. de Furuhjelm] by A. M. Clive Bayley, and a biographical note by Lily Wolffson. N.Y., Century Co., 1895. pp. [x], 318, port. front.

4. Vera Barantzova (*Nigilistka, Geneva, 1892*); from the Russian, with an introduction and a memoir of the author, by Sergius Stepniak and William Westall. London, Ward & Downey, 1895. pp. xxi, 281.

5. Vera Vorontzoff; rendered into English by Anna von Rydings-värd (Baroness von Proschwitz). Boston & N.Y., Lamson, Wolffe, (1896). pp. ix, 197.

KRAVCHINSKIĬ (Sergeĭ Mikhailovĭch) 1852–95 (Sergeĭ Stepnyak, *pseud.*).

The story of a kopeck (*Skazka o kopeĭke, Geneva, 1873*), *in* A22 (Voynich: The humour of Russia, 1895).

KRȲLOV (Ivan Andreevich) 1768–1844.

(*Krȳlov's fables were published in 9 books, 1809–43*).

1. Krilof and his fables, by W. R. S. Ralston. London, Strahan, 1869 (Jan.). pp. xlii, 180, illus.

Prose translations of 93 fables. Further impression: *1869 (May) ("new ed.").*

*——. N.Y., G. Routledge & sons, 1869.

——. 3rd ed., greatly enlarged. London, Strahan, 1871. pp. xlii, 268, illus.

Contains 148 fables.

——. 4th ed. London, Paris, & N.Y., Cassell, 1883. pp. xlii, 268, illus.

New impression of 3rd ed.

2. Krilof's fables, illustrating Russian social life; tr. from the
Russian [by J. Long] for the Calcutta weekly "Englishman".
Calcutta, pr. at the "Englishman" Press, 1869. pp. 46.
Prose translations of 70 fables.

3. Krilof's original fables; tr. by I. Henry Harrison. London,
Remington, 1883. pp. xxxii, 228, tables.
Verse translations of 149 fables.

4. Russian fables [prose translations of 20 fables, *in* Stickney
(J.H.): A child's version of Aesop's fables, with a supple-
ment containing fables from La Fontaine and Krilof. Boston,
Ginn, 1886. pp. xvii, 204, front. illus. (Classics for Children)].

LAZHECHNIKOV (Ivan Ivanovich) 1792–1869.

1. The heretic (*Basurman, 1838*); tr. from the Russian by Thomas
B. Shaw. Edinburgh & London, W. Blackwood & sons, 1844.
3 vols.
*——. London, H. Bohn, 1844. 3 vols.
*——. N.Y., Harper & brothers, 1864.

2. The palace of ice (*Ledyanoĭ dom, 1835*); tr. from the French of
Alexandre Dumas by H. L. Williams jr. N.Y., E. D. Long,
[1860]. pp. 149.
A translation of Dumas' French version La maison de glace (1860).

3. [*The palace of ice*] The Russian gipsy, or, The palace of ice,
by Alexandre Dumas. London, H. Lea, [1860]. pp. 334.
——. [*another impression*]. London, C. H. Clarke, [1861].
(Dumas' Historical Library, vol. 9).
——. [*another impression*]. London, Routledge, 1873. (Routledge's Railway Library, no. 584).

[4.]†[*The palace of ice*] The Russian gipsy, or, The palace of ice,
by Alexandre Dumas. N.Y., G. Munro, [1877]. pp. 26,
illus. (Seaside Library, vol. 8, no. 151).
†[——]. ——. [*reprint, with title* "The Russian gypsy"]. N.Y.,
G. Munro's sons, [1896]. pp. 227. (Seaside Library, Pocket
Edition, no. 2063).

LERMONTOV (Mikhail Yur'evich) 1814–41.

1. The Circassian boy (*Mtsȳri, 1840*); tr. [into verse] through
the German [of Friedrich Bodenstedt (1852)] from the Russian
by S. S. Conant. Boston, J. R. Osgood, 1875. pp. 87.

2. The demon (*Demon, 1842*); tr. [into verse] from the Russian
by Alexʳ. Condie Stephen. London, Trübner, 1875. pp.
85, front.
*Further impressions: 1881 ("2nd ed."); *1886 ("3rd ed.").*

3. The demon; tr. [into verse] from the Russian by Francis Storr. London, Rivington, Percival, 1894. pp. 43.

4. [*A hero of our time*] (*Geroĭ nashego vremeni, 1840*): Sketches of Russian life in the Caucasus, by a Russe, many years resident amongst the various mountain tribes. London, Ingram, Cooke, 1853. pp. 315, front., plts. (Illustrated Family Novelist).

   A free and expanded version, with changed names. The section Taman is omitted.

5. A hero of our own times; from the Russian; now first tr. into English. London, D. Bogue, 1854 (first half of June). pp. 231, front.

6. The hero of our days; from the Russian by Theresa Pulszky. London, T. Hodgson, [1854] (latter half of June). pp. [viii], [9]–232. (Parlour Library, no. 112).

   The section Fatalist is omitted.

7. A hero of our time; tr. from the Russian, with life and introduction, by R. I. Lipmann. London, Ward & Downey, 1886. pp. xxviii, 272.

   The section Fatalist is omitted.

   *——. [*another impression*]. London, Vizetelly, 1887. (Vizetelly's One-Volume Novels).

   *——. new ed. London, Vizetelly, 1888. pp. 312. (Celebrated Russian Novels).

8. Russian reader: Modern hero, with English translation by Ivan Nestor-Schnurmann. Cambridge, Univ. Press, 1899. pp. xx, 403.

   Russian and English text on facing pages. The section Fatalist is omitted.

   ——. [*American issue*]. N.Y., Macmillan, 1899.

   [*A hero of our time: extract*] Taman, *in* A21 (Tales from the Russian, 1891).

MACHTET (Grigoriĭ Aleksandrovich) 1852–1901

Vae victis (*Mȳ pobedili, 1884*): a sketch of Siberian life, *in* A18 (Russian Stories, vol. II. 1892).

MARKEVICH (Boleslav Mikhaĭlovich) 1822–84.

1. The neglected question (*Zabȳtȳĭ vopros, 1872*); tr. by the Princesses Ouroussoff. London, H. S. King, 1875 [*i.e.* 1874]. 2 vols.

MARLINSKIĬ (A.) *pseud., see* BESTUZHEV (Aleksandr Aleksandrovich).

MEREZHKOVSKIĬ (Dmitriĭ Sergeevich) 1865–1914.

1. †Julian the apostate (*Yulian Otstupnik, 1895*); tr. by Charles Johnston. Philadelphia, H. Altemus, [1899]. pp. 454, plts.
   The first part of the trilogy Christ and Antichrist.

MIKULICH (V.) *pseud.*, *see* **VESELITSKAYA** (Lidiya Ivanovna).

NEKRASOV (Nikolaĭ Alekseevich) 1821–77.

1. Морозъ красный-носъ: Red-nosed frost (*Moroz, krasnȳi-nos, 1864*): tr. in the original meters from the Russian [by J. Sumner Smith]. Boston, Ticknor, 1886. pp. 120, port. front.
   Russian and English text on facing pages.
   *——. 2nd ed., emended. Boston, Ticknor, 1887.

ORLOVSKIĬ (K). *pseud.*, *see* **GOLOVIN** (Konstantin Fedorovich).

OSTROVSKIĬ (Aleksandr Nikolaevich) 1823–86.

A domestic picture (*Semeĭnaya kartina, 1847*) *and* Incompatibility of temper (*Ne soshlis' kharakterami, 1858*) [*plays*], *in* A22 (Voynich: The humour of Russia, 1895).

1. The storm (*Groza, 1860*); tr. by Constance Garnett. London, Duckworth, 1899. pp. x, 119. (Modern Plays, ed. by R. Brimley Johnson and N. Erichsen).
   †——. [*American issue*]. Chicago, C. H. Sergel, 1899. (Modern Plays).

POLEVOĬ (Petr Nikolaevich) 1839–1902.

1. *Russian fairy tales, from the "Skazki" of Polevoi (*Narodnȳya russkiya skazki, 1874*), by R. Nisbet Bain. London, Lawrence & Bullen, 1892. pp. 268, front., plts.
   24 of the tales Polevoĭ rewrote for children from the folk-tales collected by Afanas'ev.
   ——. 2nd ed. London, Lawrence & Bullen, 1893. pp. viii, 264, front., plts.
   *——. Chicago, Way & Williams, 1895.

POTAPENKO (Ignatiĭ Nikolaevich) 1856–1929.

1. The curse of talent (*Proklyataya slava, 1893*; [tr. by William Gaussen] [*in* Browne (G.F.) *ed.* Memorials of a short life: a biographical sketch of W. F. A. Gaussen. London, T. F. Unwin, 1895. pp. 263, port. front.].

2. A father of six (*Shestero, 1891*), and An occasional holiday (*Redkiĭ prazdnik, 1881*); tr. from the original by W. Gaussen. London, T. F. Unwin, 1893. pp. 254. (Pseudonym Library, no. 26).
†——. [*reprint*]. N.Y., Cassell, [1893]. pp. 241. (The "Unknown" Library, no. 26).

3. The general's daughter (*General'skaya doch', 1891*); [tr. by W. Gaussen]. London, T. F. Unwin, 1892. pp. 261. (Pseudonym Library, no. 17).
†——. [*reprint*]. N.Y., Cassell, [1892]. pp. 321. (Sunshine Series, no. 126 extra).

4. A Russian priest (*Na deĭstvitel'noĭ sluzhbe, 1890*); [tr. by W. Gaussen]. London, T. F. Unwin, 1891. pp. x, 214. (Pseudonym Library, no. 7).
†——. [*reprint*]. N.Y., Cassell, [1891]. pp. ix, 285. (Sunshine Series, no. 86).

PUSHKIN (Aleksandr Sergeevich) 1799–1837.

Collections: Verse

1. *Selections from the poems of Pushkin; tr. [into verse], with critical notes and a bibliography, by Ivan Panin. Boston, Cupples & Hurd, 1888.
——. 2nd ed. [*with title* "Poems; tr. from the Russian, with introduction and notes by Ivan Panin"]. Boston, Cupples & Hurd, 1888. pp. 179.

2. Translations [into verse] from Poushkin, in memory of the hundredth anniversary of the poet's birthday by Charles Edward Turner. St. Petersburg, K. L. Ricker; London, S. Low, Marston, 1899. pp. [ix], 328, port. front.

Collections: Prose

3. The captain's daughter (*Kapitanskaya dochka, 1836*), and The queen of spades (*Pikovaya dama, 1834*). London, J. Blackwood, [1858]. pp. 200. (Blackwood's London Library, no. 20).
   Also issued as no. 13 of Blackwood's London Library; and (c.1885?) as no. 40 of Blackwood's Library of Evening Reading.

4. The prose tales; tr. from the Russian by T. Keane. London, G. Bell & sons, and N.Y., 1894. pp. 402.
   The American edition was published by Macmillan.
   Contains: The captain's daughter (*Kapitanskaya dochka, 1836*); Dubrovsky (*Dubrovskiĭ, 1841; written 1832–33*); Queen of spades (*Pikovaya dama, 1834*); Amateur peasant girl (*Barȳshnya krest'yanka, 1831*); The shot (*Vȳstrel, 1831*); The snowstorm (*Metel', 1831*); The postmaster (*Stantsionnyĭ smotritel', 1831*); The coffin-maker (*Grobovshchik, 1831*); Kirdjali (*Kirdzhali, 1834*).

The prose tales; tr. from the Russian by T. Keane. London, G. Bell & sons, 1896. pp. 466. (Bohn's Standard Library).

Contains the same stories as the 1894 edition above, with the addition of The Egyptian nights (*Egipetskie nochi, 1837*) *and* Peter the Great's negro (*Arap Petra Velikogo, 1834; written 1827*).

5. The queen of spades, and other stories; with a biography; tr. from the Russian by Mrs. Sutherland Edwards. London, Chapman & Hall, 1892, etc. pp. viii, 283, illus.

    Contains: The queen of spades; The pistol-shot; The snow-storm; The undertaker (*Grobovshchik, 1831*); The postmaster; The lady rustic (*Barÿshnya krest'yanka, 1831*); Kirdjali; History of the village of Goryukhina (*Istoriya sela Gorokhina, 1837*); Peter the Great's negro; Gipsies (*Tsÿgane, 1827*).

6. Russian romance; tr. by Mrs. J. Buchan Telfer (nee Moura-vieff). London, H. S. King, 1875. pp. 293.

    Contains: The captain's daughter; The lady-rustic; The pistol shot; The snow-storm; The undertaker; The station-master (*Stantsionnÿi smotritel', 1831*); The moor of Peter the Great.

*——. [*another impression*]. London, K. Paul, 1880.

Individual Works

The Bakchesarian fountain (*Bakhchisaraïskiï fontan, 1824*), *in* A12 (Lewis: The Bakchesarian fountain and other poems, 1849).

7. †The captain's daughter (*Kapitanskaya dochka, 1836*), or, The generosity of the Russian usurper Pugatscheff; from the Russian by G. C. Hebbe. N.Y., C. Müller, 1846. pp. 48.

8. The captain's daughter; tr. from the Russian by J. F. Hanstein. London, pr. & publ. for the author [!] by F. Hollinger, 1859. pp. vi, 151.

9. [*The captain's daughter*] Marie: a story of Russian love; from the Russian by Marie H. de Zielinska. Chicago, Jansen, McClurg, 1877. pp. 209.

    Further impression: *1880 ("new ed.").

10. *The captain's daughter: a tale of the time of Catherine II of Russia; from the Russian; tr. by Madame Jean Igelström and Mrs. Percy Easton. London, City of London Co., 1883 (April). pp. 244.

11. *The captain's daughter; from the Russian [by E. C. Price]. N.Y., G. Munro, [1883]. pp. 28. (Seaside Library, vol. 87, no. 1758).

    †——. [*reprint*]. N.Y., G. Munro, 1883. pp. 101. (Seaside Library, Pocket Edition, no. 149).

12. *The captain's daughter: a novel; literally tr. from the Russian for the use of students by Stuart H. Godfrey. Calcutta, Thacker, Spink, 1886.

13. [*The captain's daughter*] The daughter of the commandant: a Russian romance; tr. by Mrs. Milne Home. London, Eden, Remington, 1891. pp. [vii], 280.

Dubrovsky (*Dubrovskiĭ, 1841; written 1832–33*), in A21 (Tales from the Russian, [1891]).

14. Eugene Onéguine (*Evgeniĭ Onegin, 1825–32*): a romance of Russian life in verse; tr. [into verse] from the Russian by Lieut.-Col. Spalding. London, Macmillan, 1881. pp. xxiv, 276.

   *——. [*American issue*]. N.Y., Macmillan, 1881.

The shot (*Vȳstrel, 1831*); tr. by T. Keane, in A20 (Stories by Foreign Authors: Russian, 1898).

RȲLEEV (Kondratiĭ Fedorovich) 1795–1826.

1. Voinarofskyi, and other poems by K. F. Relaieff; tr. [into verse] from the Russian by T. Hart-Davies. Calcutta, Thacker, Spink, 1879. pp. 109.
   ——. new and enlarged ed. [*with title* "The poems of K. F. Relaieff"]. London, Remington, 1886, &c. pp. 145.

SALIAS DE TURNEMIR (Elizaveta Vasil'evna) *grafinya* 1815-92 (Evgeniya Tur, *pseud.*).

1. The Shalonski family (*Sem'ya Shalonskikh, 1880*): a tale of the French invasion of Russia, by Eugène Toor; tr. from the Russian by Charles James Cooke. London, Remington, 1882. pp. 254.

SALIAS DE TURNEMIR (Evgeniĭ Andreevich) *graf* 1840–1908.

1. Kiriak, or, The hut on hen's legs (*Izbushka na kur'ikh nozhkakh, 1876*), by Count Sailhas; [tr. from the Russian by Mrs. Sutherland Edwards]. London, J. M. Dent, 1896. pp. 205. (Odd Volumes, no. 2).

SALTYKOV (Mikhail Evgrafovich) 1826–89 (Saltykov-Shchedrin, *pseud.*).

The eagle as Mecaenas (*Orel-metsenat, 1886*). The recollections of Onésime Chenapan (*from Mneniya znatnȳkh inostrantsev o pompadurakh, 1873*), *and* The self-sacrificing rabbit (*Samootverzhennȳĭ zayats, 1883*) [*3 stories*], in A22 (Voynich: The humour of Russia, 1895).

30 SALTYKOV

1. Tchinovnicks: sketches of provincial life (*Gubernskie ocherki, 1856–57*), from the memoirs of the retired Conseiller de Cour Stchedrin (Saltikow); tr., with notes, from the Russian by Frederic Aston. London, L. Booth, 1861. pp. vii, 240.
   Selections from Provincial sketches.

SLEPTSOV (Vasiliĭ Alekseevich) 1836–78.
   Choir practice (*Spevka, 1862*), in A22 (Voynich: The humour of Russia, 1895).

SOKHANSKAYA (Nadezhda Stepanovna) 1825–84 (N. Kokhanov-skaya, *pseud*).
1. The rusty linchpin (*Gaĭka, 1856*), and Luboff Archipovna (*Posle obeda v gostyakh, 1858*); after the Russian of Mme. Kokhanovsky by M. M. S[teel] and J. L. E[dmonds]. Boston, D. Lothrop, 1887. pp. 296. (The Round World Series).

SOLLOGUB (Vladimir Aleksandrovich) *graf* 1814–82.
1. The tarantas (*Tarantas, 1845*): travelling impressions of young Russia; [tr. by F. von Rosenstrauch]. London, Chapman & Hall, 1850. pp. viii, 196, front., plts.

STEPNYAK (Sergeĭ) *pseud.*, see **KRAVCHINSKIĬ** (Sergeĭ Mik-haĭlovich).

SUMAROKOV (Aleksandr Petrovich) 1718–77.
1. Demetrius the Impostor (*Dimitriĭ Samozvanets, 1771*): a tragedy; tr. from the Russian [by A. G. Evstaf'ev]. London, pr. by J. Nichols & son for J. Booth, 1806. pp. vii, [8]–76.

TOLSTOĬ (Alekseĭ Konstantinovich) *graf* 1817–75.
1. The death of Ivan the Terrible (*Smert' Ioanna Groznago, 1866*): a tragedy; tr. [into verse] from the Russian (with the author's permission) by I. Henry Harrison. London, F. B. Kitto, 1869. pp. xxxi, 144.

2. Prince Serebrenni (*Knyaz' Serebryanyĭ, 1862*); tr. from the Russian by Princess Galitzine. London, Chapman & Hall, 1874. 2 vols.

3. †[*Prince Serebryani*] The terrible czar: a romance of the time of Ivan the Terrible; tr. by Capt. H. Clare Filmore. London, S. Low, Marston, 1892. 2 vols.
   Further impressions: 1892 ("2nd ed.") 2 vols.; *1893 ("3rd ed." in 1 vol.); *1894 ("4th ed.").

4. †Prince Serebryani: an historical novel of the times of Iván the Terrible and of the conquest of Siberia; tr. from the Russian by Jeremiah Curtin. N.Y., Dodd, Mead, 1892. pp. xxvi, 430.
——. [English issue]. London, B. F. Stevens, [1892].

TOLSTOĬ (Lev Nikolaevich) graf 1828–1910.

Collections

1. *The novels and other works; [edited by Nathan Haskell Dole]. N.Y., C. Scribner's sons, 1899–1902. 22 vols.

   Translated by Dole, Hapgood and others. Also known as the International Edition.

2. †Childhood, boyhood, youth; tr. from the Russian by Isabel F. Hapgood. [also, What to do? thoughts evoked by the census of Moscow.] N.Y., T. Y. Crowell, [1888]. 2 vols. in 1.

   Each volume also issued separately (see 43 and 117).

3. Christ's Christianity; tr. from the Russian. London, K. Paul, Trench, 1885. pp. x, 384.

   Contains: pt. 1, How I came to believe [My confession]; pt. 2, What I believe; pt. 3, The spirit of Christ's teaching (A commentary on the essence of the Gospel) [from The Gospel in brief]. Pts. 1 and 3 were also published together (see 24).

4. †Church and state, and other essays; including: Money [from What to do?]; Man and woman: their respective functions; The mother [from What to do?]; A second supplement to the Kreutzer sonata. Boston, B. R. Tucker, 1891. pp. 169.

   Church and state, and Money, are translated by Victor Yarros, the other 3 essays by George Schumm.

5. The Cossacks and other stories. London, Vizetelly, 1887, &c. pp. viii, [9]–320. (Vizetelly's Russian Novels).

   Contains: The Cossacks; The prisoner of the Caucasus; Recollections of Sebastopol [tr. from the French of 1886 by F. D. Millet]; Three deaths.

6. *Essays, letters, and miscellanies. N.Y., T. Y. Crowell, 1900.

7. The first step: an essay on the morals of diet; to which are added two stories [The empty drum, and How an imp paid for a crust: Russian folk-tales retold]; tr. by Aylmer Maude; with an introduction by William E. A. Axon. Manchester, A. Broadbent, 1900. pp. 78.

8. The Gospel of humaneness: selections from the writings of Count Lyof N. Tolstoĭ. London, Ideal Publishing Union, 1897. pp. viii, [9]–117. (Vegetarian Jubilee Library, vol. 6).

   Contains: My confession [extracts]; The spirit of Christ's teaching [extracts]; The Kreutzer sonata [tr. by B. R. Tucker] [extracts]; A visit to a slaughterhouse [from The first step]; Alcohol and tobacco [Why do men intoxicate themselves?]. The first 2 pieces are in the same translation as 3.

9. †Gospel stories; tr. from the Russian by Nathan Haskell Dole. N.Y., T. Y. Crowell, [1890]. pp. 243.

Contains: If you neglect the fire, you don't put it out; Where love is, there God is also; A candle; The two pilgrims; Texts for woodcuts (The devil's persistent, but God is resistant; Little girls wiser than old men; Two brothers and gold; Ilyás); The three mendicants; Popular legends (How the little devil earned a crust of bread; The repentant sinner; A seed as big as a hen's egg; Does a man need much land?); The godson; The long exile [*God sees the truth, but waits*]; What men live by.

10. In pursuit of happiness; tr. from the Russian by Mrs. Aline Delano. Boston, D. Lothrop, [1887]. pp. 193, front., plts.

Contains: Where there is love, there is God; How much land a man needs; The two pilgrims; Illyàs.

11. †The invaders and other stories; tr. from the Russian by Nathan Haskell Dole. N.Y., T. Y. Crowell, [1887]. pp. 343.

Also issued with A Russian proprietor and other stories (*see* 12).
Contains: The invaders; The wood-cutting expedition; An old acquaintance; Lost on the steppe, or, The snowstorm; Polikushka; Kholstomir, a story of a horse.

——. [*English issue*]. London, W. Scott, 1889. (Uniform edition).

12. *The invaders and other stories; tr. by N. H. Dole. [*also,* A Russian proprietor and other stories; tr. by N. H. Dole]. N.Y., T. Y. Crowell, [1889]. 2 vols. in 1.

Each volume also issued separately (*see* 11 *and* 28).

13. Iván Ilyitch and other stories; tr. from the Russian by Nathan Haskell Dole. N.Y., T. Y. Crowell, [1887]. pp. xi, 311.

Further impression: *[*1889*] (new cheap ed.). Also issued with* Family happiness (*see* 15).
Contains: The death of Iván Ilyitch; If you neglect the fire, you don't put it out; Where love is, there God is also; A candle; Two old men; Texts for woodcuts (The devil's persistent, but God is resistant; Little girls wiser than old men; Two brothers and gold; Ilyás); The three mendicants; Popular legends (How the little devil earned a crust of bread; The repentant sinner; A seed as big as a hen's egg; Does a man need much land?); The godson; Skazka [*Ivan the fool*].

——. [*English issue*]. London, W. Scott, 1889, &c. (Uniform edition).

14. *Iván Ilyitch and other stories; tr. from the Russian by Nathan Haskell Dole. N.Y., T. Y. Crowell, [1887]. pp. xi, 129.

Possibly contains the first three stories in 13.

15. *Iván Ilyitch and other stories; tr. by N. H. Dole. [*also,* Family happiness; tr. by N. H. Dole]. N.Y., T. Y. Crowell, [1889]. 2 vols. in 1.

Each volume also issued separately (*see* 13 *and* 53).

16. Ivan the fool, and three other parables. London, W. Scott, [1895] &c. pp. [vii], 115, 2 fronts.

> Vol. V (*in some issues called IV*) *in a series containing also* 37, 36, 34 *and* 81. Ivan the fool *is adapted from Dole's translation.*

17. Ivan the fool, or The old devil and the three small devils; also A lost opportunity [*If you neglect the fire, you don't put it out*], and Polikushka; tr. from the Russian by Count Norraikow. N.Y., C. L. Webster, 1891. pp. 172, illus.
    *———. [*with title* "The old devil and the three little devils; also, A lost opportunity, and Polikushka"]. London, Temple Publ. Co., 1892. pp. 204.

18. The Kreutzer sonata. [*also*, Family happiness; [tr. by N. H. Dole]]. London, W. Scott, [1890]. 2 vols. in 1. (Uniform edition).

> *Issued also with comprehensive title page, and imprint* "London, N.Y. & Melbourne, W. Scott". *Each volume also issued separately* (*see* 77 *and* 53).

19. *The Kreutzer sonata, and other stories; tr. by Benj. R. Tucker. N.Y., J. S. Ogilvie, [1890]. pp. 208.

> *Contains:* The Kreutzer sonata; Ivan the fool; A lost opportunity [*If you neglect the fire, you don't put it out*]; Polikushka; The candle; Lessons of the Kreutzer sonata.

Letters, *in* 6 (1900).

20. Letters on war. Maldon, Essex, Free Age Press, 1900. pp. 40. ([Free Age Press cheap editions of Tolstoy, no. 11]).

> *Reprinted from The New Order.*

21. Letters to friends on the personal Christian life. Maldon, Essex, Free Age Press, 1900. pp. 40. ([Free Age Press cheap editions of Tolstoy, no. 8]).

22. Life *is* worth living, and other stories; tr. from the Russian by Count Norraikow. N.Y., C. L. Webster, 1892. pp. 208, illus.

> *Contains:* Life *is* worth living [*What men live by*]; Two old men [*Two pilgrims*]; God is love [*Where love is, there God is also*]; The candle.

34

23. †The long exile and other stories for children; tr. from the Russian by Nathan Haskell Dole. N.Y., T. Y. Crowell, [1888]. pp. vi, 363.

Also issued with The physiology of war *and* Power and liberty, *both translated by Huntington Smith (see 27).*

Contains: The long exile [*God sees the truth but waits*]; What men live by; The repentant sinner; Yermak, the conqueror of Siberia; Bear-hunting worse than slavery; Stories of my dogs; Early days; Scenes from common life; Stories from physics; Tales from zoology; Stories from botany; Fables paraphrased from the Indian, and imitations; from the New speller [*the New ABC*]; School scenes at Yasnaya Polyana. *All except* What men live by, The repentant sinner, From the New speller, *and* School scenes at Yasnaya Polyana *are taken from* The ABC (*Azbuka, 1872*).

——. [*English issue*]. London, W. Scott, [1889]. (Uniform edition).

Has a port. front. not in the American edition.

Miscellanies, *in* 6 (1900).

24. †My confession, and The spirit of Christ's teaching [from The Gospel in brief]; tr. from the Russian. N.Y., T. Y. Crowell, [1887]. pp. x, 242.

Said by Morse to be translated by Hapgood. Further impression: *[1889] (new cheap ed.).*
Also issued with What I believe (*see 3*).

——. [*reprint*]. London, W. Scott, [1889]. pp. xii, 252. (Uniform edition).

25. My husband and I [*Family happiness*] and other stories. London, Vizetelly; N.Y., [etc.], Brentanos, 1887. pp. 332. (Vizetelly's Russian Novels).

Contains: My husband and I; The death of Ivan Iliitch; Polikouchka; Two generations [*Two hussars*]; The romance of a horse [*Kholstomir*]; A snow storm.
Also issued by Lovell in New York as 3 separate volumes (see 28, 88 and 33).

26. †My husband and I [*Family happiness*] and The death of Ivan Ilitch. N.Y., J. W. Lovell, [1888]. pp. [7]–132. (Lovell's Library, no. 1110).

Reissue of part of 25 (see also 88 and 33).

The old devil and the three small devils, etc., *see* 17 (Ivan the fool, etc.).

On flogged and floggers, *see* 86.

27. *The physiology of war: Napoleon and the Russian campaign [*extracts from War and peace*]; tr. from the 3rd French ed. by Huntington Smith. [*also*] Power and liberty [*the second epilogue to War and peace*]; tr. from the French by Huntington Smith. [*also*] The long exile and other stories; tr. by N. H. Dole. N.Y., T. Y. Crowell, 1888. 3 vols. in 1.

Each volume also issued separately (see 107, 106 and 23); The physiology of war and Power and liberty also issued together (see 108).

Popular legends; tr. by Dole, *in* 13 (1887 &c.), 15 (1889) *and* 9 (1890).

28. A Russian proprietor and other stories; tr. from the Russian by Nathan Haskell Dole. N.Y., T. Y. Crowell, [1887]. pp. vii, 349.

> *Also issued with* The invaders and other stories (*see* 12).
> *Contains:* A Russian proprietor; Lucerne, from the recollections of Prince Nekhliudof; Recollections of a scorer; Albert; Two hussars; Three deaths; A prisoner in the Caucasus.

——. [*English issue*]. London, W. Scott, 1888 &c. (Uniform edition).

29. *Sebastopol; tr. by Isabel F. Hapgood. [*also*, The Cossacks; tr. by Nathan Haskell Dole]. N.Y., T. Y. Crowell, [1889]. 2 vols. in 1.

> *Each volume also issued separately* (*see* 96 *and* 47).

30. Some social remedies: socialism, anarchy, Henry Georgism and the land question, communism, etc.; collected from the recent and unpublished writings of Leo Tolstoy. Christchurch, Hants, Free Age Press, 1900. pp. 40. ([Free Age Press cheap editions of Tolstoy, no. 7]).

> *Issued also with imprint* "Maldon, Essex, Free Age Press, 1900.".

31. Stop and think! [tr. from Tolstoĭ's French version by E. J. W. Warren]; also, A letter on the Peace conference [tr. by Aylmer Maude]. London, Brotherhood Publ. Co., 1899. pp. [vi], 31. (East and West Series.).

Texts for woodcuts; tr. by Dole, *in* 13 (1887 &c.), 15 (1889) *and* 9 (1890).

32. Thoughts on God [extracted from Tolstoĭ's diaries, private letters, etc.; translation edited by Vladimir Tchertkoff]. Maldon, Essex, Free Age Press, 1900. pp. 39. ([Free Age Press cheap editions of Tolstoy, no. 10]).
——, *in* 38 (1898).

33. †Two generations [*Two hussars*] and other stories. N.Y., J. W. Lovell, [1888]. pp. [203]–332. (Lovell's Library, no. 1124).

> *Reissue of part of* 25 (*see also* 26 *and* 89).
> *Contains:* Two generations; The romance of a horse [*Kholstomir*]; A snow storm.

34. The two pilgrims; If you neglect the fire, you don't put it out: two stories. London, W. Scott, [1894]. pp. [vii], 121, 2 fronts.

> *Vol. III in a series containing also* 37, 36, 81 *and* 16. *The translations are adaptations of Dole's. Further impression:* [*1895*] (*rev. ed.*).

35. Vicious pleasures: sequel to the Kreutzer sonata; [tr. from the French of Ély Halpérine (1891) by W. M. T.]. Complete edition unabridged. London, The Temple Co., [1896]. pp. vi, 169. (The After Dinner Series, no. [1]).

> *Contains:* The relations of the sexes [*Sequel to the Kreutzer sonata, & On the relations of the sexes*]; Alcohol and tobacco [*Why do men intoxicate themselves?*]; Drunkenness amongst the governing classes; Labour [*Toil*]; Church and state. *W.M.T. is probably W. M. Thomson.*

36. What men live by; What shall it profit a man? [*How much land does a man need?*]: two stories. London, W. Scott, [1894] &c. pp. [vii], 125, 2 fronts.

> *Vol. II in a series containing also 37, 34, 81 and 16. The translations are adaptations of Dole's.*

37. Where love is, there God is also; The godson: two stories. London, W. Scott, [1894] &c. pp. [vii], 95, 2 fronts.

> *Vol. I in a series containing also 36, 34, 81 and 16. The translations are adaptations of Dole's.*

38. The writings of Leo Tolstoy (collected and verified by V. Tchertkoff). The New Order, Supplements, nos. 1–12 (Feb.– Dec. 1898). pp. 93.

> *Contains:* no. 1, The work of Guy de Maupassant; nos. 2–3, The story of Ivan the fool, *and* Thoughts on God; nos. 4–12, What is art?

Individual Works

ABC (*Azbuka, 1872*) [*extracts*]; tr. by Dole, *in* 23 (1888 &c.) *and* 27 (1888).

Albert (*Al'bert, 1858*); tr. by Dole, *in* 28 (1887 &c.) *and* 12 (1889).

Alcohol and tobacco, *see* Why do men intoxicate themselves?

Anna Karenina (*Anna Karenina, 1875–77*)

39. Anna Karénina; tr. by Nathan Haskell Dole. N.Y., T. Y. Crowell, [1886]. pp. viii, 5–773.
   Further impression: *1889 ("new ed.").

——. [*English issue*]. London, Vizetelly, [1886] &c. pp. xvi, [5]–769. (Vizetelly's One-Volume Novels, no. 20).

> *Has a different introduction from the American edition, and the Glossary is transferred from the end to the preliminary matter.*

——. [*another impression*]. London, W. Scott, [1889]. 2 vols., paged continuously. (Uniform edition).

——. [*another impression*]. London, W. Scott, [1892] &c. pp. 769, [5], port. front., plts.

40. †Anna Karenina; tr. by F. K. W. N.Y., T. Y. Crowell, [1889]. 2 pts. in 1 vols.

41. †Anna Karénine; tr. by A. C. Townsend. N.Y., F. M. Lupton, [1892]. pp. 250. (Souvenir Series, no. 65).

The archbishop and the three old men, *see* The three mendicants.

Bear-hunting worse than slavery (*Okhota pushche nevoli, 1872*) [*from the ABC*]; tr. by Dole, *in* 23 (1888 &c.) *and* 27 (1888). A candle (*Svechka, 1886*); tr. by Dole, *in* 13 (1887 &c), 15 (1889) *and* 9 (1890); tr. by Tucker, *in* 19 (1890); tr. by Norraikow, *in* 22 (1892).

Childhood, Boyhood, Youth (*Detstvo, 1852; Otrochestvo, 1854; Yunost', 1857*).

42. Childhood and youth: a tale; tr. from the Russian by Malwida von Meysenbug. London, Bell & Daldy, 1862, pp. xi, 270.
    Issued in 2 different publisher's casings, one brown and one green.

43. Childhood, boyhood, youth; tr. from the Russian by I. F. Hapgood. N.Y., T. Y. Crowell, [1886] etc. pp. ix, 381, port. front.
    Also issued with What to do? (*see* 2).
    ———. [*English issue*]. London, Vizetelly, 1888 &c. pp. 381, port. front.
    Omits translator's preface.
    ———. [*reprint*]. London, W. Scott, [1889]. pp. ix, 388. (Uniform edition).

44. Boyhood, adolescence, youth; tr. by Constantine Popoff. London, E. Stock, 1890. pp. viii, 480.
    Further impression: 1894 (cheaper ed., in paper covers, with title "Boyhood").
    ———. [*another impression, with title* "Boyhood: a story"]. London, Brotherhood Publ. Co., 1895.

---

45. The Christian teaching (*Khristianskoe uchenie, Purleigh, 1898*); tr. by V. Tchertkoff. London, H. Marshall & son, 1898 (Aug.). pp. xii, 85.
    ———. [*reprint*]. London, Brotherhood Publ. Co., 1898 (Sept.). pp. vii, [8]–64. (The Writings of Leo Tolstoy, ed. by V. Tchertkoff, vol. 1, no. 1).
    "First appeared in six nos. of The New Age, July–August 1898. Now completely revised."
    ———. [*reprint*]. N.Y., F. A. Stokes, [1898]. pp. xiv, 210.

Christianity and patriotism, *see* Patriotism and Christianity.

Church and state; tr. by Yarros, *in* 4 (1891); by Thomson, *in* 35 (1896).

The Cossacks (*Kazaki, 1863*).

46. †The Cossacks: a tale of the Caucasus in 1852; tr. from the Russian by Eugene Schuyler. N.Y., C. Scribner's sons, 1878. pp. 313.

   Further impression: 1878 ("2nd ed.").

   ——. [*reprint*]. London, S. Low, Marston, Searle & Rivington, 1878. 2 vols.

   ——. rev. ed. N.Y., W. S. Gottsberger, 1887. pp. viii, [5]–313.

47. †The Cossacks: a tale of the Caucasus in the year 1852; from the Russian by Nathan Haskell Dole. Authorised translation. N.Y., T. Y. Crowell, [1888] (Oct.). pp. 350.

   Also issued with Sebastopol (see 29).

   ——. [*English issue*]. London, W. Scott, 1888 (Dec.). (Uniform edition).

48. †The Cossacks; tr. by Mrs. Laura E. Kendall. N.Y., G. Munro, [1888]. pp. 162. (Seaside Library, Pocket Edition, no. 1090).

   The Cossacks, *in* 5 (1887 &c.).

---

49. †The death of Ivan Iliitch (*Smert' Ivana Il'icha, 1886*). N.Y., G. Munro, [1888]. pp. 90. (Seaside Library, Pocket Edition, no. 1071).

   Possibly the same translation as in 25 and 26.

   The death of Ivan Il'ich; tr. by Dole, *in* 13 (1887 &c.), 14 (1887) *and* 15 (1889); another tr., *in* 25 (1887) *and* 26 (1888).

   The devil's persistent, but God is resistant (*Vrazh'e lepko, a Bozh'e krepko, 1885*); tr. by Dole, *in* 13 (1887 &c.), 15 (1889) *and* 9 (1890).

   Does a man want much land? *see* How much land does a man need?

50. The dominion of darkness (*Vlast' t'mȳ, 1887*): a drama in five acts; tr. from the original Russian. London, Vizetelly, 1888. pp. 96.

   ——. [*reprint*], Chicago, C. H. Sergel, [1890]. pp. 116. (Sergel's Columbian Library).

   Drunkenness amongst the governing classes (*Prazdnik prosveshcheniya 12-go yanvarya, 1889*); tr. by Thomson, *in* 35 (1896).

   Early days [*2 stories from The ABC, 1872*]; tr. by Dole, *in* 23 (1888 &c.) *and* 27 (1888).

   Elias, *see* Illyàs.

51. [*The emigration of the Doukhobortsi*] The persecution of the Doukhobortsi (*O pomoschchi Dukhoboram, 1898*). London, reprinted from the Daily Chronicle, 1898. broadsheet (printed on both sides).

A letter from Tolstoĭ.

——. [*another impression, with title* "The emigration of the Doukhobortsi". London, Brotherhood Publ. Co., [1898].

The empty drum (*Skazka o pustom barabane, 1891; written 1886*): a Russian folk-tale retold; tr. by Maude, *in* 7 (1900).

Fables paraphrased from the Indian, and imitations (*Basni peredelannyya s indiĭskago, i podrazheniya, 1872*) [*from The ABC*]; tr. by Dole, *in* 23 (1888 &c.) *and* 27 (1888).

Family Happiness (*Semeĭnoe schast'e, 1859*).

52. Katia; tr. from the French [of Auguste-Henri de la Nautte, comte d'Hauterive (1878)]. Authorized ed. N.Y., W. S. Gottsberger, 1887. pp. 193.

53. †Family happiness: a romance; from the Russian by Nathan Haskell Dole. Authorized translation. N.Y., T. Y. Crowell, [1888]. pp. 129.

Also issued with Ivan Ilyitch and other stories (*see* 15).

——. [*English issue*]. London, W. Scott, 1894.

Also issued with The Kreutzer sonata (*see* 18).

54. *My husband and I. N.Y., F. F. Lovell, 1888. (Household Library, no. 115).

Possibly the same translation as in 25 *and* 26.

†——. N.Y., G. Munro, [1888]. pp. 105. (Seaside Library, Pocket Edition, no. 1066).

55. †The romance of marriage; tr. Alexina Loranger. Chicago, Laird & Lee, 1890. pp. 171. (The Pastime Series, no. 45).

Family happiness, *in* 25 (1887) *and* 26 (1888).

———

The first step (*Pervaya stupen', 1892*): an essay on the morals of diet; tr. by Maude, *in* 7 (1900).

A preface written for Howard Williams's The ethics of diet.

——. [*extract*]. A visit to a slaughter-house; *in* 8 (1897).

56. The four Gospels harmonised and translated by Leo Tolstoy (*Soedinenie i perevod chetyrekh Evangeliĭ, Geneva, 1892–94; written 1881–82*); in three parts; tr. from the original manuscript into English at the request of the author. Croydon, Brotherhood Publ. Co.; London, W. Scott, 1895–6. pts. 1 & 2 only.

Part 3 was never published.

The four Gospels harmonised and translated, *see also* The
Gospel in brief (a shortened version of it).

The Fruits of Enlightenment (*Plodȳ prosveshcheniya, 1890*).

57. The fruits of enlightenment: a comedy in four acts; tr. by E. J.
Dillon. [Act 4 only]. London, W. Heinemann, 1890. pp. 29.
The fruits of enlightenment: a comedy in four acts; tr. from
the Russian by E. J. Dillon; with an introduction by Arthur W.
Pinero. London, W. Heinemann, 1891 (Aug.) &c. pp. viii,
276, port. front.

58. The fruits of culture: a comedy in four acts; tr. by George
Schumm. Boston, Mass., B. R. Tucker, 1891 (Feb.). pp. 185.

[59.]†The fruits of englightenment: a comedy in four acts. Authorized ed. N.Y., U.S. Book Co., [1891]. pp. 149. (Lovell's
Westminster Series, No. 27).

*——. N.Y., G. Munro, [1891]. (Seaside Library, no. 1835).

God is love, *see* Where love is, there God is also.

God sees the truth, but waits (*Bog pravdu vidit, da ne skoro
skazhet, 1872*) [*from The ABC*]; tr. by Dole, *in* 23 (1888 &c.),
27 (1880) *and* 9 (1890).

60. *The godson (*Krestnik, 1886*); tr. by N. H. Dole. London, W.
Scott, [*c*.1889].

> *Traced only from an advertisement in another of Scott's editions of
> Tolstoĭ.*

——. *in* 13 (1887 &c.), 15 (1889), 9 (1890) *and* 37 (1895).

The Gospel in Brief (*Kratkoe izlozhenie Evangeliya, Geneva, 1890;
written 1882–83*).

61. The Gospel in brief; tr. from the Russian original, embodying
the author's last alterations and revisions. Croydon, Brotherhood Publ. Co.; London, W. Scott, 1896 &c. pp. xi, 226.

> *A shortened version of* The four Gospels harmonized and translated,
> *consisting of the actual translation, with the addition of a foreword and
> conclusion, and the omission of the textual notes and commentaries.*

†——. [*American issue*]. N.Y., T. Y. Crowell, [1896].

62. [*The section "A recapitulation"*] The spirit of Christ's teaching.
Purleigh, Free Speech Publ. House, 1899. pp. 48. (The
Writings of Leo Tolstoy, ed. by V. Tchertkoff, vol. 2).

[——] The spirit of Christ's teaching, *in* 3 (1885) *and* 24 (1887);
[extracts] *in* 8 (1897).

A grain as big as a hen's egg, *see* A seed as big as a hen's egg.

63. *Guy de Maupassant; tr. from the Russian; conformed to the original by V. Tchertkoff. London, Brotherhood Publ. Co., 1898. pp. 32. (East and West Series).

   A translation of the preface to Nikiforov's Russian translation of Manpassant's Mont-Oriol (1894).

   ——, *in* 38 (1898).

   How an imp paid for a crust (*Kak chertёnok krayushku vȳ bȳkupal, 1886*); tr. by Dole, *in* 13 (1887 &c.), 15 (1889) *and* 9 (1890); tr. by Maude, *in* 7 (1900).

   How I came to believe, *see* My confession.

How Much Land Does a Man Need? (*Mnogo-li cheloveku zemli nuzhno, 1886*).

64. *What shall it profit a man? tr. by N. H. Dole. London, W. Scott, 1891.

   ——, *in* 13 (1887 &c.), 15 (1889), 9 (1890) *and* 36 (1894 &c.).

65. Does a man want much land? London, J. Clarke, 1892. pp. 31.

   How much land does a man need? tr. by Delano, *in* 10 (1887).

———

How the little devil earned a crust of bread, *see* How an imp paid for a crust.

66. *If you neglect the fire, you don't put it out (*Upustish' ogon', ne potushish', 1886*); tr. by N. H. Dole. London, W. Scott, [c.1889].

   Traced only from an advertisement in another of Scott's editions of Tolstoĭ.

   ——, *in* 13 (1887 &c.), 15 (1889), 9 (1890) *and* 34 (1894 &c.).

   [*If you neglect the fire, you don't put it out*] A lost opportunity; tr. by Tucker, *in* 19 (1890); tr. by Norraikow, *in* 17 (1891).

   Illyàs (*Il'yas, 1886*); tr. by Delano, *in* 10 (1887); tr. by Dole, *in* 13 (1887 &c.), 15 (1889) *and* 9 (1890).

   The invaders (*Nabeg, 1853*); tr. by Dole, *in* 11 (1887 &c.) *and* 12 (1889).

Ivan the Fool (*Skazka ob Ivane durake, 1886*).

67. *Ivan the fool. N.Y., J. S. Ogilvie, 1896. (Dora Thorne Series, no. 101).

   Possibly translated by B. R. Tucker (see 19).

68. The story of Ivan the fool, and his two brothers Simeon the warrior and Taras the stout, and of his dumb sister, Malania the spinster, and of the old devil and the three devilkins; tr., Englished, and conformed to the original by several hands. London, Brotherhood Publ. Co., 1898. pp. 31. (New Order Reprint no. 1).

   ——, *in* 38 (1898).

Ivan the fool; tr. by Dole, *in* 13 (1887 &c.), 15 (1889) *and* 16 (1895 &c.); tr. by Tucker, *in* 19 (1890); tr. by Norraikow, *in* 17 (1891 &c.).

———

Katia, *see* Family happiness.

Kholstomir (*Kholstomer, 1886; written 1863 and revised 1885*), a story of a horse; tr. by Dole, *in* 11 (1887 &c.) *and* 12 (1889); another tr., *in* 25 (1887) *and* 33 (1888).

The Kingdom of God is Within You (*Tsarstvo Bozhie vnutri vas, Berlin, 1893–94*).

69. "The kingdom of God is within you": Christianity, not as a mystic religion, but as a new theory of life; tr. from the Russian by Constance Garnett. London, W. Heinemann, 1894 (Feb.-March). 2 vols.
——. [*reprint*]. cheap ed. London, W. Heinemann, 1894. pp. xvi, 528.
†——. [*reprint*]. N.Y., Cassell, [1894]. pp. x, 368.

70. The kingdom of God is within you, or Christianity, not as a mystical doctrine, but as a new life-conception; authorised translation from the original Russian MS. by A. Delano. London, W. Scott, 1894 (March) &c. pp. viii, 376.

———

The Kreutzer Sonata (*Kreĭtserova sonata, 1891*).

71. The Kreutzer sonata; [tr. from the Russian by H. Sutherland Edwards]. London, Eden, Remington, 1890 (June). pp. 230.

72. †The Kreutzer sonata; tr. by Benj. R. Tucker. Boston, B. R. Tucker, 1890 (June). pp. 143.
Further impression: 1890 ("4th ed.").
†——. [*another impression*]. N.Y., J. S. Ogilvie, [1890]. (Sunset Series, no. 114).
——, *in* 19 (1890); [*extracts*] *in* 8 (1897).

73. The Kreutzer sonata; tr. by William M. Thomson. London, W. M. Thomson, [1890] (Oct.). pp. 238.
——. [*another impression*]. London, Temple Co., [1896].

74. †The Kreutzer sonata; tr. from the original manuscript by Frederic Lyster. N.Y., Pollard, 1890. pp. 118. (Pollard's Popular Publications, no. 1).

[75.]*The Kreutzer sonata. Chicago, C. H. Sergel, [1890]. pp. 170. (International Library, no. 1).

[76.]*The Kreutzer sonata. London, Macqueen, 1896. pp. 232.
Possibly Edwards's translation (cf. 71).

[77.]*The Kreutzer sonata. London, W. Scott, 1898. pp. 158.
Also issued with Family happiness (*see* 18).

The Kreutzer sonata, A sequel to (*Posleslovie k Kreĭtserova sonata, Berlin, 1890; Moscow, 1891*) (The relations of the sexes); tr. by Thomson, *in* 35 (1896).

The Kreutzer sonata, A second supplement to; tr. by Schumm, *in* 4 (1891).

Labour, *see* Toil.

A landlord's morning, *see* A Russian proprietor.

Lessons of the "Kreutzer sonata"; tr. by Tucker, *in* 19 (1890).

A letter on the Peace conference (*Po povodu konferentsii v Gaage, 1899*); tr. by Maude, *in* 31 (1899).

78. Life (*Ozhizhni, 1888 (censored), Geneva 1891; written 1887, parts publ. 1890*); authorised translation by Isabel F. Hapgood. N.Y., T. Y. Crowell, [1888]. pp. 295, port. front.
——. [*English issue*]. London, W. Scott, 1889. pp. 295. (Uniform edition).

Life *is* worth living, *see* What men live by.

Little girls wiser than old men (*Debchenki umnee starikov, 1885*); tr. by Dole, *in* 13 (1887 &c.), 15 (1889) *and* 9 (1890).

The long exile, *see* God sees the truth, but waits.

Lost on the steppe, *see* The snowstorm.

A lost opportunity, *see* If you neglect the fire, you don't put it out.

Lucerne (*Lyutsern, 1857*), from the recollections of Prince Nekhliudof; tr. by Dole, *in* 28 (1887 &c.) *and* 12 (1889).

Man and woman: their respective functions; tr. by Schumm, *in* 4 (1891).

Master and Man (*Khozyain i rabotnik, 1895*).

79. Master and man; tr. by A. Hulme Beaman. London, Chapman & Hall, 1895 (April). pp. 125.
——. [*reprint*]; with an introduction by W. D. Howells. N.Y., D. Appleton, 1895 (June). pp. xv, 165.

80. Master and man: a story; rendered from the Russian into English by S. Rapoport and John C. Kenworthy. London, W. Scott, [1895] (May–June). pp. vii, 147, 2 fronts.
Vol. IV (or V; see note to 16) in a series containing also 37, 36, 34 and 16. Rapoport provided a bald translation and Kenworthy rewrote it.
——. [*reprint*]. N.Y., T. Y. Crowell, [1895]. pp. 64.

81. Master and man; tr. by Hettie E. Miller. Chicago, E. A. Weeks, [1895]. pp. 117. (Melbourne Series, no. 34).

82. Master and man; tr. from the Russian by Yekaterína Alexándrovna Ludwig and George Bruce Halsted. Austin, Tex., The Neomon (Corner & Fontaine), 1895. pp. 172. (Neomonic Series, no. 2).

[83.]*Master and man; tr. from the original Russian. Chicago, F. T. Neely, 1895.
    †——. London, N.Y., F. T. Neely, [1899]. pp. 155, port. front. (Neely's Booklet Library, no. 7).

Meeting a Moscow acquaintance in the detachment, *see* An old acquaintance.

Money, *see* What to do?

The morning of a landowner, *see* A Russian proprietor.

The mother, *see* What to do?

84. [*My confession*] (*Ispoved'*, *Geneva*, *1884*; *written 1880–82*) How I came to believe ("My confession" [*sic*]. Maldon, Free Age Press, 1900. pp. 64. ([Free Age Press cheap editions of Tolstoy, no. 3]).
    A revision of the 1885 translation (see 3, etc.).
    [——] ——, *in* 3 (1885) *and* 24 (1887); [*extracts*] *in* 8 (1897).
My husband and I, *see* Family happiness.

My religion, *see* What I believe.

[The new ABC] (*Novaya Azbuka, 1875*) The new speller [*extracts*] tr. by Dole *in* 23 (1888 &c.) *and* 27 (1888).

An old acquaintance (*Vstrecha v otryade s moskovskim znakomȳm, 1856*); tr. by Dole, *in* 11 (1887 &c.) *and* 12 (1889); another tr. [?] *in* A20 (Stories by Foreign Authors: Russian. 1898).

The old devil and the three little devils, *see* Ivan the fool.

85. On flogged and floggers (*Golod ili ne golod? 1898*); with some comments by Jaakoff Prelooker and a poem by Minnie M'Kean. Reprinted from and published by the "Anglo-Russian", London, 1899. pp. 16. (Russian Reformation Society, no. 1).
    Consists mainly of comments.

On the relations of the sexes (*Ob otnosheniyakh mezhdu, 1890*); tr. by Thomson, *in* 35 (1896).

86. Patriotism and Christianity (*Khristianstvo i patriotizm, Geneva, 1895*). London, W. Reeves, [1896]. pp. 54. (Bijou Library, no. 5).

> *Reprinted from The Daily Chronicle.*

Patriotism and Christianity; to which is appended "A reply to criticisms of the work", and "Patriotism, or peace?": a letter called forth by the Venezuelan dispute between England and the United States; with a note to English readers by John C. Kenworthy. London, W. Scott, 1896. pp. 72.

> Patriotism and Christianity *is printed from the same plates as the Reeves edition above; the remainder is in a different fount.* "A reply to criticisms" *is reprinted from The New Age,* "Patriotism, or peace?" *from The Daily Chronicle.*

87. Patriotism and government (*Patriotizm i pravitel'stvo, 1900*); tr. by Aylmer Maude. Maldon, Free Age Press, 1900. pp. 39. ([Free Age Press cheap editions of Tolstoy, no. 12]).

Patriotism, or peace? (*Patriotizm ili mir? 1896*), *in* 86 (1896).

The persecution of the Doukhobortsi, *see* The emigration of the Doukhobortsi.

The physiology of war, *see* War and peace [*extracts*].

88. †Polikouchka (*Polikushka, 1863*). N.Y., J. W. Lovell, [1888]. pp. [133]–202. (Lovell's Library, no. 1113).

> *Reissue of part of* 25 (*see also* 26 *and* 33).

†——. [*reprint*]. N.Y., G. Munro, [1888]. pp. 91. (Seaside Library, Pocket Edition, no. 1069).

Polikushka; tr. by Dole, *in* 11 (1887 &c.) *and* 12 (1889); tr. by Tucker, *in* 19 (1890); tr. by Norraikow, *in* 17 (1891).

Popular legends; tr. by Dole, *in* 13 (1887 &c.), 15 (1889) *and* 9 (1890).

Power and liberty, *see* War and peace [*second epilogue*].

The power of darkness, *see* The dominion of darkness.

The prisoner of the Caucasus (*Kavkazkiĭ plennik, 1872*) [*from The ABC*]; tr. by Dole, *in* 28 (1887 &c.) *and* 12 (1889); another tr., *in* 5 (1887 &c.).

The raid, *see* The invaders.

Recollections of a scorer (*Zapiski markera, 1855*); tr. by Dole, *in* 28 (1887 &c). *and* 12 (1899).

Recollections of Sebastopol, *see* Sebastopol.

The relations of the sexes, *see* The Kreutzer sonata, A sequel to, *and* On the relations of the sexes.

46   TOLSTOĬ

89. Religion and morality (*Religiya i nravstvennost'*, *1895*).
Maldon, Essex, Free Age Press, 1900. pp. 40. ([Free Age
Press cheap editions of Tolstoy, no. 9]).

A revision of the translation first published in The Contemporary Review.

The repentant sinner (*Kayushchiĭsya greshnik*, *1886*); tr. by
Dole, *in* 13 (1887 &c.), 23 (1888 &c.), 27 (1888), 15 (1889) *and*
9 (1890).

Resurrection (*Voskresen'e*, *St. Petersburg*, *1899* (*censored ed.*);
Purleigh, *1899* (*complete*).).

90. †Resurrection: a novel; tr. by Louise Maude. London,
Brotherhood Publ. Co., 14 April 1899–10 March 1900. pp.
495. (13 parts, for binding into 3 vols.). (New Order Extras).
——. London, Brotherhood Publ. Co., 1900 (June). pp. 495.
The 13 parts bound and issued as one volume.

——. [*reprint*]. London, F. R. Henderson, 1900 (March). pp.
ix, 565, front., plts.
Published from the same address as the Brotherhood Publishing Co.
*——. [*reprint*]. N.Y., Grosset & Dunlap. [1900]. pp. viii,
519, illus.
†——. [——]. [*another impression*]. N.Y., Dodd, Mead, 1900.
pp. viii, 519, front., plts.

91. †Resurrection (The awakening); tr. by Henry Britoff. N.Y.,
J. S. Ogilvie, 1900. pp. vi, [7]–535, port. front., plts.

92. †The awakening (The resurrection); tr. by William E. Smith.
N.Y., Street & Smith, [1900]. pp. 317, port front., plts.

The romance of a horse, *see* Kholstomir.

The romance of marriage, *see* Family happiness.

A Russian proprietor (*Utro pomeshchika*, *1856*); tr. by Dole,
in 28 (1887 &c.) *and* 12 (1889).

Scenes from common life [*10 stories from The ABC*, *1872*]; tr.
by Dole, *in* 23 (1888 &c.) *and* 27 (1888).

School scenes at Yasnaya Polyana; tr. by Dole, *in* 23 (1888 &c.)
and 27 (1888).

Extracts from 2 articles: Yasno-Polyanskaya shkola za noyabr',
dekabr', mesyatsȳ (1862) *and* Komu u kogo uchit'sya pisat' (1862)

Sebastopol (*Sevastopol'skie razskazȳ*, *1855–56*).

93. Sebastopol; tr. from the French [anonymous version of 1886]
by Frank D. Millet; with introduction by W. D. Howells.

N.Y., Harper & bros., 1887. pp. 241, port. front.
Issued in 2 different publisher's casings, one brown and one blue.
——, *in* 5 (1887 &c.).

94. †Sebastopol; tr. by Mrs. Laura E. Kendall. N.Y., G. Munro,
[1888]. pp. 137. (Seaside Library, Pocket Edition, no. 1108).

95. †Sevastopol; tr. from the original Russian by Isabel F. Hapgood; authorized ed. N.Y., T. Y. Crowell, [1888]. pp. 262.
Also issued with The Cossacks (*see* 29).
——. [*English issue*]. London, W. Scott, [1890]. (Uniform
edition).

————

A second supplement to the Kreutzer sonata, *see* The Kreutzer
sonata, A second supplement to.

A seed as big as a hen's egg (*Zerno s kurinoe yaĭtso, 1886*); tr. by
Dole, *in* 13 (1887 &c.), 15 (1889) *and* 9 (1890).

96. *Shaker-Russian correspondence between Count Leo Tolstoi
and Elder F. W. Evans. Mt. Lebanon, Columbia County,
N.Y., 1891. pp. 7.

A short account of the Gospels, *see* The Gospel in brief.

97. The slavery of our times (*Rabstvo nashego vremeni, Purleigh,
1900*); tr. from the Russian MS. by Aylmer Maude; with
introduction by translator. Maldon, Essex, Free Age Press,
1900. pp. 127, port. front. ([Free Age Press cheap editions of
Tolstoy, no. 4]).
*——. [*reprint*]. N.Y., Dodd, Mead, 1900. pp. xxxi, 186,
port. front.
†——. [——]. [*another impression*]. N.Y., E. C. Walker,
[1900].

A snowstorm (*Metel', 1856*); tr. by Dole, *in* 11 (1887 &c)
and 12 (1889); another tr., *in* 25 (1887) *and* 33 (1888).

The spirit of Christ's teaching, *see* The Gospel in brief [the
section "A recapitulation"].

Stop and think! (*Ne-delanie, 1893*); tr. by Warren, *in* 31 (1899).

Stories from botany [*from The ABC, 1872*]; tr. by Dole, *in* 23
(1888 &c.) *and* 27 (1888).

Stories from physics [*from The ABC, 1872*]; tr. by Dole, *in* 23
(1888 &c.) *and* 27 (1888).

Stories of my dogs [*from The ABC, 1872*]; tr. by Dole, *in* 23
(1888 &c.) *and* 27 (1888).

Strider, *see* Kholstomir.

Tales from zoology [*from The ABC, 1872*]; tr. by Dole, *in* 23 (1888 &c.) *and* 27 (1888).

Texts for woodcuts (*Tekstȳ k lubochnȳm kartinam, 1885–86*); tr. by Dole *in* 13 (1887 &c.), 15 (1889) *and* 9 (1890).

Three deaths (*Tri smerti, 1859*); tr. by Dole, *in* 28 (1887 &c.) *and* 12 (1889); another tr., *in* 5 (1887 &c.).

98. [*The three mendicants*] (*Tri startsa, 1886*) The archbishop and the three old men; tr. from the Russian by Rosamond Venning. London & Sydney, Eden, Remington, 1893. pp. 34.

The three mendicants; tr. by Dole, *in* 13 (1887 &c.), 15 (1889) *and* 9 (1890).

Three parables (*Tri pritchi, 1895*), *in* 16 (1899).

Toil (*Trudolyubie ili torzhestvo Zemledel'tsa, 1888*).

99. †The suppressed book of the peasant Bondareff: Labor, the divine command; made known, augmented and edited by Count L. Tolstoï; tr. by Mary Cruger. N.Y., Pollard, 1890. pp. 160. (Pollard's Popular Publications, no. 2).

"The work and theory of Bondareff" *by Tolstoï is followed by Bondareff's own book*, "Labor".

*——. Chicago, Laird & Lee, 1890. (Pastime Series, no. 44).

[100].*Toil. Chicago, C. H. Sergel, 1890.

Toil; tr. by Thomson, *in* 35 (1896).

———

101. *The triumph of labour. London, Brotherhood Publ. Co., [*c.*1898]. pp. 16.

Traced only from an advertisement in another of the Brotherhood Publishing Co.'s editions of Tolstoï.

Two brothers and gold (*Dva brata i zoloto (1886)*; tr. by Dole, *in* 13 (1887 &c.), 15 (1889) *and* 9 (1890).

102. †[*Two hussars*] (*Dva gusara, 1856*) Two generations. N.Y., G. Munro, 1888 &c. pp. 104. (Seaside Library, Pocket Edition, no. 1073).

Two hussars; tr. by Dole, *in* 28 (1887 &c.) *and* 12 (1889); another tr., *in* 25 (1887) *and* 33 (1888).

Two old men, *see* The two pilgrims.

103. *The two pilgrims (*Dva starika, 1886*); or, Love and good deeds; tr. by N. H. Dole. London, W. Scott, 1889.

——, *in* 13 (1887 &c.), 15 (1889), 9 (1890) *and* 34 (1894 &c.).

The two pilgrims; tr. by Delano, *in* 10 (1887); tr. by Norraikow, *in* 22 (1892).

A visit to a slaughter-house, *see* The first step.

War and peace (*Voĭna i mir, 1865–69*).

104. War and peace. London, Vizetelly, 1886. 3 vols.

Omits philosophical passages and the second epilogue (see 118, 119 and 120). Further impression: 1887 &c. ("2nd ed.").

†———. [*with title* "War and peace: a historical novel; tr. into French [1885] by a Russian lady, and from the French by Clara Bell; revised and corrected in the United States."]. N.Y., W. S. Gottsberger, 1886. 3 pts. in 6 vols.

†———. [———]. N.Y., Harper & bros., [1886]. 3 vols. (Franklin Square Library, nos. 508, 521 and 521A).

105. War and peace; from the Russian by Nathan Haskell Dole; authorized tr. N.Y., T. Y. Crowell, 1889. 4 vols.

Also issued as 4 vols. in 2.

———. [*English issue*]. London, W. Scott, [1889]. 4 vols. (Uniform edition).

Omits the preface to the American edition. Also issued as 4 vols. in 2 [1897].

106. †[*Second epilogue*] Power and liberty; tr. from the French by Huntington Smith. N.Y., T. Y. Crowell, [1888]. pp. 132.

Also issued with The physiology of war (see 108), and with The physiology of war and The long exile and other stories (see 27).

107. †[*extracts*] The physiology of war: Napoleon and the Russian campaign; tr. from the 3rd French ed. by Huntingdon Smith. N.Y., T. Y. Crowell, [1888]. pp. ix, 190, port. front., map.

Also issued with Power and liberty (see 108), and with Power and liberty and The long exile and other stories (see 27).

108. [*extracts*] The physiology of war: Napoleon and the Russian campaign; and, Power and liberty [second epilogue to War and peace]; tr. from French by Huntington Smith. London, W. Scott, [1889]. 2 vols. in 1. (Uniform edition).

Each volume also issued separately (see 107 and 106); also issued with The long exile and other stories (see 27).

What I Believe (*V chëm moya vera?, 1884 (banned)*).

109. †My religion; tr. from the French [anonymous translation of 1884 by Huntington Smith]. N.Y., T. Y. Crowell, [1885]. pp. xii, 274.

*———. rev. ed. N.Y., T. Y. Crowell, [1885].

———. [*English issue*]. London, W. Scott, 1889. (Uniform edition).

110. What I believe; tr. from the Russian by Constantine Popoff.
London, E. Stock, 1885. pp. iv, 236.
——. *[American issue].* N.Y., W. S. Gottsberger, 1886, &c.
*——. *[another impression].* London, Brotherhood Publ. Co.,
1895.
What I believe; *in* 3 (1885).

What is Art? (*Chto takoe iskusstvo? 1898*).

111. What is art? tr. from the Russian by Aylmer Maude. London,
Brotherhood Publ. Co., 1898. 3 pts., paged continuously.
(The New Order, Extra Issues, Jan., March and May 1898).
> *Declared by Tolstoï to be the first complete and correct edition (the*
> *Russian edition was mutilated by the censor).*

——, *in* 38 (1898).
——; [2nd ed.] tr. from the Russian original by Aylmer Maude;
embodying the author's last alterations and revisions. London, Brotherhood Publ. Co., 1898 (June). pp. xvi, 237.
†——. ——, *[reprint].* N.Y., T. Y. Crowell, [1898]. pp. 203,
port. front.
——. 3rd ed. London, Brotherhood Publ. Co., 1898. pp.
xvi, 237. port. front.
——; tr. from the original Russian MS., with an introduction,
by Alymer Maude. London, W. Scott, [1899] (April). pp.
xl, 237. (Scott Library, no. 106).
> *Identical with 3rd ed. above, with the addition of a long introduction*
> *by Maude.*

——; tr. from the Russian original by Aylmer Maude, embodying the author's last alterations and revisions, with an
index of names and a new introduction by the translator. 4th
ed. London, Brotherhood Publ. Co., 1899. pp. xl, 243, port.
front.

112. †What is art? tr. from the Russian by Charles Johnston.
Philadelphia, H. Altemus, 1898 (Aug.) pp. iii, 298.

What is to be done? *see* What to do?

What Men Live By (*Chem lyudi zhivȳ, 1882*).

113. †What people live by; tr. by Mrs. Aline Delano. Boston, D.
Lothrop, 1886 &c. pp. 83, illus.

114. *What men live by; tr. from the Russian by Nathan Haskell
Dole. N.Y., T. Y. Crowell, [1888].
*——. London, W. Scott, 1889.
——, *in* 23 (1888 &c.), 27 (1888), 9 (1890 &c.) *and* 36 (1894 &c.).

115. *Life is worth living. N.Y., J. S. Ogilvie, 1896. (Dora Thorne Series, no. 102).

> *Possibly tr. by Norraikow (see below).*

Life *is* worth living; tr. by Norraikow, *in* 22 (1892).

What shall it profit a man? *see* How much land does a man need?

What To Do? (*Tak chto-zhe nam delat'? Christchurch, 1902; written 1882–86; fragments publ. Moscow, 1885–86*).

116. What to do? thoughts evoked by the census of Moscow; tr. from the Russian by Isabel F. Hapgood. N.Y., T. Y. Crowell, [1887]. pp. [vii], 273.

> *With omissions due to the censorship of the original Russian.*

117. †What to do? thoughts evoked by the census of Moscow; a new and authorized translation from the unabridged Russian manuscript. N.Y., T. Y. Crowell, [1888]. pp. v, 244.

> *Has an introduction by N. H. Dole. Also issued with* Childhood, boyhood and youth (*see* 2).

——. [*English issue*]. London, W. Scott, [1889]. pp. 244. (Uniform edition).

> *Omits the introduction by N. H. Dole.*

——. [*extract from ch.* 40] The mother; tr. by Schumm, *in* 4 (1891).

——. [*extract*]. (*Den'gi! publ. separately in Geneva, 1886–87*) Money; tr. by Yarros, *in* 4 (1891).

---

118. †Where love is, there God is also (*Gde lyubov, tam i Bog, 1885*); tr. from the Russian by Nathan Haskell Dole. N.Y., T. Y. Crowell, [1887]. pp. 19.

*——. London, W. Scott, 1889.

——, *in* 13 (1887 &c.), 15 (1889), 9 (1890) *and* 37 (1894 &c.).

Where love is, there God is also; tr. by Delano, *in* 10 (1887); tr. by Norraikow, *in* 22 (1892).

119. Why do men intoxicate themselves (*Dlya chego lyudi odurmanivayutsya? 1891*); tr. from the German [of R. Löwenfeld (1891)] by M.S.S. London & Sydney, Eden, Remington, 1892. pp. 80.

[*Why do men intoxicate themselves?*] Alcohol and tobacco; tr. by Thomson, *in* 35 (1896); another tr., *in* 8 (1897).

The wood-cutting expedition (*Rubka lesa, 1855*); tr. by Dole, *in* 11 (1887 &c.) *and* 12 (1889).

The work of Guy de Maupassant, *see* Guy de Maupassant.

52

TOLSTOĬ

Work While Ye Have the Light (*Khodite v svete, Geneva, 1892*).

120. Work while ye have the light; tr. from the Russian by E. J. Dillon; [introduction by Edmund Gosse]. London, W. Heinemann, 1890 (Nov.). pp. [xxiv], 218. (Heinemann's International Library).
　*——. Chicago, C. H. Sergel, 1890. (Sergel's Columbian Library).
　*——. N.Y., G. Munro, [1890]. (Seaside Library, Pocket Edition, no. 1639).

　　From Jan. 1890 to Oct. 1892 the Seaside Library was controlled by J. W. Lovell.

　†——. Authorized ed. N.Y., United States Book Co., [1890]. pp. 170. (Lovell's Westminster Series, no. 22).

　　The United States Book Co. was established in July 1890 with J. W. Lovell as organiser.

　*——: a tale of the early Christians. N.Y., International Book Co., 1890.

　　The International Book Co. was a subsidiary of the United States Book Co.

　*——. St. Louis, Mo., & N.Y., Waverly, 1890. (World Library, no. 6).
　*——. London, W. Scott, [c.1890].

　　Traced only from an advertisement in another of Scott's editions of Tolstoĭ.

　*——. [*another impression*]. new ed. London, Brotherhood Publ. Co., 1895. pp. 218.

　　Omits Gosse's introduction.

121. Work while ye have the light: a story of the early Christians; a new unabridged translation from the Russian MS., containing the author's latest corrections and additions. Maldon, Free Age Press, 1900. pp. 39. ([Free Age Press cheap editions of Tolstoy's writings, no. 2]).

———

Yermak, the conqueror of Siberia (*Ermak,*) *1872* [*from The ABC*]; tr. by Dole, *in* 23 (1888 &c.) *and* 27 (1888).

N.B. *The Brotherhood Publishing Co. acted during the 1890s as a distributor for various works of Tolstoĭ published previously by Walter Scott and others.*

TUR (Evgeniya) *pseud., see* **SALIAS DE TURNEMIR** (Elizaveta Vasil'evna) *grafinya.*

TURGENEV (Ivan Sergeevich) 1818–83.

1. The novels; tr. by Constance Garnett. London, Heinemann, 1894–99. 15 vols. 1, Rudin (1894); 2, A house of gentlefolk (1894); 3, On the eve (1895); 4, Fathers and children (1895); 5, Smoke (1896); 6–7, Virgin soil (1896); 8–9, A sportsman's sketches (1896); 10, Dream tales [Clara Militch, Phantoms, The song of triumphant love, The dream] and Prose poems (1897); 11, The torrents of spring, etc. [First love, Mumu] (1897); 12, A Lear of the steppes and other stories [Faust, Acia] (1898); 13, The diary of a superfluous man and other stories [A tour in the forest, Yakov Pasinkov, Andrei Kolosov, A correspondence] (1899); 14, A desperate character and other stories [A strange story, Punin and Baburin, Old portraits, The brigadier, Pyetushkov] (1899); 15, The Jew and other stories [An unhappy girl, The duellist, Three portraits, Enough] (1899).

> Rudin *and* A house of gentlefolk *were issued in the Pioneer Series.*

——. [*American issue*]. N.Y., Macmillan, 1894–99.

Andrei Kolosov (*Andreĭ Kolosov, 1844*); tr. by Garnett, *in* 1 (v. 13) (1899).

Annals of a sportsman, *see* A sportsman's sketches.

2. [*Asya*] (*Asya, 1858*) Annouchka; tr. from the French of the author's own translation [1869] by Franklin Abbott. Boston, Cupples, Upham, 1884. pp. 111.

> *Turgenev merely supervised the translation into French.*

Asya; tr. by Gersoni, *in* 24 (1886); tr. by Garnett, *in* 1 (v. 12) (1898).

The brigadier (*Brigadir, 1868*); tr. by Garnett, *in* 1 (v. 14) (1899).

Clara Militch (*Klara Milich, 1883*); tr. by Garnett, *in* 1 (v. 10) (1897).

.A correspondence (*Perepiska, 1856*); tr. by Garnett, *in* 1 (v. 13) (1899).

A daughter of Russia, *see* An unfortunate woman.

A desperate character (*Otrȳvki iz vospominaniĭ svoikh i chuzhikh, 1881*); tr. by Garnett, *in* 1 (v. 14) (1899).

The diary of a superfluous man (*Dnevnik lishnego cheloveka, 1850*); tr. by Gersoni, *in* 8 (1884); tr. by Garnett, *in* 1 (v. 13) (1899).

Dimitiri Roudine, *see* Rudin.

The dream (*Son, 1877*); tr. by Garnett, *in* 1 (v. 10) (1897).

3. *[The duellist] (Bret'er, 1847) [also, Furcht vor der Liebe, by L. Laistner, and Der Dachs auf Lichtmess, by W. H. Riehl] The ruffian. Chicago, Schick, [1887]. (Overland Library, no. 13).

> Probably a translation of Bret'er, from the German; the Overland Library was a series of translations of German translations.

The duellist; tr. by Garnett, in 1 (v. 15) (1899).

The dumb door-porter, see Mumu.

Enough (Dovol'no, 1865); tr. by Garnett, in 1 (v. 15) (1899).

4. Fathers and sons (Ottsȳ i deti, 1862): a novel; tr. from the Russian with the approval of the author, by Eugene Schuyler. N.Y., Leypoldt & Holt, 1867. pp. viii, 248. (Leisure Hour Series, no. [3]). (Uniform edition).

> † Reissued in 1872 with the imprint "H. Holt".

——. [another impression]. London, N.Y., Ward, Lock, [1883] &c. (Select Library of Fiction). (Uniform edition).

*——. N.Y., H. Holt, 1883. (Leisure Moment Series).

*——. N.Y., G. Munro, 1883. (Seaside Library).

Fathers and children; tr. by Garnett, in 1 (v. 4) (1895).

Faust (Faust, 1856); tr. by Garnett, in 1 (v. 12) (1898).

5. First love (Pervaya lyubov', 1860), and Punin and Babúrin; tr. from the Russian by permission of the author, with a biographical introduction, by Sidney Jerrold. London, W. H. Allen, 1884. pp. [xi], 237, port. front.

First love; tr. by Garnett, in 1 (v. 11) (1897).

6. †Ghosts (Prizraki, 1864) [tr. from the French (1869), in Tales for a stormy night: translations from the French. Cincinnati, R. Clarke, 1891. pp. vii, 279. (Contains 4 other stories, by Balzac, Mérimée, and Daudet)].

[Ghosts] Phantoms; tr. by Garnett, in 1 (v. 10) (1897).

A house of gentlefolk, see A nest of gentlefolk.

The Jew (Zhid, 1847); tr. by Garnett, in 1 (v. 15) (1899).

A Lear of the steppe (Stepnoĭ korol' Lir, 1870); tr. by Browne, in 21 (1874); tr. by Garnett, in 1 (v. 12) (1898).

7. [Mumu] (Mumu, 1854) The dumb door-porter: a tale imitated from the Russian of Tourguenieff; [based on X. Marmier's French translation (1858) in Sala (G.A.): The two prima donnas [an original story] and The dumb door-porter. London, Tinsley bros., 1862. pp. viii, 462.].

8. *Mumu, and The diary of a superfluous man; tr. from the Russian by Henry Gersoni. N.Y., Funk & Wagnalls, 1884. pp. 131. (Standard Library Series, no. 107).

——. [*English issue*]. London, Funk & Wagnalls, 1884.
——. 2nd ed. N.Y., Funk & Wagnalls, 1884. pp. [vii], [5]–131. (Standard Library Series. no. 107).

Contains an additional introduction.

Mumu; tr. by Garnett, *in* 1 (v. 11) (1897); another tr.? *in* A20 (Stories by Foreign Authors: Russian. 1898).

9. [*A nest of gentlefolk*] (*Dvoryanskoe gnezdo, 1859*) Liza; tr. from the Russian by W. R. S. Ralston. London, Chapman & Hall, 1869. 2 vols.
   †[——] ——. [*reprint, with title* "Liza, or, 'A nest of nobles': a novel"]. N.Y., H. Holt, 1872 &c. pp. 318. (Leisure Hour Series, no. [9]). (Uniform edition).

   Reissued in 1873 with the imprint "Holt & Williams".

   [——] ——. ——. [*another impression*, with title "Liza, or, A noble nest"]. London, N.Y., Ward, Lock, [1884]. pp. [iii], [17]–318. (Uniform edition).
   [*A nest of gentlefolk*] A house of gentlefolk; tr. by Garnett, *in* 1 (v. 2) (1894).
   Old portraits (*Starye portrety, 1881*); tr. by Garnett, *in* 1 (v. 14) (1899).

10. On the eve (*Nakanune, 1860*): a tale; tr. from the Russian by C. E. Turner. London, Hodder & Stoughton, 1871. pp. vi, 306.
    †——. [*reprint*]. American edition, with amendments. N.Y., Holt & Williams. 1873. pp. vi, 272. (Leisure Hour Series, no. [12]). (Uniform edition).

    *Reissued in 1875 with the imprint "H. Holt".

    On the eve; tr. by Garnett, *in* 1 (v. 3) (1895).

    Phantoms, *see* Ghosts.

11. Poems in prose (*Stikhotvoreniya v proze, 1882*); [tr. from the French]. Boston, Cupples, Upham, 1883. pp. 120, port. front.
    ——. [*another impression*]. 2nd ed. N.Y., London, G. P. Putnam's sons, [*c.*1887]. pp. 120, port. front.

12. [*Poems in prose*] Senilia: poems in prose, being meditations, sketches, &c.; English version, with introduction and biographical sketch of the author, by S. J. MacMullan. Bristol, Arrowsmith; London, Simpkin, Marshall, Hamilton, Kent, [1890]. pp. xxiv. 153.

    Based on the German version of W. Lange (1883) and the Danish version of I. Heilbuth.

    Prose poems; tr. by Garnett, *in* 1 (v. 10) (1897).

13. †Punin and Babwin [*sic, for Baburin*] (*Punin i Baburin, 1874*); tr. by George W. Scott. N.Y., G. Munro, 1882. pp. 18. (Seaside Library, vol. 59, no. 1207).

Punin and Baburin; tr. by Jerrold, *in* 5 (1884); tr. by Garnett, *in* 1 (v. 14) (1899).

Pyetushkov (*Petushkov, 1848*); tr. by Garnett, *in* 1 (v. 14) (1899).

14. [*Rudin*] (*Rudin, 1856*) Dimitri Roudine: a novel; tr. from the French and German versions. (Reprinted from Every Saturday). N.Y., Holt & Williams, 1873. pp. 271. (Leisure Hour Series, no. [21]). (Uniform edition).

> *Reissued in the same year with the imprint "H. Holt".*

[——] ——. [*another impression*]. London, Ward, Lock, 1883. (Select Library of Fiction). (Uniform edition).

Rudin; tr. by Garnett, *in* 1 (v. 1) (1894).

The ruffian, *see* The duellist.

Russian life in the interior, *see* A sportsman's sketches.

Senilia, *see* Poems in prose.

15. Smoke (*Dȳm, 1867*), or, Life at Baden: a novel. London, R. Bentley, 1868. 2 vols.

16. Smoke: a Russian novel; tr. from the author's French version [1868] by Wm. F. West. (Reprinted from The Week). N.Y., Holt & Williams, 1872. pp. 291. (Leisure Hour Series, no. [2]). (Uniform edition).

> *The French version was actually by Mérimée, with the assistance of Turgenev.*

——. [*another impression*]. London, Ward, Lock, [1883]. (Select Library of Fiction). (Uniform edition).

Smoke; tr. by Garnett, *in* 1 (v. 5) (1896).

17. †The song of triumphant love (*Pesn' torzhestvuyushcheĭ lyubvi, 1881*); adapted by Marian Ford. Also, Wild Jack, and Merga's petticoat, [original stories] by Katherine S. Macquoid. N.Y., G. Munro, 1882 &c. pp. 17. (Seaside Library, vol. 72, no. 1463).

The song of triumphant love; tr. by Garnett, *in* 1 (v. 10) (1897).

18. [*A sportsman's sketches*] (*Zapiski okhotnika, 1847–52*) Russian life in the interior, or, The experiences of a sportsman; edited by James D. Meiklejohn. Edinburgh, A. & C. Black, 1855. pp. vii, 428.

> *A version of E. Charrière's French translation (1854), itself embroidered.*

19. [*A sportsman's sketches*] Annals of a sportsman; tr. from the authorized French edition [of H. Delaveau (1858)] by Franklin Pierce Abbott. N.Y., H. Holt, 1885. pp. xii, 311. (Leisure Hour Series, no. [164]).

20. [*A sportsman's sketches*] Tales from the note-book of a sportsman; tr. from the Russian by Edward Richter. Series 1. London, Lamley, 1895. pp. 11, 247.

    Uniform with 22. Two volumes were announced, but the second never appeared.

    A sportsman's sketches; tr. by Garnett, *in* 1 (v. 8–9) (1896).

21. Spring floods (*Veshnie vodȳ, 1872*); tr. by Mrs. Sophie Michell Butts. [*also*] A Lear of the steppe; tr. from the French [1873] by William Hand Browne. N.Y., H. Holt, 1874. pp. 219. (Leisure Hour Series, no. 33). (Uniform edition).

    The number in the series is not given in some copies.

22. Spring floods; tr. from the Russian by Edward Richter. London, Lamley, 1895 &c. pp. 247.

    Uniform with 20.

    [*Spring floods*] Torrents of spring; tr. by Garnett, *in* 1 (v. 11) (1897).

    A strange story (*Strannaya istoriya, 1869*); tr. by Garnett, *in* 1 (v. 14) (1899).

    Tales from the note-book of a sportsman, *see* A sportsman's sketches.

    Three portraits (*Tri portreta, 1846*); tr. by Garnett, *in* 1 (v. 15) (1899).

    Torrents of spring, *see* Spring floods.

    A tour in the forest (*Poezdka v poles'e, 1857*); tr. by Garnett, *in* 1 (v. 13) (1899).

23. †[*An unfortunate woman*] (*Neschastnaya, 1869*) A daughter of Russia; tr. by George W. Scott. N.Y., G. Munro, 1882. pp. 17. (Seaside Library, vol. 60, no. 1216).

24. An unfortunate woman, and Ass'ya; tr. from the Russian by Henry Gersoni. N.Y., London, Funk & Wagnalls, 1886 &c. pp. 190. ([Standard Library, no. 142]).

25. The unfortunate one: a novel; tr. from the Russian by A. R. Thompson. London, Trübner, 1888. pp. 134.

    An unhappy girl; tr. by Garnett, *in* 1 (v. 15) (1899).

26. Virgin soil (*Nov'*, *1877*); tr. with the author's sanction from the French version, by T. S. Perry. N.Y., H. Holt, 1877. pp. 315. (Leisure Hour Series).

    Actually translated from French and German versions.

    ——. [*another impression*]. London, N.Y., Ward, Lock, [1883]. pp. 315. (Uniform edition).

27. Virgin soil; tr. by Ashton W. Dilke. London, Macmillan, 1878 &c. pp. v [i.e. iv], 348.

    Virgin soil; tr. by Garnett, *in* 1 (v. 6–7) (1896).

28. The watch (*Chasȳ*, *1876*): an old man's story [*in* The bridal march, from the Norwegian of Björnson, and The watch, from the Russian of Ivan Turgenieff; tr. by J. Evan Williams. London, Digby, Long, 1893. pp. 175].

    Yakov Pasinkov (*Yakov Pasȳnkov*, *1855*); tr. by Garnett, *in* 1 (v. 13) (1899).

USPENSKIĬ (Gleb Ivanovich) 1843–1902.

The steam chicken (*Parovoĭ tsȳplenok*, *1888*), *and* A trifling defect in the mechanism (*Malen'kie nedostatki mekhanizma*, *1881*), *in* A22 (Voynich: The humour of Russia. 1895).

USPENSKIĬ (Nikolaĭ Vasil'evich) 1837–89.

Porridge (*Rabotnik*, *1862*), *and* The village schoolmaster (*Sel'skiĭ uchitel'*, *1867*), *in* A22 (Voynich: The humour of Russia. 1895.).

VESELITSKAYA (Lidiya Ivanovna) 1857–1936 (V. Mikulich, *pseud.*).

1. Mimi's marriage (*Mimochka nevesta*, *1883*): a sketch; tr. from the Russian. London, T. F. Unwin, 1893. pp. 239. (Pseudonym Library, no. 29).

VOLKHOVSKIĬ (Feliks Vadimovich) 1846–1914.

1. A china cup, and other stories for children. London, T. F. Unwin, 1892. pp. 176, front. (The Children's Library, vol. 2).

    Contains: A china cup (*Farforovaya chashka*, *1884*); How Scarlet-comb the cock defended the right (*Kak petushok Krasnȳi Grebeshok za pravdu postoyal*); The tiny screw (*Vintik*); The dream (*Son*, *1886*); Browny (*Serko*); The old sword's mistake (*Oshibka starogo mecha*); 'My own' (*Lesnaya pomeshchitsa*); The tale about how all these tales came to light (*Kak vse èti skazki poyavilis' na svet bozhiĭ*).

    The "new life" (*Noch' na novȳĭ god*): a Siberian story, *in* A17 (Russian Stories, vol. I, 1892).

ZAGOSKIN (Mikhail Nikolaevich) 1789–1852.

1. Tales of three centuries; tr. from the Russian by Jeremiah Curtin. Boston, Little, Brown, 1891. pp. xxvii, 355.

   Contains: An evening on the Hopyor (*Vecher na Khopr, 1834*); The three suitors (*Tri zhenikha, 1835*); Kuzma Roschin (*Kuz'ma Roshchin, 1836*).

2. †The young Muscovite (*Yuriǐ Miloslavskiǐ, 1829*), or, The Poles in Russia; paraphrased, enlarged and illustrated by Frederick Chamier and by the author of "A key to both houses of Parliament". London, J. Cochrane & J. M'Crone, 1833. 3 vols.

   "Improved", and with "new incidents" added.

   ——; edited by captain Frederick Chamier. London, J. Cochrane & J. M'Crone, 1834. 3 vols.

   On title-page of British Museum copy, after "Chamier", is an MS. note "and written by Colin Mackenzie, esqr, author of "The clubs of London" &c." (Mackenzie was a friend of Sir Walter Scott). "The clubs of London" is attributed by D.N.B. to Charles Marsh, and by Allibone to W. H. Leeds, who wrote several well-informed reviews of Russian literary works, and who, Gleb Struve suggests, may be the translator of this work. (See Amer. Slav. E. Europ. Rev., v. 8, 1949, p. 306).

   †——. N.Y., Harper & bros., 1834. 2 vols.

CHRONOLOGICAL LIST OF FIRST APPEARANCES OF TRANSLATIONS

The first appearance of each translation both in England and the United States is included; translations which had already appeared in another country are enclosed in square brackets (e.g., square brackets round a U.K. entry indicate that the translation had previously been published in the U.S.A.).

An asterisk preceding an entry marks the first appearance of a work in translation in book (as opposed to periodical) form; where there are two or more translations of the same work in the same year, and I have not been able to establish definite priority, I have marked them all in this way.

Titles of works are standardized for convenience of comparison, and are not necessarily those used on the actual volumes.

Tolstoĭ refers always to L. N. Tolstoĭ (A. K. Tolstoĭ is referred to as Tolstoĭ (A. K.)).

1793	UK	*Catherine II. Ivan Czarowitz (anon.).

1803 UK *Karamzin. Flor Silin (Feldborg?).
    *   ,,   Julia (Feldborg?).
    *   ,,   Lisa (Feldborg?).
    *   ,,   Natalia (Feldborg?).
    *   ,,   Travels (Feldborg).

      Russia *   ,,   Julia (Hawkins).

1806 UK *Sumarokov. Demetrius the Impostor (Evstaf'ev).

1821 UK *Specimens of the Russian poets [pt. 1] (Bowring).

1822 USA [Specimens of the Russian poets [pt. 1] (Bowring)].

1823 UK *Specimens of the Russian poets, pt. 2 (Bowring).

1826 UK Poetical translations from the Russian language (Saunders).

1831 UK *Bulgarin. Ivan Vyzhigin (Ross).

1832 USA [Bulgarin. Ivan Vyzhigin (Ross)].

1833 UK *Zagoskin. The young Muscovite (Chamier).

1834 USA [Zagoskin. The young Muscovite (Chamier)].

1835 Russia The talisman and other pieces (Borrow).
               Targum (Borrow).

1844 UK *Lazhechnikov. The heretic (Shaw).

1846 USA   *Bestuzhev. The Tartar chief (Hebbe).
            *Pushkin. The captain's daughter (Hebbe).

1849 USA   The Bakchesarian fountain and other poems (Lewis).

1850 UK   *Sollogub. The tarantas (Rosenstrauch).

1853 UK   *Lermontov. A hero of our time (anon.).

1854 UK   *Gogol'. Dead souls (Lach-Szyrma).
            Lermontov. A hero of our time (anon.).
                  ,,   ,, ,, ,,. ,,   ,, (Pulszky).

1855 UK   *Turgenev. A sportsman's sketches. (Meiklejohn).

1857 UK   Russian popular tales (Dietrich).
            *Griboedov. Woe from wit (Benardaky).

1858 UK   Pushkin. The captain's daughter (anon.).
            *   ,,   The queen of spades (anon.).

1859 UK   Pushkin. The captain's daughter (Hanstein).

1860 UK   *Gogol'. Christmas Eve (Tolstoy).
            *   ,,   Taras Bul'ba (Tolstoy).
            *Lazhechnikov. The palace of ice (anon.).

     USA   *   ,,   ,,   ,,   ,, (Williams).

1861 UK   *Saltykov. Provincial sketches (selections) (Aston).

1862 UK   *Tolstoĭ. Childhood, boyhood, youth (Meysenbug).
            *Turgenev. Mumu (Sala).

1864 USA   [Lazhechnikov   The heretic (Shaw)].

1867 USA   *Turgenev. Fathers and sons (Schuyler).

1868 UK   *Turgenev. Smoke (anon.).

1869 UK/USA *Krȳlov. Krilof and his fables (Ralston).
     UK   *Tolstoĭ (A. K.). The death of Ivan the Terrible (Harrison).
            *Turgenev. A nest of gentlefolk (Ralston).
     India *Krȳlov. Fables (Long).

1871 UK   *Turgenev. On the eve (Turner).
     India *Aksakov. Memoirs of the Aksakof family (anon.).

1872 USA   [Turgenev. A nest of gentlefolk (Ralston)].
                 ,,   Smoke (West).

1873 UK   Russian folk-tales (Ralston).
     USA   [Turgenev. On the eve (Turner)].
            *   ,,   Rudin (anon.).

1874 UK   Slavonic fairy tales (Naaké).
            *Markevich. The neglected question (Ouroussoff).
            *Tolstoĭ (A. K.). Prince Serebryani (Golitsyn).

1874 USA   *Turgenev. A Lear of the steppe (Browne).
      *   „   Spring floods (Butts).

1875 UK   *Lermontov. The demon (Stephen).
               *Pushkin. The amateur peasant-girl (Telfer).
                     „   The captain's daughter (Telfer).
               *   „   Peter the Great's negro (Telfer).
               *   „   The shot (Telfer).
               *   „   The snow-storm (Telfer).
               *   „   The station-master (Telfer).
               *   „   The undertaker (Telfer).

      USA   *Lermontov. The novice (Conant).

1876 USA   [Slavonic fairy tales (Naaké)].

1877 USA   [Russian folk-tales (Ralston)].
               Pushkin. The captain's daughter (Zielinska).
               *Turgenev. Virgin soil (Perry).

1878 UK/USA   *Tolstoĭ. The Cossacks (Schuyler).
      UK   Turgenev. Virgin soil (Dilke).
      Germany Translations from Russian and German poets (Baratynskaya).

1879 India   *Rȳleev. Voinarofskyi and other poems (Davies).

1881 UK/USA   *Dostoevskiĭ. The house of the dead (Thilo).
               *Pushkin. Evgeniĭ Onegin (Spalding).

1882 UK   *Salias de Turnemir (E. V.) grafinya. The Shalonski family
               (Cooke).

      USA   *Turgenev. Punin and Baburin (Scott).
               *   „   The song of triumphant love (Ford).
               *   „   An unfortunate woman (Scott).

1883 UK   Krȳlov. Original fables (Harrison).
               Pushkin. The captain's daughter (Igelström & Easton).
               [Turgenev. Fathers and sons (Schuyler)].
               [„   Rudin (anon.)].
               [„   Smoke (West)].
               [„   Virgin soil (Perry)].
      USA   Pushkin. The captain's daughter (Price).
               *Turgenev. Poems in prose (anon.).

1884 UK/USA   *Turgenev. The diary of a superfluous man (Gersoni).
                     „   Mumu (Gersoni).

      UK   *Turgenev. First love (Jerrold).
                     „   Punin and Baburin (Jerrold).

      USA   *Turgenev. Asya (Abbott).

1885 UK   *Tolstoĭ. My confession (anon.).
               *   „   The spirit of Christ's Christianity (from The Gospel
                             in brief) (anon.).
               *   „   What I believe (Popoff).
               *   „   „   „   „   (anon.).
      USA   *Tolstoĭ. What I believe (Smith).
               Turgenev. A sportsman's sketches (Abbott).

1886 UK/USA *Dostoevskiĭ. Crime and punishment (anon.).
                *Tolstoĭ. Anna Karenina (Dole).
                *   ,,   War and peace (Bell).
                Turgenev. Asya (Gersoni).
                      ,,   An unfortunate woman (Gersoni).

        UK   *Dostoevskiĭ. Injury and insult (Whishaw).
                Lermontov. A hero of our time (Lipmann).
                [Rȳleev. Poems (Davies)].

        USA   The epic songs of Russia (Hapgood).
                *Chernyshevskiĭ. What's to be done? (Dole & Skidelsky).
                *   ,,   ,, ,,   ,,   (Tucker).
                *Gogol'. The cloak (Hapgood).
                    ,,   Dead souls (Hapgood).
                *   ,,   How the two Ivans quarrelled (Hapgood).
                *   ,,   Old-fashioned farmers (Hapgood).
                *   ,,   The portrait (Hapgood).
                *   ,,   St. John's Eve (Hapgood).
                    ,,   Taras Bul'ba (Hapgood).
                Krȳlov. Russian fables (Stickney).
                *Nekrasov. Red-nosed frost (Smith).
                Tolstoĭ. Childhood, boyhood, youth (Hapgood).
                [,,   What I believe (Popoff)].
                *   ,,   What men live by (Delano).

        India   Pushkin. The captain's daughter (Godfrey).

1887 UK/USA Dostoevskiĭ. The house of the dead (Edwards).
                *   ,,   The idiot (Whishaw).
                *Tolstoĭ. The death of Ivan Il'ich (anon.).
                *   ,,   Family happiness (anon.).
                *   ,,   Kholstomir (anon.).
                *   ,,   Polikushka (anon.).
                *   ,,   Sebastopol. (Millet).
                *   ,,   The snowstorm (anon.).
                *   ,,   Two hussars (anon.).

        UK   Russian lyrics in English verse (Wilson).
                *Dostoevskiĭ. The friend of the family (Whishaw).
                *   ,,   The gambler (Whishaw).
                *Gogol'. The calash (anon.).
                [,,   The cloak (Hapgood)].
                [,,   Dead souls (Hapgood)].
                [,,   How the two Ivans quarrelled (Hapgood)].
                *   ,,   The king of the gnomes (anon.).
                [,,   Old-fashioned farmers (Hapgood)].
                [,,   The portrait (Hapgood)].
                [,,   St. John's Eve (Hapgood)].
                [,,   Taras Bul'ba (Hapgood)].
                Tolstoĭ. The Cossacks (anon.).
                *   ,,   The prisoner of the Caucasus (anon.).
                *   ,,   Three deaths (anon.).
             ?[Turgenev. Poems in prose (anon.)].

        USA   *Korolenko. Easter Eve (Delano).
                *   ,,   The forest soughs (Delano).
                *   ,,   The old bellringer (Delano).
                *   ,,   The Saghalien convict (Delano).
                *   ,,   Sketches of a Siberian tourist (Delano).
                *   ,,   The vagrant (Delano).
                *Sokhanskaya. Luboff Archipovna (Steel & Edmonds).
                *   ,,   The rusty linchpin (Steel & Edmonds).

1887 UK/USA Tolstoï. Albert (Dole.)
       *   ,,   The candle (Dole).
       *   ,,   The death of Ivan Il'ich (Dole).
       *   ,,   The devil's persistent, but God is resistant (Dole).
       *   ,,   Family happiness (anon.).
       *   ,,   The godson (Dole).
       *   ,,   How an imp paid for a crust (Dole).
       *   ,,   How much land does a man need? (Delano).
       *   ,,   ,,   ,,   ,,   ,,   ,,   ,, (Dole).
       *   ,,   If you neglect the fire, you don't put it out (Dole).
       *   ,,   Ilyas (Delano).
       *   ,,   ,, (Dole).
       *   ,,   The invaders (Dole).
       *   ,,   Ivan the fool (Dole).
       *   ,,   Kholstomir (Dole).
       *   ,,   Little girls wiser than old men (Dole).
       *   ,,   Lucerne (Dole).
       [,,   My confession (anon.)].
       *   ,,   An old acquaintance (Dole).
       *   ,,   Polikushka (Dole).
       *   ,,   The prisoner of the Caucasus (Dole).
       *   ,,   Recollections of a scorer (Dole).
       *   ,,   The repentant sinner (Dole).
       *   ,,   A Russian proprietor (Dole).
       *   ,,   A seed as big as a hen's egg (Dole).
       *   ,,   The snowstorm (Dole).
       [,,   The spirit of Christ's teaching (from The Gospel in brief) (anon.)].
       *   ,,   Three deaths (Dole).
       *   ,,   The three mendicants (Dole).
       *   ,,   Two brothers and gold (Dole).
       *   ,,   Two hussars (Dole).
       *   ,,   The two pilgrims (Delano).
       *   ,,   ,,   ,,   ,, (Dole).
       *   ,,   What to do? (Hapgood).
       *   ,,   Where love is, there God is also (Delano).
       *   ,,   ,,   ,,   ,,   ,,   ,,   ,, (Dole).
       *   ,,   The wood-cutting expedition (Dole).
      *Turgenev. The duellist (anon.).

1888 UK/USA Tolstoï. The Cossacks (Dole.)

      UK   *Dostoevskiï. The permanent husband (Whishaw).
       *   ,,   Uncle's dream (Whishaw).
       *Golovin. Nadia (Langenau).
       [Tolstoï. Albert (Dole)].
       [,,   Childhood, boyhood, youth (Hapgood)].
       *   ,,   The dominion of darkness (anon.).
       [,,   Lucerne (Dole)].
       [,,   The prisoner of the Caucasus (Dole)].
       [,,   Recollections of a scorer (Dole)].
       [,,   A Russian proprietor (Dole)].
       [,,   Three deaths (Dole)].
       [,,   Two hussars (Dole)].
       Turgenev. An unfortunate woman (Thompson).

      USA   Gogol'. Taras Bul'ba (Curtin).
       Pushkin. Selections from his poems (Panin).
       Tolstoï. The ABC (extracts) (Dole).
          ,,   Bear-hunting worse than slavery (Dole).
          ,,   The Cossacks (Kendall).
          ,,   Family happiness (Dole).

1888 USA   *Tolstoĭ.   God sees the truth, but waits (Dole).
         *   ,,   Life (Hapgood).
         *   ,,   The new ABC (extracts) (Dole).
         *   ,,   School scenes at Yasnaya Polyana (Dole).
           ,,   Sebastopol (Hapgood).
           ,,   ,,   (Kendall).
           ,,   Two hussars (anon.).
         *   ,,   War and peace (extracts: The physiology of war) (Smith).
         *   ,,   War and peace (second epilogue) (Smith).
           ,,   What men live by (Dole).
           ,,   What to do? (Dole?)
         *   ,,   Yermak (Dole).

1889 UK/USA Tolstoĭ.   War and peace (Dole).

     UK   *Garshin.   Mad love (anon.).
           [Tolstoĭ.   The ABC (extracts) (Dole)].
         [,,   Bear-hunting worse than slavery (Dole)].
         [,,   The candle (Dole)].
         [,,   The death of Ivan Ilʹich (Dole)].
         [,,   The devil's persistent, but God is resistant (Dole)].
         [,,   God sees the truth, but waits (Dole)].
         [,,   The godson (Dole)].
         [,,   How an imp paid for a crust (Dole)].
         [,,   How much land a man needs (Dole)].
         [,,   If you neglect the fire, you don't put it out (Dole)].
         [,,   Ilyas (Dole)].
         [,,   The invaders (Dole)].
         [,,   Ivan the fool (Dole)].
         [,,   Kholstomir (Dole)].
         [,,   Life (Hapgood)].
         [,,   Little girls wiser than old men (Dole)].
         [,,   The new ABC (extracts) (Dole)].
         [,,   An old acquaintance (Dole)].
         [,,   Polikushka (Dole)].
         [,,   The repentant sinner (Dole)].
         [,,   School scenes at Yasnaya Polyana (Dole)].
         [,,   A seed as big as a hen's egg (Dole)].
         [,,   The snowstorm (Dole)].
         [,,   The three mendicants (Dole)].
         [,,   Two brothers and gold (Dole)].
         [,,   The two pilgrims (Dole)].
         [,,   War and peace (extracts: The physiology of war) (Smith)].
         [,,   War and peace (second epilogue) (Smith).
         [,,   What I believe (Smith)].
         [,,   What men live by (Dole)].
         [,,   What to do? (Dole?).
         [,,   Where love is, there God is also (Dole)].
         [,,   The wood-cutting expedition (Dole)].
         [,,   Yermak (Dole)].

    USA   Tolstoĭ.   Anna Karenina (F.K.W.).

1890 UK/USA Myths and folk-tales of the Russians, etc. (Curtin).
          *Korolenko.   The blind musician (Stepnyak & Westall).
          *Tolstoĭ.   Work while ye have the light (Dillon).

     UK   Tales and legends from the land of the Tsar (Hodgetts).
          Tolstoĭ.   Childhood, boyhood, youth (Popoff).
         [,,   Family happiness (Dole)].

1890 UK   *Tolstoĭ. The fruits of enlightenment (Act 4 only) (Dillon).
                *   „   The Kreutzer sonata (Edwards).
                      „   „   „   „   (Thomson).
                [„   Sebastopol (Hapgood)].
                Turgenev. Poems in prose (MacMullan).

      USA   *Korolenko. The blind musician (Delano).
                Tolstoĭ. The candle (Tucker).
                      „   The dominion of darkness (anon.).
                      „   Family happiness (Loranger).
                      „   If you neglect the fire, you don't put it out (Tucker).
                      „   Ivan the fool (Tucker).
                *   „   The Kreutzer sonata (Lyster).
                *   „   „   „   „   (Tucker).
                *   „   Lessons of the Kreutzer sonata (Tucker).
                      „   Polikushka (Tucker).
                *   „   Toil (Cruger).

      India   *Gogol'. The inspector-general (Davies).

1891 UK/USA *Danilevskiĭ. The princess Tarakanova (Muchanov).
                *Grigorovich. The cruel city (Pierson).
                *Potapenko. A Russian priest (Gaussen).

      UK   Rhymes from the Russian (Pollen).
                Tales from the Russian (Edwards?).
                *Grigorovich. New Year's Eve (Edwards?).
                Lermontov. Taman (*from* A hero of our time) (Edwards?).
                Pushkin. The captain's daughter (Home).
                *   „   Dubrovsky (Edwards?).
                *Tolstoĭ. The fruits of enlightenment (Dillon).

      USA   *Korolenko. In bad society (Stepnyak & Westall).
                *   „   In two moods (Stepnyak & Westall).
                *Tolstoĭ. Church and state (Yarros).
                [„   The fruits of enlightenment (Dillon?)].
                      „   „   „   „   (Schumm).
                      „   If you neglect the fire, you don't put it out (Norraikow).
                      „   Ivan the fool (Norraikow).
                *   „   Man and woman (Schumm).
                      „   Money (*from* What to do?) (Yarros).
                *   „   The mother (Schumm).
                      „   Polikushka (Norraikow).

                *   „   A second supplement to the Kreutzer sonata
                              (Schumm).
                *   „   Shaker-Russian correspondence.
                *Turgenev. Ghosts (anon.).
                *Zagoskin. An evening on the Hopyor (Curtin).
                *   „   Kuzma Roschin (Curtin).
                *   „   The three suitors (Curtin).

1892 UK/USA Gogol'. The inspector-general (Sykes).
                *Potapenko. The general's daughter (Gaussen).
                Tolstoĭ (A. K.). Prince Serebryani (Curtin).

      UK   Russian Stories, vols. I & II.
                [Targum & The talisman (Borrow)].
                *Garshin. Wounded in battle (anon.).
                [Gogol'. The inspector-general (Davies)].
                *Korolenko. Easter Eve (Gaussen).
                      „   In bad society (anon.).
                [„   „   „   „   (Stepnyak & Westall)].

1892 UK   [Korolenko. In two moods (Stepnyak & Westall)].
           *   ,,   Makar's dream (anon.).
              ,,   The Saghalien convict (Gaussen).
        *Machtet. Vae victis (anon.).
        *Polevoĭ. Russian fairy tales (Bain).
        Pushkin. The amateur peasant-girl (Edwards).
           *   ,,   Gipsies (Edwards).
           *   ,,   History of the village of Goryukhina (Edwards).
           *   ,,   Kirdjali (Edwards).
              ,,   Peter the Great's negro (Edwards).
              ,,   The queen of spades (Edwards).
              ,,   The shot (Edwards).
              ,,   The snowstorm (Edwards).
              ,,   The undertaker (Edwards).
        Tolstoĭ. (A. K.). Prince Serebryani (Filmore).
        Tolstoĭ. How much land does a man need? (anon.).
        [,,   If you neglect the fire, you don't put it out
                    (Norraikow)].
        [,,   Ivan the fool (Norraikow)].
        [,,   Polikushka (Norraikow)].
        *   ,,   Why do men intoxicate themselves? (M.S.S.).
        *Volkhovskiĭ. A china cup and other stories (anon.).
        *   ,,   The new life (anon.).

      USA   Tolstoĭ. Anna Karenina (Townsend).
              ,,   A candle (Norraikow).
              ,,   The two pilgrims (Norraikow).
              ,,   What men live by (Norraikow).
              ,,   Where love is, there God is also (Norraikow).

1893 UK/USA *Potapenko. A father of six (Gaussen).
             *   ,,   An occasional holiday (Gaussen).
      UK   *Garshin. A coward (Voynich).
             *   ,,   From the memoirs of private Ivanov (Voynich).
             *   ,,   An occurrence (Voynich).
             *   ,,   The scarlet flower (Voynich).
        *Kostromitin. The last day of the carnival (Sosnin).
        Tolstoĭ. The three mendicants (Venning).
        *Turgenev. The watch (Williams).
        *Veselitskaya. Mimi's marriage (anon.).

      USA   Russian folksongs (Lineva).

1894 UK/USA *Dostoevskiĭ. Poor folk (Milman).
             *Goncharov. A common story (Garnett).
             Pushkin. The amateur peasant-girl (Keane).
               ,,   The captain's daughter (Keane).
               ,,   Dubrovsky (Keane).
               ,,   Kirdjali (Keane).
               ,,   The queen of spades (Keane).
               ,,   The shot (Keane).
               ,,   The snowstorm (Keane).
               ,,   The station-master (Keane).
               ,,   The undertaker (Keane).
             *Tolstoĭ. The kingdom of God is within you (Garnett).
             Turgenev. A nest of gentlefolk (Garnett).
               ,,   Rudin (Garnett).

      UK   Lermontov. The demon (Storr).
            Tolstoĭ. The kingdom of God is within you (Delano).
      USA   *Karazin. The two-legged wolf (Lanin).

1895 UK/USA *Gogol'. A madman's diary (Voynich).
       *   „   Marriage (Voynich).
              *Gorbunov. At the police inspector's (Voynich).
       *   „   Before the justice of the peace (Voynich).
       *   „   A seventeenth century letter from Ems (Voynich).
       *   „   "La traviata" (Voynich).
              *Kravchinskiĭ. The story of a kopeck (Voynich).
              *Ostrovskiĭ. A domestic picture (Voynich).
       *   „   Incompatibility of temper (Voynich).
              *Saltykov. The eagle as Mecaenas (Voynich).
       *   „   The recollections of Onésime Chenapan (Voynich).
       *   „   The self-sacrificing rabbit (Voynich).
              *Sleptsov. Choir practice (Voynich).
              *Tolstoĭ. Master and man (Beaman).
                „   „   „   „ (Rapoport & Kenworthy).
              Turgenev. Fathers and sons (Garnett).
                „   On the eve (Garnett).

       UK   ?The epic songs of Russia (Hapgood).
              *Kovalevskaya. Recollections of childhood (Bayley).
       *   „   „   „   (Cossel).
       *   „   Vera Barantzova (Stepnyak & Westall).
              *Potapenko. The curse of talent (Gaussen).
              *Tolstoĭ. The four Gospels harmonised (anon.).
              Turgenev. A sportsman's sketches (Richter).
                „   Spring floods (Richter).

       USA   *Kovalevskaya. Recollections of childhood (Hapgood).
              [Polevoĭ. Russian fairy tales (Bain)].
              *Tolstoĭ. Master and man (Ludwig & Halsted).
       *   „   „   „   „ (Miller).

1896 UK/USA *Tolstoĭ. The Gospel in brief (anon).
              Turgenev. Smoke (Garnett).
                „   A sportsman's sketches (Garnett).
                „   Virgin soil (Garnett).

       UK   *Pushkin. The Egyptian nights (Keane).
                „   Peter the Great's negro (Keane).
              *Salias de Turnemir (E. A.) *graf.* Kiriak (Edwards).
              Tolstoĭ. Church and state (Thomson).
       *   „   Drunkenness amongst the governing classes
                         (Thomson).
                „   On the relations of the sexes (Thomson).
       *   „   Patriotism and Christianity (anon.).
       *   „   Patriotism, or peace? (anon.).
       *   „   A sequel to the Kreutzer sonata (Thomson).
                „   Toil (Thomson).
                „   Why do men intoxicate themselves? (Thomson).

       USA   Kovalevskaya. Vera Barantzova (Rydingsvärd).
              Tolstoĭ. What men live by (Norraikow??).

1897 UK/USA *Turgenev. Clara Militch (Garnett).
       *   „   The dream (Garnett).
                „   First love (Garnett).
                „   Ghosts (Garnett).
                „   Mumu (Garnett).
                „   Poems in prose (Garnett).
                „   The song of triumphant love (Garnett).
                „   Spring floods (Garnett).

       UK   *Tolstoĭ. A visit to a slaughter-house (*from* The first step)
                         (anon.).

1897 UK   Tolstoĭ. Why do men intoxicate themselves? (anon.).

      France   Stories from the folklore of Russia (Blumenthal).

1898 UK/USA *Tolstoĭ. The Christian teaching (Chertkov).
              *   „   What is art? (Maude).
              Turgenev. Asya (Garnett).
              *   „   Faust (Garnett).
                   „   A Lear of the steppe (Garnett).

      UK   *Tolstoĭ. The emigration of the Doukhobortsi (anon.).
              *   „   Guy de Maupassant (ed. Chertkov).
                   „   Ivan the fool (anon.).
              *   „   The triumph of labour (anon.).

      USA   *Tolstoĭ. What is art? (Johnston).

1899 UK/USA Lermontov. A hero of our time (Nestor-Schnurmann).
              *Ostrovskiĭ. The storm (Garnett).
              *Turgenev. Andrei Kolosov (Garnett).
              *   „   The brigadier (Garnett).
              *   „   A correspondence (Garnett).
              *   „   A desperate character (Garnett).
                   „   The diary of a superfluous man (Garnett).
                   „   The duellist (Garnett).
              *   „   Enough (Garnett).
              *   „   The Jew (Garnett).
              *   „   Old portraits (Garnett).
                   „   Punin and Baburin (Garnett).
              *   „   Pyetushkov (Garnett).
              *   „   A strange story (Garnett).
              *   „   Three portraits (Garnett).
              *   „   A tour in the forest (Garnett).
                   „   An unhappy woman (Garnett).
              *   „   Yakov Pasinkov (Garnett).

      UK   *Bestuzhev. Ammalat Bey (Gordon).
              *   „   The snow of Shah-Dagh (Gordon).
              *Pushkin. Translations (of his poems) (Turner) (also pub-
                         lished in Russia).
              *Tolstoĭ. A letter on the Peace conference (Maude).
              *   „   On flogged and floggers (anon.).
              *   „   Resurrection (Maude) (1899–1900).
                   „   The spirit of Christ's teaching (*from* The Gospel
                         in brief) (ed. Chertkov).
              *   „   Stop and think! (Warren).
              *   „   Three parables (anon.).

      USA   *Merezhkovskiĭ. Julian the Apostate (Johnston).
               Tolstoĭ. Works (Dole, Hapgood & others).

1900 UK/USA *Tolstoĭ. The slavery of our times (Maude).

      UK   *Tolstoĭ. The empty drum (Maude).
                   „   The first step (Maude).
                   „   How an imp paid for a crust (Maude).
              *   „   Letters on war (anon.).
              *   „   Letters to friends on the personal Christian life
                         (anon.).
              *   „   Patriotism and government (Maude).
              *   „   Religion and morality (anon).

1900 UK   *Tolstoï.   Some social remedies (anon.).
              *   ,,   Thoughts on God (ed. Chertkov).
                   ,,   Work while ye have the light (anon.).
      USA   *Tolstoï.   Letters (anon.).
                   ,,   Resurrection (Britoff).
              [,,   ,,   (Maude)].
                   ,,   ,,   (Smith).

INDEX OF TRANSLATORS

Form of Reference:

A=Collections and Anthologies.
Tolstoĭ refers always to L. N. Tolstoĭ. (A. K. Tolstoĭ is referred to as Tolstoĭ (A. K.)).
<*German*, <*French*, etc.=translated from the German, French, etc.

Biographical References:

Allibone: Critical dictionary of English literature.
Boase: Boase's Modern English biography.
DAB: Dictionary of American biography.
DNB: Dictionary of national biography.
WWW: Who was who.
WWA: Who was who in America.
(Reference is generally made only to the fullest sources.)

Abbott (Franklin Pierce): Turgenev 2, 19 (*both* <*French*).
Aston (Frederic): Saltykov.

Bain (Robert Nisbet) 1854–1909 (*DNB*): Polevoĭ.
Baratynskaya (Anna Davydovna) *knyazhna* Abamelik: A1.
Bayley (Annie Margaret Clive) 1852– : Kovalevskaya 1 (<*Swedish*).
Beaman (Ardern George Hulme) 1857–1929 (*WWW*): Tolstoĭ 79.
Bell (*Mrs.* Clara Courtenay) *née* Poynter, 1834– : Tolstoĭ 104 (<*French*).
Benardaki (Nikolaĭ Dmitrevich): Griboedov.
Blumenthal (Verra Xenophontovna de) *née* Kalamatiano: A2.
Borrow (George) 1803–81 (*DNB*): A3–5.
Bowring (*Sir* John) 1792–1872 (*DNB, Boase*): A6, 7; Derzhavin 1.
Britoff (Henry): Tolstoĭ 91.
Browne (William Hand) 1828–1912 (*WWA*): Turgenev 21 (<*French*).
Butts (*Mrs.* Sophie) *née* Michell: Turgenev 21.

Chamier (Frederick) 1796–1870 (*DNB, Boase*): Zagoskin 2.
Chertkov (Vladimir Grigor'evich) 1854– : Tolstoĭ 32, 38, 45, 62, 63.
   (*Chertkov supervised and edited these translations, which were done by various members of the Tolstoyan community at Maldon (and later at Christchurch*)).
Conant (Samuel Stillman) 1831– (*Allibone*): Lermontov 1 (<*German*).
Cooke (Charles James): Salias de Turnemir (E. V.).
Cossel (Louise von): Kovalevskaya 2.
Cruger (Mary) 1834–1908 (*WWA*): Tolstoĭ 99.
Curtin (Jeremiah) 1840?–1906 (*DAB*): A8; Gogol' 9; Tolstoĭ(A.K.)4; Zagoskin1.

Davies (Thomas Hart-): Gogol' 6; Rȳleev.
Delano (*Mrs.* Aline P.) *née* Kuz'michova, 1845– : Korolenko 2, 4; Tolstoĭ 10, 70, 113.
Dilke (Ashton Wentworth) 1850–83 (*DNB, Boase*): Turgenev 27.
Dillon (Emile Joseph) 1854–1933 (*DNB*): Tolstoĭ 57, 120.
Dole (Nathan Haskell) 1852–1935 (*DAB*): Chernyshevskiĭ 1; Tolstoĭ 1, 9, 11, 12, 13, 14, 15, 16, 18, 23, 27, 28, 29, 34, 36, 37, 39, 47, 53, 60, 64, 66, 103, 105, 114, 117?, 118.
Donovan (*Mrs.* Alexina) *née* Loranger, *see* Loranger.

Easton (*Mrs.* Percy): Pushkin 10.
Edmonds (Jane Loring): Sokhanskaya.

Edwards (Henry Sutherland) 1828-1906 (*DNB*): Dostoevskiĭ 4 (<*French*); Tolstoĭ 71, 76?
Edwards (*Mrs.* Margaret Sutherland) *née* Watson: A21?; Pushkin 5; Salias de Turnemir (E. A.).
Elrington (John Battersby) (*Allibone*): Karamzin 2?
Evstaf'ev (Alekseĭ Grigor'evich) 1783-1857: Sumarokov.

Feldborg (Andreas Andersen) 1782-1838 (*see note to Karamzin 2 for biographical reference*): Karamzin 2?, 3 (<*German*).
Filmore (Henry Clare) 1861-   : Tolstoĭ (A. K.) 3.
Ford (Marian): Turgenev 17 ("*adapted*").

Galitzine (Mariya) *Princess, see* Golitsyn.
Garnett (*Mrs.* Constance) *née* Black, 1862-1946: Goncharov; Ostrovskiĭ; Tolstoĭ 69; Turgenev 1.
Gaussen (William Frederick Armytage) 1863-93: A18; Potapenko 1, 2, 3, 4.
Gersoni (Henry) 1844-97 (*Allibone*): Turgenev 8, 24.
Godfrey (Stuart Hill) 1861-1941 (*WWW*): Pushkin 12.
Golitsyn (Mariya) *knyazhna*: Tolstoĭ (A. K.) 2.
Gordon (*Sir* Home Seton Charles Montagu), *12th bart.*, 1871-1956: Bestuzhev 1 (<*French*).

Halsted (George Bruce) 1853-1922 (*DAB*): Tolstoĭ 82.
Hanstein (J. F.): Pushkin 8.
Hapgood (Isabel Florence) 1850-1928 (*DAB*): A10; Gogol' 2, 3, 5, 8; Kovalevskaya 3; Tolstoĭ 1, 2, 24?, 29, 43, 78, 95, 116.
Harrison (John Henry) 1829-1900 (*Boase*): Krȳlov 3; Tolstoĭ (A. K.) 1.
Hart-Davies (Thomas), *see* Davies.
Hawkins (Ann P.): Karamzin 1 (<*French*).
Hebbe (Gustaf Clemens) 1804-93: Bestuzhev 2; Pushkin 7.
Hodgetts (Edith M. S.): A11.
Home (*Mrs.* Mary Pamela Milne-): Pushkin 13.

Igelström (*mme* Jean): Pushkin 10.

Jerrold (Sidney) 1857-   (*Allibone*): Turgenev 5.
Johnston (Charles) 1867-1931 (*WWA*): Merezhkovskiĭ; Tolstoĭ 112.

Keane (T.): A20; Pushkin 4.
Kendall (*Mrs.* Laura E.): Tolstoĭ 48, 94.
Kenworthy (John Coleman): Tolstoĭ 80 (*rewrote Rapaport's translation*).
Kravchinskiĭ (Sergeĭ Mikhaĭlovich) 1852-95 (Sergius Stepnyak, *pseud.*) (*Chambers Encycl.*): Korolenko 1, 3; Kovalevskaya 4.

Lach-Szyrma (Krystyn) 1790 *or* 91-1866 (*Boase*): Gogol' 4.
Langenau (   ) *Baroness*: Golovin.
Lanin (Boris): Karazin.
Lansing (*Mrs.* Jennie H.) *née* Stickney, *see* Stickney.
Leeds (William Henry) 1786-1866 (*Allibone*): Zagoskin?
Lewis (William David) 1792-1881 (*DAB, Allibone*): A12.
Lineva (Evgeniya Eduardovna) 1854-   : A13.
Lipmann (R. I.): Lermontov 7.
Long (James) 1814-87: Krȳlov 2.
Loranger (Alexina) *afterwards Mrs.* Donovan: Tolstoĭ 55.
Ludwig (Yekaterina Alexandrovna): Tolstoĭ 82.
Lyster (Frederic): Tolstoĭ 74.

MacMullan (S. J.): Turgenev 12 (<*German & Danish*).
Maude (Aylmer) 1858-1938 (*DNB, Annual Register*): Tolstoĭ 7, 31, 87, 97, 111.
Maude (*Mrs.* Louise) *née* Shanks, 1855-1939 (*DNB, under Aylmer Maude*): Tolstoĭ 90.

Meiklejohn (James D.): Turgenev 18 (<*French*).
Meysenbug (Malwida von) 1816–1903: Tolstoĭ 42.
Michell (Sophie), *see* Butts (*Mrs.* Sophie) *née* Michell.
Miller (Hettie E.): Tolstoĭ 81.
Millet (Francis Davis) 1846–1912 (*DAB, Encycl. Brit.*): Tolstoĭ 5, 93 (*both* <*French*).
Milman (Lena): Dostoevskiĭ 7.
Muchanov (Ida de): Danilevskiĭ.

Naaké (John Theophilus): A14.
Nestor-Schnurmann (Ivan), *see* Schnurmann.
Norraikow (Adolphus) *graf*: Tolstoĭ 17, 22, 115?

Ourousoff, *the Princesses:* Markevich.

Panin (Ivan) 1855–   (*Allibone*): Pushkin 1.
Perry (Thomas Sergeant) 1845–1928 (*DAB*): Turgenev 26 (<*French*).
Pierson (Ernest De Lancey): Grigorovich.
Pollen (John) 1848–   : A15.
Popoff (Constantine): Tolstoĭ 44, 110.
Price (E. C.): Pushkin 11.
Proschwitz (Anna Maria von Rydingsvärd, *baroness von*), *see* Rydingsvärd.
Pulszky (Terézia) *née* Walder, 1815–   (*Allibone*): Lermontov 6.

Ralston (William Ralston Shedden) 1828–89 (*DNB, Boase*): A16; Krȳlov 1; Turgenev 9.
Rapoport (S.) [=Angelo Solomon Rappoport, 1871–1950?]: Tolstoĭ 80.
Richter (Edward): Turgenev 20, 22.
Rosenstrauch (Friedrich von): Sollogub.
Ross (George): Bulgarin.
Rydingsvärd (Anna Maria von) *baroness* von Proschwitz, 1856–   : Kovalevskaya 5.

S. (M. S.): Tolstoĭ 119 (<*German*).
Sala (George Augustus Henry) 1828–92 (*DNB, Boase*): Turgenev 7 (<*French*).
Saunders (W. H.): A19.
Schnurmann (Ivan Nestor-): Lermontov 8.
Schumm (George): Tolstoĭ 4, 58.
Schuyler (Eugene) 1840–90 (*DAB*): Tolstoĭ 46; Turgenev 4.
Scott (George W.): Turgenev 13, 23.
Shaw (Thomas Budd) 1813–62 (*DNB, Boase*): Lazhechnikov 1.
Skidelsky (Simon S.) 1862–   : Chernyshevskiĭ 1.
Smith (Huntington) 1857–   : Tolstoĭ 27, 106, 107, 108, 109, (*all* <*French*).
Smith (J. Sumner): Nekrasov.
Smith (William E.): Tolstoĭ 92.
Sosnin (J.): Kostromitin.
Spalding (Henry) 1840–   : Pushkin. 14.
Steel (Mary M.): Sokhanskaya.
Stephen (*Sir* Alexander Condie) 1850–1908 (*DNB*): Lermontov 2.
Stepnyak (Sergius) *pseud.*, *see* Kravchinskiĭ.
Stickney (Jennie H.) *afterwards Mrs.* Lansing: Krȳlov 4.
Storr (Francis): Lermontov 3.
Sykes (Arthur Alkin): Gogol′ 7.

Tchertkoff (Vladimir Grigorevich), *see* Chertkov.
Telfer (*Mrs.* John Buchan) *née* Mouravieff: Pushkin 6.
Thilo (Marie von): Dostoevskiĭ 3.
Thompson (Alfred Robert) (*Allibone*): Turgenev 25.
Thomson (William M.): Tolstoĭ 35, 73.
Tolstoy (George): Gogol′ 1.
Townsend (A. C.): Tolstoĭ 41.

RUSSIAN LITERATURE
THEATRE AND ART

RUSSIAN LITERATURE THEATRE AND ART

A Bibliography of works in
English, published 1900–1945

by

AMREI ETTLINGER, Ph.D.

JOAN M. GLADSTONE, B.A. (Lond.)

PREFACE

THE following bibliography is designed to serve two purposes. We wanted to make the approach to Russian and Soviet literature easier for the general reader, and to provide at the same time a basis for serious research work in the literary field.

The bibliography, which does not claim to be completely exhaustive, has been limited to books and pamphlets published between 1900 and 1945. As it is concerned mainly with Russian and Soviet literature and kindred subjects, the material had to be restricted, and many aspects of Russian and Soviet culture, such as music, had to be left out. Our object has been to supplement Mr. P. Grierson's admirable compilation, *Books on Soviet Russia, 1917–42*, published in 1943, to which we would refer all readers who are looking for information on the political, sociological and historical life of Russia. There is room for a future publication to cover the period before 1900, and a host of material in periodicals. Articles in periodicals are quoted here only when reference seemed absolutely necessary.

As to the practical use of the bibliography, we hope that the material is arranged clearly enough for finding items quickly. Round brackets designate the name of the series in which a book has been published, or may contain the abbreviation of a title which has been quoted before in full. Square brackets are used for more detailed information about the character of a book, particularly in the case of collections. In the section "Individual Russian Authors", collected works are noted before separate works.

For transliteration, the scheme of the Washington Library of Congress has been followed with certain modifications.

Owing to war conditions, not all the books mentioned have been available, and in a number of cases it has not been possible to verify details of contents, etc.

Our warmest thanks for untiring interest and constant help are due to Dr. W. Bonser, Professor J. Lavrin, and last, but not least, to Professor S. Konovalov.

AMREI ETTLINGER.
JOAN M. GLADSTONE.

December, 1945.

CONTENTS

6

ABBREVIATIONS

anon.	anonymous(ly).
c.	circa.
comp.	compiled.
cont.	continued.
ed.	edition, edited.
Engl.	English.
ibid.	ibidem.
ill.	illustrated.
incl.	including.
Ld.	London.
ltd.	limited.
n.d.	no date.
N.Y.	New York.
Oxf.	Oxford.
pl.	plates.
pp.	pages.
pseud.	pseudonym.
pt.	part.
repr.	reprint(ed).
rev.	revised.
transl.	translation, translated.
Univ. Pr.	University Press.
U.S.A.	for : published in the United States, publisher unknown.
VOKS.	Soviet Union Society for Cultural Relations with Foreign Countries.
vol(s).	volume(s).

I. GENERAL BIBLIOGRAPHY

BAKER (E. A.) and PACKMAN (J.): *A guide to the best fiction*, Engl. and American, incl. transl. from foreign languages. New ed. 634 pp. Ld. Routledge, 1932.

BRISTOL PUBLIC LIBRARY: *Russia, a select reading list*. 27 pp. Bristol, 1942.

CAMPBELL (J. M.): *Selected list of Russian books*; comp. for the Free Public Library Commission of Massachusetts. (Foreign book list, 7.) N.Y. 1916.

Commercial Year Book of the Soviet Union. See: Soviet Union Year Book.

DOMINCOVICH (H. A.): *Russian literature for the Engl. classroom.* Engl. Journal, December, 1942.

GRIERSON (P.): *Books on Soviet Russia, 1917–1942*; a bibliography and a guide to reading. 354 pp. Ld. Methuen, 1943.

KERNER (R. J.): *Slavic Europe*; a selected bibliography in the Western European languages, comprising history, languages and literatures. (Harvard Bibliographies. Library series, 1.) 402 pp. Cambridge, Mass. Harvard Univ. Pr., 1918.

MARTIANOFF (N. N.): *Books available in Engl. by Russians and on Russia.* 4th ed. 48 pp. N.Y. Martianoff, 1942.

MARTIANOFF (N. N.) and STERN (M. A.): *Almanac of Russian artists in America.* 249 pp. Ill. N.Y. Martinanoff, 1932.

MOHRENSCHILDT (S. von): *Books in Engl. on Russian literature, 1917–42.* Russian Review, autumn 1942.

Soviet Union Year Book, 1930. Comp. and ed. by A. A. Santalov and L. Segal. 670 pp. Ld. Allen & Unwin, 1930. [Contains: Who's Who in literature.]

U.S.S.R. Handbook. 643 pp. Ld. Gollancz, 1936. [Contains: a chapter on literature, and a Who's Who.]

WRIGHT (C. T. H.): *A classified list of books relating to Russia and Russian affairs*, mostly published in England since 1910. 23 pp. 1917.

II. STUDIES IN RUSSIAN LITERATURE

GENERAL WORKS

BARING (M.) : *Landmarks in Russian literature.* 299 pp. 3rd ed. Ld. Methuen, 1916.
—— *The mainsprings of Russia.* 328 pp. Ld. Nelson, 1914.
—— *An outline of Russian literature.* 256 pp. Ld. Williams & Norgate, 1915. 2nd ed. Oxf. Univ. Pr., 1928. Repr. Thornton Butterworth, 1929. (Home university library.)
—— *Russian essays and stories.* 295 pp. Ld. Methuen, 1908.
—— *The Russian people.* 366 pp. Ld. Methuen, 1911.
BOWRA (C. M.) : *The heritage of symbolism.* 340 pp. N.Y. Macmillan, 1943. [Contains : chapter on Blok.] 244 pp. Ld. Macmillan, 1943.
BRASOL (B. L.) : *The mighty three : Pushkin, Gogol, Dostoevsky.* A critical trilogy, with an introduction by C. A. Manning. 295 pp. N.Y. and Ld. Williams & Norgate, 1937.
BRUECKNER (A.) : *A literary history of Russia.* Ed. by E. H. Minns. Transl. from the German by H. Havelock. (Library of literary history, 9.) 558 pp. Ld. Fisher Unwin, 1908.
CHADWICK (H. M.) and CHADWICK (N. K.) : *Growth of literature,* II, pt. 1 : Russian oral literature, pp. 1–298. Cambridge Univ. Pr., 1936.
EASTMAN (M.) : *Art and the life of action ; with other essays.* 189 pp. Ld. Allen, 1935.
—— *Artists in uniform : a study of literature and bureaucratism.* 261 pp. Ld. Allen & Unwin, 1934.
ELTON (O.) : *Essays and addresses.* 275 pp. N.Y. Longmans, 1939. [Incl. essays on Pushkin and Chekhov.]
FLORES (A.) ed. : *Literature and Marxism* ; a controversy by Soviet critics. (Critics group series, 9.) 95 pp. N.Y. Critics Group, 1938.
GUTHRIE (A. L.) : *Russian literature ; a study outline.* 53 pp. N.Y., 1917.
HAPGOOD (I. F.) : *A survey of Russian literature,* with selections. 279 pp. N.Y. Chautauqua Pr., 1902.

HUTTON (J. A.): *Guidance on Russia from her literature.* 169 pp. Ld. Hodder & Stoughton, 1930.

KAUN (A. S.) and SIMMONS (E. J.) ed.: *Slavic studies*; 16 essays in honour of G. R. Noyes. 242 pp. Ithaca, Cornell Univ. Pr., 1943.

KROPOTKIN (Prince P. A.): *Russian literature.* 341 pp. N.Y. McClure, Phillips, 1905.

   With title: *Russian literature, ideals and realities.* 341 pp. Ld. Duckworth, 1915.

KUNITZ (J.): *Russian literature and the Jew; a sociological inquiry into the nature and origin of literary patterns.* 195 pp. N.Y. Columbia Univ. Pr., 1929.

LAVRIN (J.): *Studies in European literature.* 222 pp. Ld. Constable, 1929. [Essays on: Turgenev; Tolstoy and Nietzsche; Chekhov and Maupassant; Dostoevsky and Proust.]

—— *Aspects of modernism: from Wilde to Pirandello.* 247 pp. Ld. Nott, 1936. [Incl. essays on: Blok, Esenin, Rozanov.]

—— *Russian literature.* 80 pp. (Benn's sixpenny library.) Ld. Benn, 1927.

MACKIEWIECZ (M. N.): *Russian minds in fetters.* 184 pp. Ld. Allen & Unwin, 1932.

MAIS (S. P. B.): *Why we should read.* 311 pp. N.Y. Dodd, Mead & Co, 1921. [Incl. essays on: Chekhov, Dostoevsky, Gogol, Goncharov, Lermontov, Nekrasov, Pushkin, Tolstoy, Turgenev.]

MANNING (C. A.): *Ukrainian literature; studies of the leading authors.* 126 pp. N.Y. Ukrainian Nat. Association, 1944.

MASARYK (T. G.): *The spirit of Russia; studies in history, literature and philosophy.* Transl. by E. and C. Paul. 2 vols. 480, 585 pp. Ld. Allen & Unwin, 1919.

MILIUKOV (P. N.): *Outlines of Russian culture.* Ed. by M. M. Karpovich. Transl. by V. Ughet and E. Davis. 3 pts. (Pt. 2: Literature.) 126 pp. Philadelphia. Univ. of Pennsylvania Pr., 1942.

MIRSKY (Prince D. S.): *Contemporary Russian literature, 1881–1925.* (Contemporary literature series.) 372 pp. Ld. Routledge, 1933.

—— *A history of Russian literature from the earliest times to the death of Dostoevsky* (1881). 388 pp. Ld. Routledge, 1927.

—— *Modern Russian literature.* 120 pp. (The world's manuals). Ld. Oxf. Univ. Pr., 1925.

New Directions in prose and poetry, 1941. Ed. by J. Laughlin. 729 pp. Norfolk, Conn. New Directions, 1941. [Contains: pp. 515–650. Soviet Russian poetry, a survey, translations and critical essays.]

OLGIN (M. J.) : *A guide to Russian literature (1820–1917).* 323 pp. Ld. Cape, 1921. [Contains translated extracts from Russian critics, a commentary by Olgin and analysis of selected works.]

SEGAL (L.) : *The romantic movement in Russia.* 91 pp. Portsmouth, 1922.

SIMMONS (E. J.) : *English literature and culture in Russia (1553–1840).* 357 pp. (Harvard studies in comparative literature, 12.) Cambridge, Mass. Harvard Univ. Pr., 1935.

—— *Outline of modern Russian literature, 1880–1940.* 93 pp. Ithaca. Cornell Univ. Pr., 1943.

SHAKNOVSKY : *A short history of Russian literature.* Transl. with a supplementary chapter by S. Tomkeyeff. 180 pp. Ld. Kegan Paul, 1921.

SOVIET WRITERS' CONGRESS, 1934 : Problems of Soviet literature ; reports and speeches at the First Soviet Writers' Congress, by A. A. Zhdanov and others. Ed. by H. G. Scott. 279 pp. N.Y. International Publishers, 1935. Ld. Lawrence, 1936.

STEPHENS (W.) : *The soul of Russia.* 307 pp. Ld. Macmillan, 1916.

STRUVE (G.) : *Soviet Russian literature.* 270 pp. Ld. Routledge, 1935.

—— *25 years of Soviet Russian literature, 1918–1943.* New ed. of : *Soviet Russian literature.* 347 pp. Ld. Routledge, 1944.

U.S.S.R. speaks for itself. 4 pts. (in 1). Pt. 4 : *Culture and leisure.* Ld. Lawrence & Wishart, 1943.

VOYNICH (E. L.) : *The humour of Russia.* Ld. Scott, 1911. [With specimens.]

WALISZEWSKI (K.) : *A history of Russian literature.* 450 pp. (Short histories of the literatures of the world, 8.) Ld. Heinemann, 1900 ; Appleton, 1927.

WIENER (L.) : *An interpretation of the Russian people.* 248 pp. N.Y. McBride, 1915.

WILLIAMS (H. W.) : *Russia of the Russians.* 430 pp. Ld. Pitman, 1914. Repr. 1920. [Contains chapters on the press, literature, theatre.]

WOOLF (V.) : *The Russian point of view.* (*In* : The common reader. Ld. Hogarth Pr., 1925.)

YARMOLINSKY (A.) : *Russian literature.* 56 pp. (Reading with a purpose, 61.) Chicago. American Library Association, 1931.

POETRY

JARINTZOV (N.): *Russian poets and poems: classics and moderns.*
With an introduction on Russian versification. Vol. I:
Classics. 357 pp. Oxf. Blackwell, 1917. [Only vol. I seems
to have been published.]

KAUN (A. S.): *Soviet poets and poetry.* 208 pp. Berkeley. Univ.
of California Pr., 1943.

NEWMARCH (R. H.): *Poetry and progress.* Ld. Lane, 1907.

PATRICK (G. Z.): *Popular poetry in Soviet Russia.* 289 pp.
Berkeley. Univ. of California Pr., 1929. [Account of post-
revolutionary peasant poetry, with transl.]

ZNAKOMY (L.) and LEVIN (D.): *A decade of Soviet poetry.* (*In:*
New Directions in prose and poetry, 1941, pp. 621–27.)

THE NOVEL

LAVRIN (J.): *An introduction to the Russian novel.* 216 pp. Ld.
Methuen, 1942.

MIRSKY (Prince D. S.): *See:* WALPOLE (H.) and others: *Tendencies of the modern novel.*

PERSKY (S.): *Contemporary Russian novelists.* Transl. from the
French by F. Eisemann. 317 pp. 2nd ed. Ld. Palmer, 1915.

PHELPS (W. L.): *Essays on Russian novelists.* With a bibliography by A. Keogh. 322 pp. N.Y. Macmillan, 1911.

VOGÜÉ (E. M. M., vicomte de): *The Russian novel.* Transl. from
the 11th French ed. by H. A. Sawyer. 337 pp. Ld. Chapman & Hall, 1913; N.Y. 1916.

WALPOLE (H.) and others: *Tendencies of the modern novel.* Ill.
160 pp. Ld. Allen & Unwin, 1934. [Contains: MIRSKY
(Prince D. S.): *The Soviet Russian novel.*]

III. STUDIES IN RUSSIAN THEATRE
AND ART

DRAMA, THEATRE, FILM

AROSSEV (A.) comp.: *Soviet cinema; a compilation by many authors*. 312 pp. Moscow. VOKS, 1935.

BAKSHY (A.): *The path of the modern Russian stage, and other essays*. Ld. Palmer & Haywood, 1916.

BATES (A.): *Russian drama*. Ld. Historical Publishing Co., 1906.

BROWN (B. W.): *Theatre at the left*. 105 pp. U.S.A. Booke shop, 1938.

BRYHER, pseud.: *Film problems of Soviet Russia*. 140 pp. Ld. Territet, 1929.

CARTER (H.): *The new spirit in the European theatre, 1914–1924; a comparative study of the changes effected by war and revolution*. 292 pp. Ld. Benn, 1925.

—— *The new spirit in the Russian theatre, 1917–1928, and a sketch of the Russian cinema and radio*. Pl. 348 pp. N.Y. Brentano's; Ld. Shaylor, 1929.

—— *The new theatre and cinema of Soviet Russia*. 278 pp. Ld. Chapman & Dadd, 1924.

CHANDLER (F. W.): *Aspects of modern drama*. N.Y. Macmillan, 1918.

—— *Modern continental playwrights*. (Plays and playwrights series.) 711 pp. N.Y. and Ld. Harper, 1931. [Contains: bibl. of Russian authors in Engl.]

CHARQUES (R. D.) ed.: *Footnotes to the theatre*. Pl. 335 pp. Ld. Davies, 1939.

CLARK (B. H.): *A study of modern drama; a handbook . . . of the last three quarters of a century*. Rev. ed. 534 pp. N.Y. and Ld. Appleton, 1938.

COLEMAN (A. P.): *Humour in the Russian comedy from Catherine to Gogol*. (Columbia Univ. Slavonic studies, vol. 2.) 92 pp. N.Y. Columbia Univ. Pr., 1925.

DANA (H. W. L.): *Drama in wartime Russia*. N.Y. National Council of American-Soviet Friendship, 1943.

14

—— *Handbook on Soviet drama: lists of theatres, plays, operas, ballets, films, and books and articles about them.* 158 pp. N.Y. American Russian Institute, 1938.

DICKINSON (T. H.) and others: *The theatre in a changing Europe.* 492 pp. Ld. Putnam, 1938. [Contains: The Russian theatre, by J. Gregor and H. W. L. Dana.]

EFIMOVA (N. Y.): *Adventures of a Russian puppet theatre.* Transl. by E. Mitcoff. 199 pp. Birmingham, Michigan. McPharlin, 1935.

EISENSTEIN (S. M.): *The film sense.* Transl. by J. Leyda. 207 pp. Ld. Faber, 1943.

FLANAGAN (H.): *Shifting scenes of the modern European theatre.* Pl. 280 pp. Ld. Harrap, 1929.

FOVITSKY (A. L.): *Moscow Art Theatre and its distinguishing characteristics.* Ill. 48 pp. N.Y. Chernoff, 1922.

FÜLÖP-MILLER (R.) and GREGOR (J.): *Mind and face of Bolshevism, an examination of cultural life in Soviet Russia.* Transl. by F. S. Flint and D. F. Tait. 308 pp. Ld. Putnam, 1927.

—— *The Russian theatre, its character and history, with special reference to the revolutionary period.* Transl. by P. England. Ill. 136 pp. Philadelphia. Lippincott; Ld. Harrap, 1930.

GRIFFITH (H. F.) ed.: *Playtime in Russia,* by various authors. Ill. 249 pp. Ld. Methuen, 1935.

GYSEGHEM (A. van): *Theatre in Soviet Russia.* Ill. 220 pp. Ld. Faber, 1943.

HOUGHTON (N.): *Moscow rehearsals: an account of methods of production in the Soviet theatre.* Ill. 291 pp. N.Y. Harcourt Brace, 1936.

—— Slightly different ed. 313 pp. Ld. G. Allen, 1938.

KOMMISSARZHEVSKY (F. F.): *Costume of the theatre.* 178 pp. Ld. Bles, 1931.

—— *Myself and the theatre.* Ill. 205 pp. Ld. Heinemann, 1929.

LONDON (K.): *The seven Soviet arts.* Transl. by E. Bensinger. Ill. 382 pp. Ld. Faber, 1937: N.Y. Yale Univ. Pr., 1938.

MACLEOD (J.): *The new Soviet theatre.* Ill. 242 pp. Ld. Allen & Unwin, 1943.

MARKOV (P. A.): *The Soviet theatre.* (New Soviet library, 3.) 176 pp. Ld. Gollancz, 1934.

MOSCOW THEATRE FOR CHILDREN: *An album of photographs illustrating the work of the oldest professional theatre for children.* 96 pp. Ld. M. Lawrence, 1934.

NEMIROVICH—DANCHENKO (V. I.): *My life in the Russian theatre.* Transl. by J. Cournos. 358 pp. Ld. Bles, 1936.

NILSEN (V. S.) : *The cinema as a graphic art ; on a theory of representation in the cinema.* With an appreciation by S. M. Eisenstein. Transl. by S. Garry. Ill. 227 pp. Ld. Newnes, 1937.

PERRY (H. ten Eyck) : *Masters of dramatic comedy and their social themes.* 428 pp. Cambridge, Mass. Harvard Univ. Pr., 1939.

PUDOVKIN (V. I.) : *Film acting : a course of lectures delivered at the State Institute of Cinematography, Moscow.* Transl. by I. Montagu. (Filmcraft series.) 153 pp. Ld. Newnes, 1935.

—— *Film technique : 5 essays and 2 addresses.* Transl. and annotated by I. Montagu. (Filmcraft series.) 204 pp. Ld. Newnes, 1933.

ROTHA (P.) : *The film till now ; a survey of the cinema.* 362 pp. Ld. Cape, 1930.

—— *Movie parade.* 142 pp. Ld. Studio, 1936.

SAYLER (O. M.) : *Inside the Moscow Art Theatre.* Ill. 240 pp. N.Y. Brentano's, 1925 ; Ld. Brentano's, 1928.

—— *Russian players in America.* (Etched text and pictures.) Ltd. ed. U.S.A. Wall, 1923.

—— *Russian theatre under the revolution.* 273 pp. Boston. Little, Brown, 1920.

—— *Russian theatre.* 364 pp. Ld. and N.Y. Brentano's, 1922. [Enlarged ed. of above.]

SHALIAPIN (F. I.) : *Pages from my life ; an autobiography.* Transl. by H. M. Buck. Rev. and enlarged ed. by K. Wright. 345 pp. N.Y. Harper, 1927.

—— With title : *Man and mask ; forty years in the life of a singer.* Transl. P. Mégroz. 413 pp. Ld. Gollancz, 1932.

SMIRNOV (A. A.) : *Shakespeare : a Marxist interpretation.* Transl. by S. Volochova and others : special ed. for the New Theatre League. (Critics group series, 2.) 95 pp. N.Y. Critics Group, 1936.

STANISLAVSKY (K.) [pseud. of K. S. Alekseev] : *An actor prepares.* Transl. by E. R. Hapgood. 313 pp. Ld. Bles, 1936.

—— *My life in art.* Transl. by J. J. Robbins. 586 pp. Ld. Bles, 1924.

The theatre in the U.S.S.R. Published by the Soviet Union Society for Cultural Relations with Foreign Countries. (VOKS), vol. 6. Ill. 108 pp. Moscow, 1934.

VOLKOV (N.) : *Moscow theatre.* Issued in English by Intourist for the second annual theatre festival. 86 pp. Moscow, 1934.

WEIR (A. E.): *Thesaurus of the arts: drama, music . . . painting, screen . . . literature, sculpture, architecture, ballet.* N.Y. 1943.

WIENER (L.): *Contemporary drama of Russia.* (Contemporary drama series.) N.Y. Little, 1924.

ZELIKSON (M.) comp.: *The artist of the Kamerni theatre: 1914–1934.* Ill. 212 pp. Moscow, 1935.

BALLET

AMBROSE (K.): *Ballet-lovers' pocket book.* 64 pp. Ld. Black, 1943.

ANTHONY (G.): *Massine. See:* MASSINE.

—— *Russian ballet; camera studies.* With an introduction by A. Haskell. Ltd. ed. Pl. 32 pp. Ld. Bles, 1939.

Ballet Russe; the heart of ballet music. Ill. 96 pp. N.Y., c. 1942.

BEAUMONT (C. W.): *Complete book of ballets; a guide to the principal ballets of the 19th and 20th century.* Pl. 900 pp. Ld. Putnam, 1938.

—— *Design for the ballet.* Ed. by C. G. Holme. Special winter number of the *Studio.* 152 pp. Ld. Studio Ltd., 1937.

—— New rev. ed. 156 pp. Ld. Studio, 1939.

—— *Diaghilev. See:* DIAGHILEV (S.).

—— *The Diaghilev ballet. See:* DIAGHILEV (S.).

—— *Five centuries of ballet design.* Pl. 136 pp. Ld. Studio Ltd., 1939.

—— *Fokine. See:* FOKINE (M.)

—— *A history of ballet in Russia, 1613–1881.* Pl. 140 pp. Ld. Beaumont, 1930.

—— *Nijinsky. See:* NIJINSKY (V.).

—— *Pavlova. See:* PAVLOVA (A.).

—— *Short history of ballet.* Pl. (Essays on dancing and dancers, 4.) 40 pp. Ld. Beaumont, 1933.

—— *Supplement to Complete book of ballets.* Pl. 208 pp. Ld. Beaumont, 1942.

BENOIS (A.): *Reminiscences of the Russian ballet.* Transl. by M. Britnieva. Pl. 414 pp. Ld. Putnam, 1941.

BOURMAN (A.) and LYMAN (D.): *The tragedy of Nijinsky. See:* NIJINSKY (V.).

DANDRÉ (V. E.): *Anna Pavlova. See:* PAVLOVA (A.).

B

DIAGHILEV (S.):
—— BEAUMONT (C. W.): *The Diaghilev ballet in London; a personal record.* 355 pp. Ld. Putnam, 1940.
—— BEAUMONT (C. W.): *Sergei Diaghilev.* Pl. (Essays on dancing and dancers, 3.) 28 pp. Ld. Beaumont, 1933.
—— HASKELL (A. L.) and NOUVEL (W.): *Diaghileff: his artistic and private life.* Pl. 359 pp. Ld. Gollancz, 1936.
—— LIFAR (S.): *Sergei Diaghilev; his life, his work, his legend: an intimate biography.* Pl. 399 pp. Ld. Putnam, 1940.
FOKINE (M.):
—— BEAUMONT (C. W.): *Michael Fokine and his ballets.* 177 pp. Ld. Beaumont, 1935.
HASKELL (A. L.): *Ballet, a complete guide to appreciation.* Ill. (Pelican special.) 172 pp. Harmondsworth, 1938. Repr. 1943.
—— *Diaghilev. See:* DIAGHILEV (S.).
—— *Tamara Karsavina. See:* KARSAVINA (T.).
HOPPÉ (E. O.): *Studies from the Russian ballet.* Fine Art Society, n.d.
HYDEN (W.): *Pavlova. See:* PAVLOVA (A.).
IVCHENKO (V. Y.) [V. Svetlov, pseud.]: *Anna Pavlova. See:* PAVLOVA (A.).
KAMENEFF (V.): *Russian ballet through Russian eyes.* 42 pp. Ld. Russian Book Shop, 1936.
KARSAVINA (T.): *Theatre street; reminiscences.* With foreword by Sir J. M. Barrie. 341 pp. N.Y. and Ld. Heinemann, 1931.
—— HASKELL (A. L.): *Tamara Karsavina.* (Artists of the dance, 4.) 2nd ed. 36 pp. Pl. Ld. British-Continental, 1931.
LEGAT (N. G.): *Ballet russe: memoirs of N. Legat.* Transl. with a foreword by Sir P. Dukes. Dedicatory poem by J. Masefield. Pl. 67 pp. Ld. Methuen, 1939.
—— *Story of the Russian school.* Transl. by Sir P. Dukes. (Artists of the dance, 8.) Pl. 87 pp. Ld. British-Continental, 1932.
LIEVEN (Prince P. A.): *The birth of the Ballets Russes.* Transl. by L. Zarine. Pl. 377 pp. Boston. Houghton, 1936.
LIFAR (S.): *Ballet, traditional to modern.* Transl. by C. W. Beaumont. Pl. 302 pp. Ld. Putnam, 1938.
—— *Sergei Diaghilev. See:* DIAGHILEV (S.).
MASSINE (L.):
—— ANTHONY (G.): *Massine: camera studies.* With an appreciation by S. Sitwell. Pl. 33 pp. Ld. Routledge, 1939.

NIJINSKY (V.): *Diary*. Transl. and ed. by R. Nijinsky. Pl. 187 pp. N.Y. Simon & Schuster, 1936; Ld. Gollancz, 1937.
—— BEAUMONT (C. W.): *Vaslev Nijinsky*. (Essays on dancing and dancers, 2.) Ill. 28 pp. Ld. Beaumont, 1932.
—— BOURMAN (A.) and LYMAN (D.): *The tragedy of Nijinsky*. Ill. 291 pp. Hale, Wittlesley House, 1937.
—— NIJINSKY (R.): *Nijinsky*. Foreword by P. Claudel. Ill. 447 pp. N.Y. Simon & Schuster, 1934; Ld. Gollancz, 1936.
OLIVEROFF (A.): *Flight of the swan; a memory of Pavlova. See:* PAVLOVA (A.).
PAVLOVA (A.):
—— BEAUMONT (C. W.): *Anna Pavlova*. (Essays on dancing and dancers, 1.) Ill. 24 pp. Ld. Beaumont, 1932.
—— DANDRÉ (V. E.): *Anna Pavlova*. Ill. 409 pp. N.Y. Goldberger, 1933; Ld. Cassell, 1932.
—— HYDEN (W.): *Pavlova: the genius of dance*. Ill. 208 pp. Re-issue. Ld. Constable, 1934.
—— IVCHENKO (V. Y.) [pseud. V. Svetlov]: *Anna Pavlova; a choreographic portrait*. (Artists of the dance.) 40 pp. Ill. Ld. British-Continental, c. 1930.
—— OLIVEROFF (A.): *Flight of the swan: a memory of Pavlova, as told to J. Gill*. Ill. 258 pp. N.Y. Dutton, 1932.
PROPERT (W. A.): *The Russian ballet, 1921–1929*. With a preface by J. E. Blanche. Pl. 103 pp. Ld. Lane, 1931.
SCHWEZOFF (I.): *Russian somersault*. Autobiography. 414 pp. N.Y. Harper, 1936.
—— With title: *Borzoi*. Ill. 441 pp. Ld. Hodder, 1935.
STOKES (A.): *Russian ballets*. 213 pp. Ld. Faber, 1935.
TERRY (Dame E.): *Russian ballet*. Ill. Indianapolis. Bobbs, 1913.
VALOIS (N. de): *Invitation to the ballet*. Ill. 304 pp. Ld. Lane, 1937; Oxf., 1938.

FINE ARTS

APLETIN (M.) ed.: *Painting, sculpture and graphic art in the U.S.S.R.* VOKS ill. Almanac, 1934.
BUXTON (D. R.): *Russian medieval architecture, with an account of the Transcaucasian styles and their influence in the west*. Pl. 112 pp. Cambridge Univ. Pr., 1934.
CHEN (J.): *Soviet art and artists*. 106 pp. Ld. Pilot Pr., 1944.

CONWAY (Sir W. M.) : *Art treasures in Soviet Russia.* Ill. 284 pp. Ld. Arnold, 1925.

FARBMAN (M. S.) ed. : *Masterpieces of Russian painting, 11th to 18th century.* Text by A. I. Anisimov and others. Pl. 124 pp. Ld. Europa, 1930.

FREEMAN (J.) and others, ed. : *Voices of October ; art and literature in Soviet Russia.* 317 pp. Ld. Vanguard Pr., 1930.

GRINDEA (M.) : *Soviet literature, art, music.* (Today's booklets. Adam international anthology.) 48 pp. Ld. Practical Pr., 1942.

HOLME (C. G.) ed. : *Art in the U.S.S.R.* (Studio Special.) Ill. 138 pp. Ld. Studio, 1935.

KONDAKOV (N. P.) : *The Russian icon.* Transl. by E. H. Minns. Ill. 226 pp. Oxf. Clarendon Pr., 1927.

LONDON (K.) : *The seven Soviet arts.* Transl. by E. Bensinger. Ill. 382 pp. Ld. Faber, 1937 ; N.Y. Yale Univ. Pr., 1938.

LOUKOMSKY (G. K.) : *History of modern Russian painting, 1840–1940.* 184 pp. Ld. Hutchinson, 1945.

LUNACHARSKY (A. V.) : *Selected works of art from the Fine Art Museum of the U.S.S.R, with notes and introduction.* '(Art ed. of the Association of Painters of the Revolution, 1.) Pl. N.Y. Amkniga, 1930.

MILIUKOV (P. N.) : *Outlines of Russian culture*, pt. 3 : *Architecture, painting and music.* Ed. by M. Karpovich. 159 pp. Philadelphia. Univ. of Pennsylvania, 1942.

NEWMARCH (R. H.) : *The Russian arts.* Ill. N.Y. Dutton, 1916.

Soviet Literature, Art, Music. See : GRINDEA (M.).

TALBOT RICE (D.) ed. : *Russian art.* Publication in connection with the Exhibition of Russian Art, Belgrave Square, 1935. Ill. 136 pp. Ld. Guerney & Jackson, 1935.

IV. RUSSIAN LITERATURE, IN ENGLISH TRANSLATIONS, FROM THE 19TH CENTURY TO THE PRESENT TIME

ANTHOLOGIES : GENERAL

BECHHOFER (C. E.) [afterwards Roberts] ed. and partly transl. : *A Russian anthology in English.* 288 pp. Ld. Kegan Paul, 1917.

COURNOS (J.) ed. : *A treasury of Russian life and humour.* 676 pp. N.Y. Coward McCann, 1943. [Contains : prose, poetry and plays.]

FREEMAN (J.) and others, ed. : *Voices of October ; art and literature in Soviet Russia.* 317 pp. Ld. Vanguard Pr., 1930.

GANGULEE (N. N.) ed. : *The Russian horizon ; an anthology.* Foreword by H. G. Wells. 278 pp. Ld. Allen & Unwin, 1943. [Contains : quotations from prose and poetry.]

GRINDEA (M.) : *Soviet literature, art, music.* (Today's booklets. Adam international anthology.) 48 pp. Ld. Practical Pr., 1942.

GUERNEY (B. G.) ed. : *Treasury of Russian literature, being a comprehensive selection of many of the best things by numerous authors.* With a foreword and biographical and critical notes. 1,048 pp. N.Y. Vanguard, 1943.

KONOVALOV (S.). *See under :* COLLECTIONS OF SHORT STORIES.

REAVEY (G.) and SLONIM (M.) ed. and transl. : *Soviet literature : an anthology.* 430 pp. Ld. Wishart, 1933. [Contains : stories and extracts from novels and poetry. Stories and extracts from : Babel ; Bely ; Bezimensky ; Fadeev ; Fedin ; Gabrilovich ; Gladkov ; V. Ivanov ; Kataev ; Kaverin ; Leonov ; Olesha ; Pasternak ; Pilnyak ; Remizov ; Seifullina ; Semenov ; Sholokhov ; Tikhonov ; Zamyatin ; Zoshchenko. Poetry by : Akhmatova ; Bely ; Bezimensky ; Blok ; Esenin ; Gumilev ; Klebnikhov ; Mayakovsky ; Pasternak ; Selvinsky ; Tikhonov ; Tsvetaevna ; Ushakov ; Voloshin. With short biographical sketches and various essays.]

SELVER (P.) : *Anthology of modern Slavonic literature in prose and verse.* 348 pp. Ld. Kegan Paul, 1919. [Contains: Russian prose: Chekhov; Merezhkovsky; Sergeev-Tsensky; Shevchenko; Sologub. Russian poetry: Balmont; Bryusov; Gorodetsky; Hippius; V. Ivanov; Merezhkovsky; Minsky; Shevchenko; Sologub.]

Soviet Literature, Art, Music. See: GRINDEA (M.).

SPECTOR (I.) : *Golden age of Russian literature.* [An anthology.] N.Y. Lymanhouse, 1939. 258 pp. Caldwell. Caxton Printers, 1943.

UNDERWOOD (E.) : *The Slav anthology : Russian, Polish, Bohemian, Servian, Croatian.* 346 pp. Portland, Maine. Mosher, 1931.

Voices of October. See : FREEMAN (J.) and others.

VOYNICH (E. L.) : *Humour of Russia.* Ld. Scott, 1911.

WIENER (L.) ed. : *Anthology of Russian literature, from the earliest period to the present time.* 2 vols. N.Y. and Ld. Putnam, 1902–3. (Contains: bibliography of translations.]

ANTHOLOGIES : POETRY

BIANCHI (M. G. D.) ed. and transl. : *Russian lyrics and Cossack songs, done into Engl. verse.* 139 pp. N.Y. 1910.

BOWRA (C. M.) ed. : *A book of Russian verse.* Transl. by various hands. 127 pp. Ld. Macmillan, 1943. [Contains: Akhmatova; Annenski; Balmont; Baratynsky; Blok; Bryusov; Esenin; Fet; Gumilev; V. Ivanov; Kazin; Khodasevich; Khomyakov; Koltsov; Lermontov; Mandelstam; Mayakovsky; Maykov; Nekrasov; Pasternak; Polonsky; Pushkin; Sologub; Solovev; Surikov; Tolstoy; Tyuchev.]

CORNFORD (F.) and SALAMAN (E. P.) : *Poems from the Russian.* 74 pp. Ld. Faber, 1943. [Contains: Akhmatova; Balmont; Blok; Fet; Koltsov; Krylov; Lermontov; Maykov; Nekrasov; Pushkin; Tolstoy; Tyuchev.]

COXWELL (C. F.) ed. and transl. : *Russian poems.* With an introduction by D. S. Mirsky. 309 pp. Ld. Daniel, 1929. [Contains: Akhmatova; Annenski; Apukhtin; Balmont; Baratynsky; Batyushkov; Bely; Blok; Bryusov; Bunin; Fet; Glinka; Gumilev; Z. Hippius; V. Ivanov; Khomyakov; Koltsov; Krylov; Kuzmin; Lermontov; Mayakovsky; Maykov; Merezhkovsky; Minsky; Nadson; Nekrasov;

Nikitin; Ogarev; Pasternak; Pavlova; Polonsky; Pushkin; Sologub; Solovev; A. K. Tolstoy; Turgenev; Tyuchev; Voloshin; Yazykov; Zhukovsky.]

DEUTSCH (B.) and YARMOLINSKY (A.) ed. and transl.: *Modern Russian poetry.* 179 pp. Ld. Lane, 1921.

—— Same, enlarged; with title: *Russian poetry: an anthology.* 254 pp. N.Y., 1927; Ld. Lawrence, 1929. [Contains: Akhmatova; Balmont; Baratynsky; Bedny; Bely; Bezimensky; Blok; Bryusov; Bunin; Chulkov; Esenin; Ehrenburg; Fet; Gastev; Gerasimov; Gorodetsky; Z. Hippius; V. Ivanov; Kazin; Klyuev; Koltsov; Kuzmin; Lermontov; Mayakovsky; Maykov; Merezhkovsky; Minsky; Nekrasov; Oreshin; Polonsky; Pushkin; Severyanin; Sologub; Solovev; A. K. Tolstoy; Tyuchev; Voloshin.]

ELTON (O.): *Verse from Pushkin and others.* 188 pp. Ld. Arnold, 1935. [Contains: Akhmatova; Blok; Nekrasov; Pushkin; Tyuchev.]

JARINTZOV (N.): *Russian poets and poems.* Vol. 1: *Classics.* 357 pp. Oxf. Blackwell, 1917.

KAUN (A. S.): *Soviet poets and poetry.* 208 pp. Berkeley. Univ. of California Pr., 1943.

KRUP (J.): *Six poems from the Russian.* 317 pp. N.Y. Galleon Pr., 1936.

MATHESON (P. E.): *Holy Russia, and other poems.* 63 pp. Ld. Oxf. Univ. Pr., 1918. [Contains: Fet; Koltsov; Krasov; Lermontov; Nadson; Nekrasov; Nikitin; Ogarev; Pushkin; Shishkov; A. K. Tolstoy; Tyuchev; Yazykov; Zhukovsky.]

New Directions, anthology in prose and poetry. Ed. by J. Laughlin. 729 pp. Norfolk. New Directions, Connecticut, 1941. [Contains: pp. 513–650 a chapter: "Soviet Russian poetry; a survey, translations and critical essays." On poets: Bagritsky; Khodasevich; Kirsanov; Lugovskoy; Mayakovsky; Outkin; Pasternak; Selvinsky; Svetlov; Tikhonov; Zharov.]

POLLEN (J.): *Russian songs and lyrics.* 191 pp. Ld. East & West, 1916.

RUDZINSKY (B. A.) ed. and transl.: *Selections of Russian poetry.* 102 pp. Ld. Blackie, 1918.

SELVER (P.) ed. and transl.: *Modern Russian poetry.* Texts and transl. 65 pp. Ld. Kegan Paul, 1917. [Contains: Balmont; Blok; Bryusov; Bunin; Z. Hippius; Merezhkovsky; Minsky; Sologub; Solovev.]

SHELLEY (G.) ed. and transl.: *Modern poems from Russia.* 93 pp. Ld. Allen & Unwin, 1942. [Contains: Akhmatova;

Balmont; Bely; Blok; Ehrenburg; Esenin; Gumilev; Klyuev; Mayakovsky; Merezhkovsky; Pasternak; Sologub; Zharov.]

SOSYURA (V.): *Poems of Soviet Ukraine.* Transl. by M. Trommer. N.Y. Trommer, 1939.

TROMMER (M.): *Poems by women poets of Russia.*

COLLECTIONS OF SHORT STORIES

CHAMOT (A. E.) ed. and transl.: *Selected Russian short stories.* 344 pp. Ld. Oxf. Univ. Pr., 1925. (World's classics.) [Contains: Chekhov; Dostoevsky; Garshin; Gogol; Gorky; Kuprin; Lermontov; Pushkin; Turgenev.]

COURNOS (J.) ed. and transl.: *Short stories out of Soviet Russia.* 206 pp. Ld. Dent, 1929; reissued 1932. [Contains: Alekseev; Babel; V. Ivanov; Kataev; Leonov; Lidin; Pilnyak; Prishvin; Sergeev-Tsensky; A. N. Tolstoy; Zozulya.]

FEN (E.) ed. and transl.: *Modern Russian stories.* 244 pp. Ld. Methuen, 1943. [Contains: Babel; Fedin; Leonov; Neverov; Pilnyak; Romanov; A. N. Tolstoy; Zoshchenko.]

FEN (E.) ed. and transl.: *Soviet stories of the last decade.* 212 pp. Ld. Methuen, 1945. [Contains: Bramm and Grinberg; Dikovsky; Dolghih; Ehrenburg; Gorbatov; Kozhevnikov; Lidin; Malyshkin; Roonova; Shoshin; Simonov; Sokolov-Nikitov.]

FRIEDLAND (L. S.) and PIROSHNIKOFF (J. R.): *Flying Osip; stories of New Russia.* 318 pp. Ld. Unwin, 1925.

GRAHAM (S.): *Great Russian short stories.* 1,021 pp. Ld. Benn, 1929. [Contains: Afanasev; Alekseev; Andreev; Apukhtin; Babel; Bryusov; Bunin; Chekhov; Chirikov; Doroshovich; Dostoevsky; Ertel; Garshin; Gogol; Gorky; Kataev; Kuprin; Okulev; Pilnyak; Pushkin; Romanov; Sologub; Solovev; L. N. Tolstoy; Turgenev; Zhukovsky; Zoshchenko.]

KONOVALOV (S.) ed.: *Bonfire: stories out of Soviet Russia; an anthology of contemporary Russian literature.* 320 pp. Ld. Benn, 1932. [Contains: Babel; Chetverikov; Ehrenburg; Fadeev; Fedin; Fibikh; V. Ivanov; Kataev; Lebedinsky; Leonov; Lidin; Neverov; Ognev; Olesha; Pilnyak; Romanov; Semenov; Shklovsky; A. N. Tolstoy; Vesely; Yakovlev; Zamyatin; Zayaitsky; Zoshchenko.]

KOTELIANSKY (S. S.) ed. and partly transl.: *Russian short stories*. 156 pp. Ld. Allen Lane, Penguin Books, 1941. [Contains: Bunin; Chekhov; Garshin; Kuprin,]

MONTAGU (I.) and MARSHALL (H.) ed.: *Soviet short stories*; 1st series. (Life and literature in the Soviet Union, 2.) 154 pp. Ld. Pilot Pr., 1942. [Contains: Ardov; Ehrenburg; Isbach; Kerash; Lidin; Olesha; Pavstovsky; Platonov; Tynyanov; Zoshchenko.]

MONTAGU (I.) and MARSHALL (H.) ed.: *Soviet short stories, 1942–43*; 2nd series. (Life and literature in the Soviet Union, 5.) 121 pp. Ld. Pilot Pr., 1943. [Contains: Gorbatov; Isbach; Kassil; Pavstovsky; Petrov; Shpanov; Sholokhov; Simonov; Sobolev; Tikhonov; Wassilevska.]

MONTAGU (I.) and MARSHALL (H.) ed.: *Soviet short stories, 1944*; 3rd series. (Life and literature in the Soviet Union.) 152 pp. Ld. Pilot Pr., 1944. [Contains: Dovzhenko; Gorbatov; Ilenkov; Kaverin; Knorre; Kozhèvnikov; Lavrenov; Simonov; Tikhonov; Trenyev.]

ROBBINS (J. J.) and KUNITZ (J.) ed. and transl.: *Azure cities: stories of New Russia*. (Modern books.) 320 pp. Ld. Mod. Bks. Ltd., 1929. [Contains: Babel; Ivanov; Liashko; Lidin; Neverov; Pilnyak; Romanov; Seifullina; Shaginian; Shishkov; A. Tolstoy; Volkov; Zoshchenko.]

RODKER (J.) ed.: *Soviet anthology; short stories by Soviet writers*. 231 pp. Ld. Cape, 1943. [Contains: Babel; Bergelson; Freirman; Gorky; Grossman; Kataev; Kaverin; Lench; Pavlenko; Pavstovsky; Pilnyak; Raskin; Slobodsky; Tikhonov; Virta; Volosov; Weissenberg; Zoshchenko.]

Russian Short Stories. 448 pp. Ld. Faber, 1943. [Contains: Andreev; Babel; Bunin; Chekhov; Dostoevsky; Garshin; Gogol; Gorky; V. Ivanov; Kataev; Kuprin; Leonov; Lermontov; Leskov; Prishvin; Pushkin; Sergeev-Tsensky; Sologub; L. N. Tolstoy; Turgenev.]

SCHWEIKERT (H. C.) ed.: *Russian short stories*. Rev. ed. Ld. Scott, 1919.

Soviet Short Stories. See: MONTAGU (I.) and MARSHALL (H.).

Soviet War Stories. 192 pp. Ld. Hutchinson, 1943; Heinemann, 1944. [Contains: Panferov; Gorbatov; Sholokhov; K. Simonov; Wassilewska.]

TOWNSEND (R. S.): *Short stories by Russian authors*. 275 pp. (Everyman's Library.) Ld. Dent, 1924. [Contains: Andreev; Chekhov; Chirikov; Gogol; Gorky; Korolenko; Kuprin; Pushkin; Sologub; L. N. Tolstoy.] Repr. 1943.

YARMOLINSKY (A.) ed.: *A treasury of great Russian short stories.*
1,018 pp. N.Y. Macmillan, 1944.

COLLECTIONS OF PLAYS

BECHHOFER (C. E.) [afterwards Roberts] transl.: *Five Russian
plays, with one from the Ukrainian.* 173 pp. Ld. Kegan
Paul; N.Y. Dutton, 1916. [Contains: Chekhov; Evreinov;
Fonvizin; Ukrainka.]
BLAKE (B.) ed.: *Four Soviet plays.* 427 pp. Ld. Lawrence &
Wishart, 1937. [Contains: Gorky; Kocherga; Pogodin;
Vishnevsky.]
Four Soviet War Plays. 208 pp. Ld. Hutchinson, 1943.
[Contains: Korneichuk; Leonov; K. Simonov.]
LYONS (E.) ed.: *Six Soviet plays.* 608 pp. Ld. Gollancz, 1935.
(Contains: Afinogenev; Bulgakov; Glebov; Kataev; Kir-
shon; Pogodin.]
NOYES (G. R.) ed. and partly transl.: *Masterpieces of the Russian
drama.* With an introduction. 902 pp. Ld. and N.Y.
Appleton, 1933. [Contains: Andreev; Chekhov; Fonvizin;
Gogol; Gorky; Griboedov; Mayakovsky; Ostrovsky;
Pisemsky; A. K. Tolstoy; L. N. Tolstoy; Turgenev.]
SAYLER (O. M.) ed.: *Moscow Art Theatre series of Russian plays.*
First series. Transl. by J. Covan. N.Y. Brentano's, 1923.
5 vols. and 1 vol. ed. [Contains: Chekhov; Gorky; A. K.
Tolstoy.]
—— Second series. N.Y. Brentano's, 1923. [Contains:
Chekhov; Dostoevsky; Ostrovsky.]

FOLK-LITERATURE, INCLUDING PROVERBS

BAIN (R. N.) ed. and transl.: *Cossack fairy tales and folk tales.*
290 pp. Ld. Lawrence & Bullen (1st ed. 1894), new ed. 1902.
—— *Russian fairy tales.* Ld. Lawrence (1st ed. 1893), 3rd ed.
1915.
BAUER–CZARNOMSKI. (F.): *Proverbs in Russian and English.*
103 pp. Ld. 1920.

BLUMENTHAL (V. de) ed.: *Folk tales from the Russian.* 153 pp. Ld. 1903.

The Book of the Bear. Being twenty-one tales newly translated by J. E. Harrison and H. Mirrlees. Ld. Nonesuch Pr., 1926.

CHADWICK (H. M.) and CHADWICK (N. K.): *The growth of literature,* vol. 2: *Russian oral literature.* Ld. Cambridge Univ. Pr., 1936.

CHADWICK (N. K.): *Russian heroic poetry.* 294 pp. Ld. Cambridge Univ. Pr., 1932.

CHAMPION (S. G.) ed.: *Racial proverbs; a selection of the world's proverbs* [in English]. 767 pp. Ld. Routledge, 1938. [Contains, pp. 255–77, a list of 790 Russian and 202 Ukrainian proverbs. Introduction by A. I. Guershoon.]

COXWELL (C. F.) ed. and transl.: *Siberian and other folk tales; primitive literature of the empire of the Tsar.* With introduction and notes. 1,056 pp. Ld. Daniel, 1925.

DOLE (N. H.) ed. and transl.: *The Russian fairy book.* 126 pp. N.Y., 1907.

ENTWISTLE (W. J.): *European balladry.* Book 2, chapter 4: 'Russian ballads.' Oxf. Clarendon Pr., 1939.

GUERSHOON (A. I.): *Certain aspects of Russian proverbs.* 204 pp. Ld. Muller, 1941. [Contains: List of 1,361 Russian proverbs in English translation.]

HAPGOOD (I. F.): *Epic songs of Russia.* Ld. (1st ed. 1886), 2nd ed. 1915.

HOUGHTON (L. S.): *The Russian grandmother's wonder tales.* 348 pp. N.Y. Scribner, 1906.

KAUN (A. S.): *Folk trends in Soviet poetry.* (*In: New Directions in prose and poetry,* pp. 569–95. 1941.)

MAGNUS (L. A.): *The heroic ballads of Russia.* [A study with prose summaries.] 210 pp. Ld. Kegan Paul, Trench, Trubner, 1921.

—— *Russian folk tales.* 350 pp. Ld. Mitford, 1915.

The tale of the armament of Igor. See: The tale of the armament of Igor.

MICHELL (R.) and others: *The chronicle of Novgorod.* Ld. 1914.

PULMAN (S.) ed. and transl.: *Children's story from Russian fairy tales and legends.* 144 pp. Philadelphia. McKay, 1925.

SEGAL (L.): *Russian proverbs and their English equivalents.* N.Y. Dutton, 1917.

ZEITLIN (I.) ed.: Skazki: *Tales and legends of old Russia.* (Contains translations of some of Pushkin's folk tales in verse.] 335 pp. N.Y. 1926.

The Tale of the Armament of Igor, a.d. 1185; a Russian historical epic. Ed. and transl. by L. A. Magnus. With rev. Russian text. (Publications of the Philological Society.) 122 pp. Ld. Oxf. Univ. Pr., 1915.

WORKS OF INDIVIDUAL AUTHORS

AFANASEV (Aleksandr), 1826–71.
  Death and the soldier. Transl. by R. Graham. (*In:* S. Graham, *Great Russian short stories*, 1929.)
AFINOGENEV (Aleksandr Nikolaevich), 1900–41.
  Distant point; a play. Transl. and adapted by H. Griffith. Songs freely adapted by G. Parsons. 95 pp. Ld. Cape & Pushkin Pr., 1941.
  Fear; a play in four acts and nine scenes. Authorised translation, by C. Malamuth. (*In:* E. Lyons, *Six Soviet plays*, 1935.)
  Fear; transl. by N. Strelsky, D. B. Colman and A. Greene. N.Y. Poughkeepsie, 1934.
  Listen, professor! A play in three acts. Acting version by P. Phillips. 78 pp. Pl. N.Y. French, 1944.
AKHAMATOVA (Anna) [pseud. of Anna Andreevna Gorenko], 1888–.
  All is plundered. (*In:* Reavey and Slonim, *Soviet Literature*, 1933.)
  Forty-seven love poems. Transl. by N. Duddington. 64 pp. Ld. Cape, 1927.
  Poems. (*In:* C. M. Bowra, *A book of Russian verse*, 1943.)
  Poems. (*In:* F. Cornford and E. P. Salaman, *Poems from the Russian*, 1943.)
  Poems. (*In:* C. F. Coxwell, *Russian poems*, 1929.)
  Poems. (*In:* G. Shelley, *Modern poems from Russia*, 1942.)
  Poem. (*In:* O. Elton, *Verse from Pushkin and others*, 1935.)
AKSAKOV (Sergei Timofeevich), 1791–1859.
  Chronicles of a Russian family. Transl. by M. C. Beverley. N.Y. Dutton; Ld. Routledge, 1924. (Broadway translations.) [Translation of the whole of *Family chronicle*, 3 chapters of *Years of childhood*, of *Bagrov, the grandson*, and the first 3 parts of *Recollections*.]
  Notes on angling. (*In:* A. Ransome, *Rod and line.* Ld. Cape, 1932. Pp. 244–86.
  Years of childhood. Transl. by J. D. Duff. 340 pp. Ld. Arnold, 1916.

—— Same. 446 pp. Ld. Oxf. Univ. Pr., 1923. (World's classics.) [Contains also: *The scarlet flower*, a short story.]

A Russian gentleman, Transl. by J. D. Duff. 209 pp. Ld. Arnold, 1917.

—— Same. 283 pp. Ld. Oxf. Univ. Pr., 1923. (World's classics.) [Transl. of *Family chronicle*.]

A Russian schoolboy. Transl. by J. D. Duff. 216 pp. Ld. Arnold, 1917.

—— Same. 288 pp. Ld. Oxf. Univ. Pr., 1924. (World's classics.) [Contains: transl. of *Recollections*, and *Butterfly collecting*.]

Biography, criticism, etc.:

OSBOURNE (E. A.) comp.: *Early translations from the Russian*: 5. S. T. Aksakov. (Bookman. Ld. 1932.)

ALDANOV (Mark) [pseud. of Mark Aleksandrovich Landau], 1888–.

The devil's bridge. Transl. by A. E. Chamot. 325 pp. N.Y. and Ld. Knopf, 1928. [Second part of the trilogy, *The ninth thermidor*.]

The fifth seal. Transl. by N. Wreden. 482 pp. N.Y. Scribner, 1943.

The key. Transl. by E. Gellibrand. 327 pp. Ld. Harrap, 1931.

The ninth thermidor. Transl. by A. E. Chamot. 377 pp. N.Y. Knopf, 1926. (First part of the trilogy.]

Saint Helena: little island. Transl. by A. E. Chamot. 193 pp. Ld. Jarrolds, 1924. [Third part of the trilogy, *The ninth thermidor*.]

ALEICHEM (Shalom) [pseud. of Shalom Rabinowitz], 1859–1916.

Jewish children. Transl. from the Yiddish by H. Berman. 268 pp. Ld. Heinemann, 1920; N.Y. Knopf, 1926.

Stempenyn. Transl. by H. Berman. Ld. Methuen, 1913.

Biography, criticism, etc.:

SAMUEL (M.)

The world of Sholom Aleichem. N.Y. Knopf, 1943.

ALEKSANDER (Irina) [pseud., of Irina Kunina.]

Running tide. Transl. by B. G. Guerney. 264 pp. N.Y. Duell, 1943.

ALEKSEEV (Gleb), 1892–.

Diphtheria. Transl. by L. Zarine. (*In*: S. Graham, *Great Russian short stories*, 1929.)

Other eyes. (*In*: J. Cournos, *Short stories out of Soviet Russia*, 1932.)

ANDREEV (Leonid Nikolaevich), 1871–1919.

Plays : *The black maskers* ; *The life of man* ; *The Sabine women.* Transl. by C. L. Meader and F. N. Scott. With an introduction by V. V. Brusyanin. Ld. Duckworth ; N.Y. Scribner, 1915.

Abyss. Transl. by J. Cournos. 31 pp. Waltham St. Lawrence. Golden Cockerell Pr., 1929.

Anathema ; a tragedy in seven scenes. Transl. by H. Bernstein. N.Y. Macmillan, 1910.

And it came to pass that the king was dead. Transl. by M. Magnus. 46 pp. Ld. Daniel, 1921.

―― Same, with title : *When the king loses his head, and other stories.* Transl. by A. J. Wolfe. N.Y. International Book Publishing Co., 1920. (Russian authors' library.)

The confessions of a little man during the great days. Transl. by R. S. Townsend. 242 pp. Ld. Duckworth, 1917. [Russian title : *The yoke of war.*]

The crushed flower, and other stories. 361 pp. Ld. Duckworth, 1917.

The dark. Transl. by L. A. Magnus and K. Walter. 52 pp. Richmond. L. & V. Woolf, 1922.

The dear departing ; a frivolous performance in one act. Transl. by J. West. 32 pp. Ld. Hendersons, 1916.

A dilemma. Transl. by J. Cournos. Philadelphia. Brown, 1910.

―― Same, with title : *Dilemma ; a story of mental perplexity.* Transl. by J. Cournos. 114 pp. N.Y. Greenberg, n.d.

He who gets slapped : a play in four acts. Transl. with an introduction by G. Zilboorg. N.Y. and Ld. Brentano's, 1922.

He who gets slapped ; a novel adapted by G. A. Carlin from L. Andreev's drama, and the Victor Seastoom photo-play. Ill. with scenes from the photo-play. 273 pp. N.Y. Grosset. 1925.

His excellency the governor. Transl. by M. Magnus. 96 pp. Ld. Daniel, 1921.

Judas Iscariot, forming with Eleazor and Ben Tobit a biblical trilogy. Transl. by W. H. Lowe. 192 pp. Ld. Griffiths, 1910.

Katerina (Yekaterina Ivanovna) ; a drama in four acts. Authorised transl. from the original MS. with a preface by H. Bernstein. N.Y. and Ld. Brentano's, 1923 and 1924.

Life of man ; a play in five acts. Transl. by C. J. Hogarth. 141 pp. N.Y. Macmillan ; Ld. Allen & Unwin, 1915.

The little angel, and other stories. 255 pp. Ld. Hodder & Stoughton, 1915. (Great Russian Fiction.)

—— Same. Transl. by W. H. Lowe. N.Y. Knopf, 1916. (Borzoi Pocket Books.)

The little angel. Repr. from the ed. published by Hodder & Stoughton, 1915. (*In:* S. Graham, *Great Russian short stories*, 1929.)

Love one's neighbour. Transl. by T. Seltzer. Boni, 1914; N.Y. Shay, 1917.

The red laugh. Fragments of a discovered manuscript. Transl. by A. Linden. 117 pp. Ld. Fisher Unwin, 1905; N.Y. Duffield, 1915.

Roerich; a monograph of a great artist. N.Y. Brentano's, 1925.

Samson in chains. [Posthumous tragedy.] Authorised transl. from the original MS. by H. Bernstein. N.Y. Brentano's, 1923.

Sashka Jigouleff. Transl. by L. Hicks. 287 pp. Ld. Jarrolds, 1926.

—— Same, with introduction by M. Gorky. 294 pp. N.Y. MacBride, 1925. (Russian Masterpieces, 2.)

Satan's diary. Transl. by H. Bernstein. N.Y. Boni & Liveright, 1920.

Savva; The life of man. Two plays. Transl. with an introduction by T. Seltzer. N.Y. Little, 1914. (Modern Drama Series.)

The seven who were hanged. Authorised transl. by H. Bernstein. N.Y. Ogilvie, 1909.

—— Same. 80 pp. Ld. Fifield, 1909.

—— Same. Transl. by H. Bernstein. 190 pp. Cleveland World publ., 1941.

Silence. Transl. by J. Cournos. Philadelphia. Brown, 1908. Also published by Frank Maurice, N.Y.

Silence, and other stories. Transl. by W. H. Lowe. 219 pp. Ld. Griffiths, 1910.

The sorrows of Belgium: a play in six scenes. Authorised transl. by H. Bernstein. 132 pp. N.Y. Macmillan, 1915.

To the stars; a drama. Transl. by M. Magnus. 84 pp. Ld. 1921. (Plays for a People's Theatre, 10.)

The waltz of the dogs; a play in four acts. Authorised transl. from the original MS. by H. Bernstein. 141 pp. Ld. Brentano's, 1924. (Printed in U.S.A.)

Biography, criticism, etc.:

GORKY (M.): *Reminiscences of Leonid Andreev.* Transl. by K. Mansfield and S. S. Koteliansky. 128 pp. Ld. Heinemann, 1931; Ld. Dulau, 1928; N.Y. Random House, 1928.

GORKY (M.) : *Reminiscences of Tolstoy, Chekhov and Andreev.*
Ld. Hogarth Pr., 1934.

KAUN (A. S.) : *Leonid Andreev; a critical study.* 361 pp. N.Y.
Huebsch. Viking Pr., 1924.

ANNENSKI (Innokenti Fedorovich), 1856–1909.
Poems. (*In :* C. M. Bowra, *A book of Russian verse,* 1943.)
Poems. (*In :* C. F. Coxwell, *Russian poems,* 1929.)

APUKHTIN (Aleksei Nikolaevich), 1841–93.
The Archive of Countess D . . . (*In :* S. Graham, *Great Russian short stories,* 1929.)
From death to life. Transl. by R. Frank and E. Huybers. N.Y.
Frank, 1917. (Gems of Russian Literature.)
Poems. (*In :* C. F. Coxwell, *Russian poems,* 1929.)

ARDOV (Victor).
Happy ending. (*In :* I. Montagu and H. Marshall, *Soviet short stories,* 1942.)

ARSENIEV (Vladimir Klavidevich), 1872–.
Dersu, the Trapper; a hunter's life in Ussuria. Transl. by M.
Burr. Ill. 352 pp. Ld. Secker & Warburg, 1939; N.Y.
Dutton, 1941.

ARTEM VESELY. *See* : VESELY (Artem).

ARTSYBASHEV (Boris Mikhailovich), 1899–.
Poor Shaydullah. Told and ill. by the author. Ld. Macmillan, 1931.
Seven Simeons; a Russian tale. Retold and ill. by the author.
Ld. Cassell, 1937.

ARTSYBASHEV (Mikhail Petrovich), 1878–1927.
Breaking point. Ld. Secker, 1915.
Jealousy. N.Y. Boni & Liveright, 1923.
The millionaire; Ivan Lande; Nina. Three novelettes. Transl. by
P. Pinkerton. Ld. Secker, 1915.
Sanine. Transl. by P. Pinkerton. Ld. Secker, 1915. New ed.
327 pp. N.Y. Viking Pr., 1926.
—— Same. Preface by E. Boyd. 380 pp. N.Y. 1931.
(Modern Library of the World's Best Books.)
The savage. Transl. by G. Cannan and A. Strindberg. N.Y. Boni
& Liveright, 1924.
Tales of the Revolution. Transl. by P. Pinkerton. Ld. Secker, 1917.
War; a play in four acts. Transl. by T. Seltzer. N.Y. Knopf 1916.
War. Transl. by P. Pinkerton and I. Ozhol. Ld. Richards, 1918.

ASH (Shalom), 1880–.
> *Three novels: Uncle Moses; Chaim Lederer's return; Judge not.*
> 3 vols. (in 1). Transl. by E. Krauch. 176, 116, 127 pp. N.Y.
> Putnam, 1938.
> *Apostle.* Transl. by M. Samuel. 804 pp. N.Y. Putnam, 1943.
> *Children of Abraham;* short stories. Transl. by M. Samuel.
> 433 pp. N.Y. Putnam, 1942.
> *The mother.* Transl. by N. Ausuebel. 357 pp. N.Y. Liveright,
> 1930.
> —— Same. Authorised transl. by E. Krauch. 295 pp. N.Y.
> Grosset, 1940. (Novels of Distinction.)
> *Mottke, the thief.* Transl. by W. and E. Muir. 314 pp. N.Y.
> Putnam, 1935.
> *Nazarene.* Transl. by M. Samuel. 698 pp. N.Y. Putnam,
> 1939.
> *Sabbatai Zevi;* a tragedy in three acts and six scenes, with a
> prologue and an epilogue. Authorised transl. by F. Whyte and
> G. R. Noyes. 131 pp. Ill. N.Y. Jewish publ., 1930.
> *Salvation.* Transl. by W. and E. Muir. 332 pp. N.Y. Putnam,
> 1934.
> *Song of the valley.* Transl. by E. Krauch. 245 pp. N.Y. Putnam,
> 1939; Ld. Routledge.
> *Three cities; a trilogy.* Transl. by W. and E. Muir. Special ed.
> 899 pp. N.Y. Putnam, 1943.
> *The war goes on.* Transl. by W. and E. Muir. 528 pp. N.Y.
> Putnam, 1936.
> —— Same, with title: *Calf of paper.* Cheap ed. Ld.
> Gollancz, 1938.
> *What I believe.* Transl. by M. Samuel. 201 pp. N.Y. Putnam,
> 1941.
> —— Same, with title: *My personal faith.* 201 pp. Ld.
> Routledge, 1942.

AVDEENKO (Aleksandr Evstigneevich).
> *I love: a novel.* Transl. by A. Wixley. 283 pp. Ld. Lawrence,
> 1935.

BABEL (Isaak Emmanuilovich), 1894–.
> *The awakening.* (*In:* G. Reavey and M. Slonim, *Soviet literature,*
> 1933.)
> *Benia Krik: a film novel.* Transl. by I. Montagu and S. S.
> Nolbandov. 96 pp. Ltd. ed. Ld. Collet, 1935.
> *The birth of a king.* (*In:* E. Fen, *Modern Russian stories,* 1943.)
> *The death of Dolgushov.* (*In:* J. Cournos, *Short stories out of
> Soviet Russia,* 1929.)

C

—— Same. (*In:* S. Konovalov, *Bonfire*, 1932.)

End of St. Ipaty. (*In:* G. Reavey and M. Slonim, *Soviet literature*, 1933.)

Gedali. (*In:* S. Konovalov, *Bonfire*, 1932.)

Karl-Yankel. Transl. by A. Brown. (*In:* J. Rodker, *Soviet anthology*, 1943.)

The letter. (*In:* J. Cournos, *Short stories out of Soviet Russia*, 1929.)

—— Same. Transl. by A. Brown. (*In:* J. Rodker, *Soviet anthology*, 1943.)

Life and adventures of Matvey Pavlichenko. Transl. by J. Harland. (*In:* S. Graham, *Great Russian short stories*, 1929.)

Red cavalry. Transl. by J. Harland. Ld. Knopf, 1929.

Salt. (*In:* J. Cournos, *Short stories out of Soviet Russia*, 1929.)

BAGRITSKY (Edouard), 1895–1934.

Poems. (*In: New Directions in prose and poetry*, 1941.)

BALMONT (Konstantin Dmitrievich), 1867–.

Poems. (*In:* C. M. Bowra, *A book of Russian verse*, 1943.)

Poems. (*In:* F. Cornford and E. P. Salaman, *Poems from the Russian*, 1943.)

Poems. (*In:* C. F. Coxwell, *Russian poems*, 1929.)

Poems. (*In:* B. Deutsch and A. Yarmolinsky, *Russian poetry*, 1929.)

Poems. (*In:* P. Selver, *Modern Russian poetry*, 1917, and his: *Anthology of modern Slavonic literature*, 1919.)

BARATYNSKY (Evgeny Abramovich), 1800–44.

Poems. (*In:* C. M. Bowra, *A book of Russian verse*, 1943.)

Poems. (*In:* C. F. Coxwell, *Russian poems*, 1929.)

Poems. (*In:* B. Deutsch and A. Yarmolinsky, *Russian poetry*, 1929.)

BASHKIRTSEVA (Maria Konstantinova), 1860–84.

Journal of a young artist. New ed. N.Y. Dutton, 1926.

Biography, criticism, etc.:

CAHUET (A.): *Moussia; the life and death of Maria Bashkirtseva.* Transl. by K. Wallis. Ill. 300 pp. N.Y. Macaulay, 1929.

BATYUSHKOV (Konstantin Nikolaevich), 1787–1855.

Dying Tasso. (*Extract in:* L. Wiener, *Russian anthology*, vol. 2, 1903.)

BEDNY (Demyan) [pseud. of Efim Alekseevich Pridvorov], 1883–.

Poems. (*In:* B. Deutsch and A. Yarmolinsky, *Russian poetry*, 1929.)

BELINSKY (Visarion Grigorevich), 1811–48.

The natural school. (*In:* L. Wiener, *Russian anthology*, 1903.)

BELY (Andrey) [pseud. of Boris Nikolaevich Bugaev], 1880–1934.
  Kotik Letaev. (*Extract in:* G. Reavey and M. Slonim, *Soviet literature*, 1933.)
  Poem: *Christ is risen.* (*Extract in:* B. Deutsch and A. Yarmolinsky, *Russian poetry*, 1929.)
  Russia. (*In:* G. Reavey and M. Slonim, *Soviet literature*, 1933.)
BERGELSON (David).
  The Russian for parallel. Transl. by S. Garry. (*In:* J. Rodker, *Soviet anthology, short stories*, 1943.)
BEZIMENSKY (Aleksandr Ilyich), 1882–.
  Poems. (*In:* G. Reavey and M. Slonim, *Soviet literature*, 1933.)
  Poem: *Village and factory*, (*In:* B. Deutsch and A. Yarmolinsky, *Russian poetry*, 1929.)
BILL–BELOTSERKOVSKY (Vladimir Naumovich), 1884–.
  Life is calling: a play in four acts. Transl. by A. Wixley. 88 pp. Ld. Lawrence & Wishart, 1938; N.Y. International Publishers, 1938.
BLOK (Aleksandr Aleksandrovich), 1880–1921.
  The collapse of humanism. Transl. by I. Berlin. (*In: The Oxford Outlook*, Oxf. Blackwell, 1931.)
  New America. (*In:* G. Reavey and M. Slonim, *Soviet literature*, 1933.)
  Poems. (*In:* C. M. Bowra, *A book of Russian verse*, 1943.)
  Poems. (*In:* F. Cornford and E. P. Salaman, *Poems from the Russian*, 1943.)
  Poems. (*In:* B. Deutsch and A. Yarmolinsky, *Russian poetry*, 1929.)
  Poems. (*In:* O. Elton, *Verse from Pushkin and others*, 1935.)
  The twelve. Transl. by C. E. Bechhofer. Ld. Chatto & Windus, 1920.
  —— Same. Transl. by B. Deutsch and A. Yarmolinsky. N.Y. Rudge, 1931.
  —— Same. (*Extract in:* G. Reavey and M. Slonim, *Soviet literature*, 1933.)
  Biography, criticism, etc.:
  BOWRA (C. M.): *Alexander Blok.* (*In his: The heritage of symbolism*, 1943.)
  LAVRIN (J.): *Alexander Blok.* (*In his: Aspects of modernism*, 1936.)
BRAMM (M.) and GRINBERG (I.).
  The friends. (*In:* E. Fen, *Soviet stories of the last decade*, 1945.)
BRYUSOV (Valery Yakovlevich), 1873–1924.
  Fiery angel: a sixteenth century romance. Transl. by I. Montagu and S. Nolbandov. 392 pp. Ld. Cayme Pr., 1930.

The marble bust. (*In:* S. Graham, *Great Russian short stories,* 1929.)

Poems. (*In:* C. M. Bowra, *A book of Russian verse,* 1943.)

Poems. (*In:* C. F. Coxwell, *Russian poems,* 1929.)

Poems. (*In:* P. Selver, *Modern Russian poetry,* 1917. *And in his: Anthology of modern Slavonic literature,* 1919.)

The republic of the southern cross, and other stories. Transl. by R. Graham. Ld. Constable, 1918. (Constable's Russian library.) [Contains: 'The republic of the southern cross'; 'Rhea Silvia'; 'The marble bust'.]

Rhea Silvia. (*In:* S. Graham, *Great Russian short stories,* 1929.)

BUGAEV (Boris Nikolaevich), *see:* BELY (Andrey) [pseud. of Boris Nikolaevich Bugaev.]

BULGAKOV (Mikhail Afanasevich), 1891–.

Days of the turbines; a play. [Based on the novel, *The white guard.*] Authorised transl. by E. Lyons. (*In:* E. Lyons, *Six Soviet plays,* 1935.)

BUNIN (Ivan Alekseevich), 1870–.

The dreams of Chang, and other stories. Transl. by B. G. Guerney. N.Y. Knopf, 1923.

—— Same. With title on cover: *Fifteen tales.* Ld. Secker, 1924.

Early passions. Ld. Pallas, 1939.

The Elaghin affair, and other stories. Selected and transl. by B. G. Guerney. 297 pp. N.Y. Knopf, 1935.

The gentleman from San Francisco, and other stories. Transl. by D. H. Lawrence, S. S. Koteliansky and L. Woolf. 86 pp. Richmond. L. & V. Woolf, 1922. 2nd ed. Ld. Hogarth Pr., 1934.

—— Same. Authorised transl. by B. G. Guerney. 313 pp. N.Y. Knopf, 1933. Repr. 1941. (Albla Books.)

Grammar of love. Transl. by J. Cournos. 221 pp. Ld. L. & V. Woolf, 1935. (U.S.A. printed.)

Mitya's love. Transl. from the French by M. Boyd. With an introduction by E. Boyd. 212 pp. N.Y. Holt, 1926.

Never-ending spring. Transl. by H. C. Matheson. (*In:* S. Graham, *Great Russian short stories,* 1929.)

Poems. (*In:* C. F. Coxwell, *Russian poems,* 1929.)

Poems. (*In:* P. Selver, *Modern Russian poetry,* 1917.)

Sunstroke. Transl. by H. C. Matheson. (*In:* S. Graham, *Great Russian short stories,* 1929.)

The village. Transl. by I. F. Hapgood. 291 pp. Ld. Secker, 1923; N.Y. Knopf, 1933.

The well of days. Transl. by G. Struve and H. Miles. 351 pp. Ld. Hogarth Pr., 1933; N.Y. Knopf, 1934.

CHEKHOV (Anton Pavlovich), 1860–1904.

The tales of Tchehov. Transl. by C. Garnett. 13 vols. Ld. Chatto & Windus; N.Y. Macmillan, 1916–1922:

Vol. 1. *The darling, and other stories.* Introduction by E. Garnett. [Contains: 'The darling'; 'Tolstoy's criticism on the darling'; 'Ariadne'; 'Polinka'; 'Anyuta'; 'The two Volodyas'; 'The trousseau'; 'The helpmate'; 'Talent'; 'An artist's story'; 'Three years'.]

Vol. 2. *The duel, etc.* [Contains: 'The duel'; 'Excellent people'; 'Mire'; 'Neighbours'; 'At home'; 'Expensive lessons'; 'The princess'; 'The chemist's wife'.]

Vol. 3. *The lady with the dog, etc.* [Contains: 'The lady with the dog'; 'A doctor's visit'; 'An upheaval'; 'Ionitch'; 'The head of the family'; 'The black monk'; 'Volodya'; 'An anonymous story'; 'The husband'.]

Vol. 4. *The party, etc.* [Contains: 'The party'; 'Terror'; 'A woman's kingdom'; 'A problem'; 'The kiss'; 'Anna on the neck'; 'The teacher of literature'; 'Not wanted'; 'Typhus'; 'A misfortune'; 'A trifle from life'.]

Vol. 5. *The wife, etc.* [Contains: 'The wife'; 'Difficult people'; 'The grasshopper'; 'A dreary story'; 'The privy councillor'; 'The man in a case'; 'Gooseberries'; 'About love'; 'The lottery ticket'.]

Vol. 6. *The witch, etc.* [Contains: 'The witch'; 'Peasant wives'; 'The post'; 'The new villa'; 'Dreams'; 'The pipe'; 'Agafya'; 'At Christmas time'; 'Gusev'; 'The student'; 'In the ravine'; 'The huntsman'; 'Happiness'; 'A malefactor'; 'Peasants'.]

Vol. 7. *The bishop, etc.* [Contains: 'The bishop'; 'The letter'; 'Easter eve'; 'A nightmare'; 'The murder'; 'Uprooted'; 'The Steppe'.]

Vol. 8. *The chorus girl, etc.* [Contains: 'The chorus girl'; 'Verotchka'; 'My life'; 'At a country house'; 'A father'; 'On the road'; 'Rothschild's fiddle'; 'Ivan Matveyitch'; 'Zinotchka'; 'Bad weather'; 'A gentleman friend'; 'A trivial incident'.]

Vol. 9. *The schoolmistress, etc.* [Contains: 'The schoolmistress'; 'A nervous breakdown'; 'Misery'; 'Champagne'; 'After the theatre'; 'A lady's story'; 'In exile'; 'The cattle dealers'; 'Sorrow'; 'On official duty'; 'The first-class passenger'; 'A tragic actor'; 'A transgression'; 'Small

fry'; 'The requiem'; 'In the coach house'; 'Panic fears';
'The bet'; 'The head-gardener's story'; 'The beauties';
'The shoemaker and the devil'.]

Vol. 10. *The horse-stealers, etc.* [Contains: 'The horse-stealers';
'Ward No. 6'; 'The Petchenyeg'; 'A dead body'; 'A
happy ending'; 'The looking-glass'; 'Old age'; 'Darkness'; 'The beggar'; 'A story without a title'; 'In trouble';
'Frost'; 'A slander'; 'Minds ferment'; 'Gone astray';
'An avenger'; 'The jeune premier'; 'A defenceless
creature'; 'An enigmatic nature'; 'A happy man'; 'A
troublesome visitor'; 'An actor's end'.]

Vol. 11. *The schoolmaster, etc.* [Contains: 'The schoolmaster';
'Enemies'; 'The examining magistrate'; 'Betrothed';
'From the diary of a violent tempered man'; 'In the
dark'; 'A play'; 'A mystery'; 'Strong impressions';
'Drunk'; 'The Marshall's widow'; 'A bad business';
'In the court'; 'Boots'; 'Joy'; 'Ladies'; 'A peculiar man';
'At the barber's'; 'An inadvertence'; 'The album'; 'Oh!
the public'; 'A tripping tongue'; 'Overdoing it'; 'The
orator'; 'Malingerers'; 'In the graveyard'; 'Hush!'; 'In
an hotel'; 'In a strange land'.]

Vol. 12. *The cook's wedding, etc.* [Contains: 'The cook's wedding'; 'Sleepy'; 'Children'; 'The runaway'; 'Grisha';
'Oysters'; 'Home'; 'A classical student'; 'Vanka'; 'An
incident'; 'A day in the country'; 'Boys'; 'Shrove
Tuesday'; 'The old house'; 'In Passion week'; 'White
brow'; 'Kashtanka'; 'A chameleon'; 'The dependents';
'Who was to blame?'; 'The bird market'; 'An adventure'; 'The fish'; 'Art'; 'The Swedish match'.]

Vol. 13. *Love, etc.* [Contains: 'Love'; 'Lights'; 'A story without
an end'; 'Mari d'Elle'; 'A living chattel'; 'The doctor';
'Too early'; 'The cossack'; 'Aborigines'; 'An enquiry';
'Martyrs'; 'The lion and the sun'; A daughter of Albion';
'Choristers'; 'Nerves'; 'A work of art'; 'A joke'; 'A
country cottage'; 'A blunder'; 'Fat and thin'; 'The
death of a government clerk'; 'A pink stocking'; 'At a
summer villa'.]

Select tales of Tchehov. Transl. by C. Garnett. 849 pp. Ld.
Chatto & Windus, 1927. [Contains: 'The lady with the dog';
'The horse-stealers'; 'The bishop'; 'In the ravine'; 'Sleepy';
'Ionitch'; 'At Christmas time'; 'My life'; 'The chorus girl';
'The new villa'; 'The teacher of literature'; 'The witch'; 'An
anonymous story'; 'The beauties'; 'A transgression';

'Gusev'; 'A woman's kingdom'; 'Mire'; 'Easter eve'; 'A dreary story'; 'A misfortune'; 'Happiness'; 'The darling'.]

Tales from Tchehov. Transl. by C. Garnett. 248 pp. Ld. Penguin Books, 1938.

The plays of Tchehov. Transl. by C. Garnett. 2 vols. Ld. Chatto & Windus; N.Y. Macmillan, 1923–24.

Vol. 1. 'The cherry orchard'; 'Uncle Vanya'; 'The seagull'; 'The bear'; 'The proposal'.

Vol. 2. 'Three sisters'; 'Ivanov'; 'A swansong'; 'An unwilling martyr'; 'The anniversary'; 'On the high road'; 'The wedding'.

Plays and stories. Transl. by S. S. Koteliansky. 360 pp. Ld. Dent, 1937. (Everyman's Library.)

Five famous plays by Anton Chekhov: 'The bear', 'The three sisters', 'The cherry orchard', transl. by J. West; 'Uncle Vanya', 'The seagull', transl. by M. Fell. 311 pp. Ld. Duckworth, 1939.

Plays. Transl. by M. Fell. N.Y., 1912. [Contains: 'Uncle Vanya'; 'Ivanov'; 'The seagull'; 'The swansong'.]

Two plays. Transl. by G. Calderon. N.Y. and Ld., 1912. [Contains: 'The seagull'; 'The cherry orchard'.]

A bear. Transl. by R. T. A. House. N.Y. Moods, 1919.

The bet, and other stories. Transl. by S. S. Koteliansky and J. M. Murry. Boston. Luce, 1915.

The cherry orchard. (*In:* O. M. Sayler, *Moscow Art Theatre series of Russian plays*, series 1, 1923.)

The black monk, and other stories. Transl. by R. E. C. Long. Ld. Duckworth, 1903; N.Y. Stokes, 1915.

In a foreign land. (*In:* P. Selver, *Anthology of modern Slavonic literature*, 1919.)

Ivanov. (*In:* O. M. Sayler, *Moscow Art Theatre series of Russian plays*, series 2, 1923.)

The jubilee. (*In:* C. E. Bechhofer, *Five Russian plays*, 1916.)

The kiss, and other stories. Transl. by R. E. C. Long. Ld. Duckworth, 1908; N.Y. Scribner, 1912.

My life. Transl. by E. R. Schimanskaya. 106 pp. Ld. King & Staples, 1943. (Modern Readers' Library.)

The pass, and other stories. Transl. by R. E. C. Long. 317 pp. N.Y. Scribner, 1912.

Russian silhouettes; more Russian stories. Transl. by M. Fell. 318 pp. N.Y. Scribner, 1915.

The shooting party. Transl. by A. E. Chamot. 244 pp. Ld. Stanley Paul, 1926.

The Steppe, and other stories. Transl. by A. Kaye. 296 pp. N.Y. Stokes, 1915.

Stories of Russian life. Transl. by M. Fell. 314 pp. N.Y. Scribner, 1914.

That worthless fellow Platonov. Transl. by J. Cournos. 279 pp. Ld. Dent, 1930.

The three sisters. (*In:* O. M. Sayler, *Moscow Art Theatre series of Russian plays,* series 1, 1923.)
—— Same. Transl. by S. Young. N.Y. French, 1941.

Uncle Vanya. (*In:* O. M. Sayler, *Moscow Art Theatre series of Russian plays,* series 1, 1923.)
—— Same. Transl. by R. Caylor. N.Y. Covici, 1930.

The wedding. (*In:* C. E. Bechhofer, *Five Russian plays,* 1916.)

The wood demon. Transl. by S. S. Kotel..ansky. 120 pp. Ld. Chatto & Windus, 1926. [The first version of Uncle Vanya.]

Letters of Anton Tchehov to his family and friends. Transl. by C. Garnett, with a biographical sketch. Ld. Chatto & Windus; N.Y. Macmillan, 1920.

Letters to Olga Leonardovna Knipper. Transl. by C. Garnett. 387 pp. N.Y. Doran; Ld. Chatto & Windus, 1926.

Letters on the short story, the drama and other literary topics. Selected and ed. by L. S. Friedland. 346 pp. Ld. Bles, 1924.

Life and letters of Anton Tchehov. Transl. and ed. by S. S. Koteliansky and P. Tomlinson. 315 pp. Ld. Cassell, 1925.

Literary and theatrical reminiscences. Transl. and ed. by S. S. Koteliansky. 248 pp. Ld. Routledge; N.Y. Doran, 1927. [Unpublished work of Chekhov, with miscellaneous essays and reminiscences by various authors.]

The note books of Anton Tchekhov, together with Reminiscences of Tchekhov, by Gorky. Transl. by S. S. Koteliansky and L. Woolf. Ld. Hogarth Pr.; N.Y. Huebsch, 1921.

Biography, criticism, etc.:

HEIFETZ: *Bibliography of Chekhov's works translated into English and published in America. Bulletin of Bibliography,* May 13, N.Y., 1929.

BARING (M.): *Plays of Anton Tchekhov.* (*In his:* Landmarks of Russian literature. Ld., 1916.)

ELTON (O.): *Chekhov.* Oxf. Clarendon Pr., 1929. (Taylorian Lecture, 1929.) Repr. in his: *Essays and addresses.* Ld. Arnold, 1939.

GERHARDI (W.): *Anton Chekhov; a critical study.* Ld. Cobden-Sanderson, 1923.

MURRY (J. M.): *Aspects of literature.* 203 pp. N.Y. Knopf, 1920. [Contains essay on Chekhov.]

MURRY (J. M.): *Discoveries: essays in literary criticism.* 313 pp. Ld. Collins, 1924. [Contains essay on Chekhov.]

SHESTOV (L.): *Anton Chekhov, and other essays.* Transl. by S. S. Koteliansky and J. M. Murry. Ld. 1916.

TOUMANOVA (N. A.): *Anton Chekhov, the voice of twilight Russia.* 239 pp. Ld. Cape, 1937.

CHETVERIKOV (D.).

Corpses. (*In:* S. Konovalov, *Bonfire,* 1932.)

CHIRIKOV (Evgeny Nikolaevich), 1864–.

Bound over. Transl. by L. Zarine. (*In:* S. Graham, *Great Russian short stories,* 1929.)

The magician. Transl. by L. Zarine (ibid.).

Marka of the pits. Transl. by L. Zarine. 223 pp. N.Y. Alston Rivers, 1930.

CHULKOV (Georgiy), 1879–.

Poems. (*In:* B. Deutsch and A. Yarmolinsky, *Modern Russian poetry,* 1923.)

CHUVOVSKY (Korney Ivanovich), 1883–.

Crocodile. With the original Russian illustrations. Transl. by B. Deutsch. 31 pp. N.Y. Lippincott, 1931; Ld. Mathews, 1932.

DANILEVSKY (Grigoriy Petrovich), 1829–90.

Moscow in flames. Transl. by A. S. Rappoport. Ld. Stanley Paul, 1917.

DIKOVSKY (Sergey).

The commandant of the isle of birds. (*In:* E. Fen, *Soviet stories of the last decade,* 1945.)

DOLGHIH (A.).

Raw stuff. (*In:* E. Fen, *Soviet stories of the last decade,* 1945.)

DOROSHEVICH (Vasiliy), 1864–.

How Hassan lost his trousers. Transl. by R. Graham. (*In:* S. Graham, *Great Russian short stories,* 1929.)

DOSTOEVSKAYA (Anna Grigorevna), 1846–1918.

The diary of Dostoevsky's wife. Ed. by R. Fülöp-Miller and F. Eckstein. Transl. from the German by M. Pemberton. 421 pp. Ld. Gollancz, 1928.

Dostoevsky portrayed by his wife: the diary and reminiscences of Mme Dostoevsky. Transl. and ed. by S. S. Koteliansky. Ld. Routledge, 1926.

DOSTOEVSKAYA (Lyubov Fedorovna), 1869–.

The emigrant. Transl. by V. Margolies. With an introduction by S. Graham. Ld. Constable, 1916.

DOSTOEVSKY (Fedor Mikhailovich), 1821–81.
The novels of Fyodor Dostoevsky. From the Russian by Constance
Garnett. Ld. Heinemann, 1912–1920. 12 vols.
Vol. 1. *The Brothers Karamazov.* 1912.
Vol. 2. *The idiot.* 1913.
Vol. 3. *The possessed.* 1913.
Vol. 4. *Crime and punishment.* 1914.
Vol. 5. *The house of the dead.* 1915.
Vol. 6. *The insulted and injured.* 1915.
Vol. 7. *A raw youth.* 1916.
Vol. 8. 'The eternal husband'; 'The double'; 'A gentle spirit'.
1917.
Vol. 9. 'The gambler'; 'Poor people'; 'The landlady'. 1917.
Vol. 10. 'White nights'; 'Notes from underground'; 'A faint
heart'; 'A Christmas tree and a wedding'; 'Polzunkov';
'A little hero'; 'Mr. Prohartchin'. 1918.
Vol. 11. 'An honest thief'; 'Uncle's dream'; 'A novel in nine
letters'; 'An unpleasant predicament'; 'Another man's
wife'; 'The heavenly Christmas tree'; 'The peasant
Marey'; 'The crocodile'; 'Bobuk'; 'The dream of a
ridiculous man'. 1919.
Vol. 12. 'A friend of the family'; 'Nyetochka Nyezhanov'. 1920.
The Brothers Karamazov. Transl. by C. Garnett. 2 vols. Ld.
Dent 1927. (Everyman's Library.)
—— Same. (*In:* O. M. Sayler, *Moscow Art Theatre of Russian
plays,* series 2, 1923.)
Buried alive. See: The house of the dead. 1911.
Crime and punishment: a Russian realistic novel. 455 pp. Ld.
Dent, 1915. (Everyman's Library.) (Repr. of 1911.)
Crime and punishment. Transl. by C. Garnett. Ill. 531 pp.
N.Y. A. S. Barnes, 1944. (Illustrated Modern Library.)
The gambler. See: Poor folk, and *The gambler.* 1915.
The grand inquisitor. [Parts 2–3, Book 5, Chapter 4 of *The Brothers
Karamazov.*] Transl. by S. S. Koteliansky. With an intro-
duction by D. H. Lawrence. 81 pp. Ld. Secker,
1935.
The house of the dead; or, Prison life in Siberia. Ld. Dent, 1911.
(Everyman's Library.) Repr. of *Buried alive,* ed. of 1881 and
1887.
The idiot. Transl. by E. M. Martin. 605 pp. Ld. Dent, 1914.
(Everyman's Library.)
—— Same. Transl. by C. Garnett. 586 pp. N.Y. Modern
Library, 1942. (Modern Library Giants.)

Letters from the underworld, and other tales. Transl. by C. J. Hogarth. Ld. Dent, 1913. (Everyman's Library.) [Contains: 'Letters from the underworld'; 'The gentle maiden'; 'The landlady'.]

A nasty story. Transl. by A. E. Chamot. (*In:* A. E. Chamot, *Selected Russian short stories,* 1925.)

—— Same. With title: *An unpleasant predicament. See: The novels of F. Dostoevsky.* Transl. by C. Garnett, vol. 11, 1919.

Poor folk, and *The gambler.* Transl. by C. J. Hogarth. Ld. Dent, 1915. (Everyman's Library.)

The possessed. 2 vols. Ld. Dent, 1931. (Everyman's Library.) Repr. of *The novels of F. Dostoevsky.* Transl. by C. Garnett, vol. 3, 1913.

Stavrogin's confession. Transl. by S. S. Koteliansky and V. Woolf. Ld. Hogarth Pr., 1922. [Contains: three unpublished chapters from *The possessed,* and the plan of *The life of a great sinner,* of which *The Brothers Karamazov* was intended to be part.]

Pages from the journal of an author. Transl. by S. S. Koteliansky and J. Middleton Murry. London and Dublin. Maunsell, 1916. (The Modern Russian Library.) Boston. Luce, 1916. [Contains: 'The dream of a queer fellow', and 'Pushkin'.]

Letters of F. M. Dostoevsky to his family and friends. Transl. from the German by Ethel C. Mayne. Ld. Chatto & Windus, 1914. [Contains: 77 letters of Dostoevsky, recollections of Dostoevsky by Grigorevich, etc., contemporary judgments of Aksakov, Turgenev, Tolstoy, etc., and a chronological table of Dostoevsky's life.]

Letters of Dostoevsky to his wife. Translated by Elizabeth Hill and Doris Mudie. Ld. Constable, 1930.

Dostoevsky: letters and reminiscences. Translated by S. S. Koteliansky and J. M. Murry. Ld. Chatto & Windus; N.Y. Knopf, 1923. 286 pp. [Contains: letters from D. to his wife and friends and reminiscences by his wife.]

New Dostoevsky letters. Translated by S. S. Koteliansky. Ld. Mandrake Pr., 1929.

Biography, criticism, etc.:

OSBOURNE (E. A.): *Russian literature and translations,* 7: *F. M. Dostoevsky.* Bookman. Ld. June, 1933.

ABRAHAM (G.): *Dostoevsky.* Ld. Duckworth, 1936. (Great Lives.)

BERDYAEV (N. A.): *Dostoevsky: an interpretation.* Transl. by D. Attwater. Ld. Sheed, 1936; N.Y. 1934.

CARR (E. H.): *Dostoevsky; a new biography*. Ld. Allen & Unwin, 1931.

DOSTOEVSKAYA (A. G.): *Dostoevsky portrayed by his wife. See*: DOSTOEVSKAYA (A. G.).

DOSTOEVSKAYA (A. G.): *The diary of Dostoevsky's wife. See*: DOSTOEVSKAYA (A. G.).

DOSTOEVSKAYA (L. F.): *Fyodor Dostoevsky; a study*. 294 pp. Yale. Univ. Pr., 1922.

GIDE (A.): *Dostoevsky*. Transl. from the French, with an introduction, by Arnold Bennett. 224 pp. Ld. Dent; N.Y. Knopf, 1926.

LAVRIN (J.): *Dostoevsky and his creation: a psychocritical study*. 189 pp. Ld. Collins, 1920.

LAVRIN (J.): *Dostoevsky: a study*. Ld. Methuen, 1943. [New ed.]

LLOYD (J. A. T.): *A great Russian realist: Fedor Dostoieffsky*. Ld. Stanley Paul, 1912.

MEIER-GRAEFFE (J.): *Dostoevsky, the man and his work*. Transl. by H. H. Marks. 406 pp. Ill. N.Y. Harcourt, 1928.

MEREZHKOVSKY (D. S.): *Tolstoy as man and artist, with an essay on Dostoevsky*. Ld. Constable, 1902.

MUCHNIC (H.): *Dostoevsky's English reputation, 1881–1936*. 219 pp. Northampton, Mass. 1939. (Smith College Studies in Modern Languages, 20.) [Contains: Bibliography of books and articles in English on Dostoevsky.]

MURRY (J. M.): *Fyodor Dostoevsky: a critical study*, 264 pp. Boston. Small, 1924.

SIMMONS (E. J.): *Dostoevski: the making of a novelist*. Cambridge, Mass. Harvard Univ. Pr.; Ld. Oxf. Univ. Pr., 1940.

SOLOVYOV (E. A.): *Dostoevsky; his life and literary activity*. Transl. by C. J. Hogarth. Ld. Allen & Unwin, 1916.

YARMOLINSKY (A.): *Dostoevsky: a life*. 447 pp. N.Y. Harcourt, 1934.

YARMOLINSKY (A.): *Dostoevsky: a study in his ideology*. N.Y., 1921.

ZERNOV (N.): *Three Russian prophets: Khomyakov, Dostoevsky, Soloviev*. 171 pp. Ld. Student, 1944.

ZWEIG (St.): *Three masters: Balzac, Dickens, Dostoevsky*. Transl. from the German by E. and C. Paul. 238 pp. N.Y. Viking Pr.; Ld. Allen & Unwin, 1930.

DOVZHENKO (Aleksandr).
> *Mother Stoyan.* (*In:* I. Montagu and H. Marshall, *Soviet short stories*, 1944.)
> *The night before the battle.* (Ibid.)

DYMOV (Osip) [pseud. of O. I. Perelman], 1878–.
> *The flight from the cross.* Transl. by G. M. Foakes. Ld. Werner Laurie, 1916.
> *Nju; an everyday tragedy.* Transl. by R. Ivan. N.Y. 1917. (Borzoi Books.)

EHRENBURG (Ilya Grigorevich), 1891–.
> *The call.* (*In:* E. Fen, *Soviet stories of the last decade*, 1945.)
> *Extraordinary adventures of Julio Jurenito and his disciples.* Transl. by U. Vanzler. 399 pp. N.Y. Covici, 1930.
> *The fall of Paris.* Transl. by G. Shelley. 382 pp. Ld. Hutchinson, 1942.
> —— With title: *The fall of Paris, seen through Soviet eyes.* Foreword by S. T. Warner. Ld. Modern Books, 1941.
> *The love of Jeanne Ney.* Transl. by H. C. Matheson. 356 pp. Ld. Davies, 1929.
> *New short stories.* (*In:* I. Montagu and H. Marshall, *Soviet short stories.* Ld. 1942.)
> *Out of chaos.* Transl. by A. Bakshy. 391 pp. N.Y. Holt, 1934. [Russian title: *The second day.*]
> *Protochny lane.* (*In:* S. Konovalov, *Bonfire*, 1932.)
> *A Soviet writer looks at Vienna.* Transl. by I. Montagu. 47 pp. Ld. Lawrence, 1934.
> *A street in Moscow.* Transl. by S. Volochova. 278 pp. Ld. Grayson, 1933.

ERSHOV (Petr Pavlovich), 1815–69.
> *Humpy.* Transl. by W. C. White. 110 pp. N.Y. Harper, 1931.
> *Little hunchback horse.* Adaptation from a poem [by Ershov] by I. Wicker. 155 pp. N.Y. Putnam, 1942.
> *Little magic horse, a Russian tale.* Transl. by T. B. Drowne. Ill. Macmillan, 1942.

ERTEL (Aleksandr Ivanovich), 1855–1908.
> *A greedy peasant*, and *A specialist.* Transl. by N. Duddington. (*In:* S. Graham, *Great Russian short stories*, 1929.)

ESENIN (Sergey), 1895–1925.
> Poems. (*In:* C. M. Bowra, *A book of Russian verse*, 1943.)
> Poems. (*In:* B. Deutsch and A. Yarmolinsky, *Russian poetry*, 1929.)

The tramp; The last village poet; My mysterious world; Tavern Moscow. (In: G. Reavey and M. Slonim, *Soviet literature,* 1933.)

EVREYNOV (Nikolai Nikolaevich), 1879–.

Chief things: a comedy for some, a drama for others. Theatre Guild acting version made from the translation by H. Bernstein and L. Randoll. 226 pp. N.Y. Doubleday, 1926.

The beautiful despot. (In: C. E. Bechhofer, *Five Russian plays* 1916.)

The corridors of the soul, a monodrama. Adapted by P. Wilde from the Vienna version of F. T. Csokor. *(In:* P. Wilde, *Contemporary one-act plays from nine countries.* Ld. Harrap, 1936.)

The merry death. (In: C. E. Bechhofer, *Five Russian plays,* 1916.)

Theatre in life. Ed. and transl. by A. I. Nazaroff. With an introduction by O. M. Sayler. 296 pp. Ld. Harrap; N.Y. Brentano's, 1927.

The theatre of the soul. Transl. by M. Potapenko and C. St. John. Ld. Hendersons, 1915.

FADEEV (Aleksandr Aleksandrovich), 1901–.

Annihilation. (In: S. Konovalov, *Bonfire,* 1932.)

The bandits, from *The last of the Udegs. (In:* G. Reavey and M. Slonim, *Soviet literature,* 1933.)

The nineteen. Transl. by R. D. Charques. 293 pp. Ld. Lawrence, 1929. [Russian title: *The rout.*]

FEDIN (Konstantin Aleksandrovich), 1892–.

The chronicle of Narovchat. (In: E. Fen, *Modern Russian stories,* 1943.)

Love and war, from *The brothers. (In:* G. Reavey and M. Slonim, *Soviet literature,* 1933.)

The orchard. (In: S. Konovalov, *Bonfire,* 1932.)

FET (Afanasy Afanasevich), afterwards Shenshin, 1820–92.

Poem: *Nocturne. (In:* P. E. Matheson, *Holy Russia,* 1918.)

Poems. *(In:* C. M. Bowra, *A book of Russian verse,* 1943.)

Poems. *(In:* F. Cornford and E. P. Salaman, *Poems from the Russian,* 1943.)

Poems. *(In:* B. Deutsch and A. Yarmolinsky, *Russian poetry,* 1929.)

FIALKO (Nathan Moisevich), 1881–.

The new city. Transl. from the Russian and rev. by the author. 153 pp. N.Y. Margent Pr., 1937.

FIBIKH (Daniel).

The execution. (In: S. Konovalov, *Bonfire,* 1932.)

FIGNER (Vera Nikolaevna), 1852–.
  Memoirs of a revolutionist. Authorised transl. by C. C. Daniels
  and G. A. Davidson. Ed. by A. Kaun. 318 pp. N.Y.
  International Publ. Co., 1927.
FRANKO (Ivan Yakovlevich), 1856–1916.
  Moses; a poem. Transl. from the Ukrainian by W. Semenyna,
  with a biographical sketch by S. Shumeyko. 93 pp. N.Y.
  United Ukrainian Organisation of the U.S., 1938.
  Voice from Ukrainia. Biographical sketch and transl. from his
  works by P. Cundy. 74 pp. Manitoba. Buffy, 1932.
FREIRMAN (R.).
  Pathless. Transl. by A. Brown. (*Extract in:* J. Rodker, *Soviet
  anthology*, 1943.)
FURMANOV (Dmitri Andreevich), 1891–1926.
  Chapayev. 483 pp. N.Y. International Publishers, 1935.
  —— Same. Cheap ed. 336 pp. Ld. Lawrence, 1936.
  —— Same. (Workers' Library.) 311 pp. Ld. Lawrence, 1941.
GABRILOVICH (Evgeny).
  The year 1930. (*In:* G. Reavey and M. Slonim, *Soviet literature*,
  1933.)
GARSHIN (Vsevelod Mikhailovich), 1855–88.
  The crimson flower. Transl. by R. Graham. (*In:* S. Graham,
  Great Russian short stories, 1929.)
  Four days. Transl. by H. C. Matheson. (*In:* S. Graham, *Great
  Russian short stories*, 1929.)
  —— Same. Transl. by S. S. Koteliansky. (*In: Russian short
  stories*, 1943.)
  The red flower. Anon. transl. 37 pp. Philadelphia. Brown, 1911.
  The signal, and other stories. Transl. by R. Smith. Ld.
  Duckworth; N.Y. Knopf, 1915. [Contains: 'Four days';
  'Nadjeda Nikolaevna'; 'The signal'.]
GASTEV (Aleksey Kapitónovich), 1882–.
  Poems. (*In:* B. Deutsch and A. Yarmolinsky, *Russian poetry*,
  1929.)
GERASIMOV (Mikhail Prokofevich), 1889–.
  Poem. (*In:* B. Deutsch and A. Yarmolinsky, *Russian poetry*,
  1929.)
  Poems. (*In:* G. Z. Patrick, *Popular poetry in Soviet Russia*, 1929.)
GERMAN (Yuri Pavlovich), 1910–.
  Alexei the gangster. Transl. by S. Garry. 288 pp. Ld.
  Routledge, 1940.
  Antonina. Transl. by S. Garry. 470 pp. Ld. Routledge, 1937.
  —— Same. With title: *Tonia.* 412 pp. N.Y. Knopf, 1938.

GLADKOV (Fedor Vasilevich), 1883–.
   Cement. Transl. by A. S. Arthur and C. Ashleigh. 311 pp. Ld.
      Lawrence, 1929.
   The ragged brigade, from *Power.* (*In:* G. Reavey and M.
      Slonim, *Soviet literature,* 1933.)
GLEBOV (Anatoliy Glebovich), 1899–.
   Inga; a play in four acts and thirteen scenes. Transl. by C.
      Malamuth. (*In:* E. Lyons, *Six Soviet plays,* 1935.)
GLINKA (Fedor Nikolaevich), 1788–1880.
   Poems. (*In:* C. F. Coxwell, *Russian poems,* 1929.)
GOGOL (Nikolay Vasilevich), 1809–52.
   The works of Nikolay Gogol. From the Russian by C. Garnett.
      6 vols. Ld. Chatto & Windus, 1922–1928.
   Vols. 1–2. *Dead souls.*
   Vol. 3. *The overcoat, and other stories.* [Contains: 'The over-
      coat'; 'The carriage'; 'The Nevsky prospect'; 'A
      madman's diary'; 'The prisoner'; 'The nose'; 'The
      portrait'.]
   Vol. 4. *Evenings on a farm near Dinkanka.*
   Vol. 5. *The government inspector, and other plays.* [Contains:
      'The government inspector'; 'Marriage'; 'The
      gamblers'; 'Dramatic sketches and fragments'.]
   Vol. 6. 'Mirogod'; 'Old-world landowners'; 'Taras Bulba';
      'Viy'; 'Tale of two Ivans'.
   Dead souls. Transl. by C. J. Hogarth. 324 pp. Ld. Dent,
      1915. (Everyman's Library.)
   —— Same. Transl. by I. F. Hapgood. Reissued. Ld. Benn,
      1929. (Essex Library.)
   —— Same. With title: *Tchitchikoff's journeys.* Transl. by I. F.
      Hapgood. Ld. Fisher Unwin, 1915. Repr. of ed. of 1886
      and 1887.
   Diary of a madman. Transl. by Prince D. S. Mirsky. Ill. 81 pp.
      Ld. Cresset Pr., 1929. Ltd. ed.
   Evenings in Little Russia. Transl. by E. W. Underwood and W. H.
      Cline. 153 pp. Evanston. Lord, 1903. [Contains: 'The fair
      of Sorotchinet'; 'An evening in May'; 'Midsummer evening'.]
   The gamblers. Transl. by A. Berkman. N.Y. Macaulay, 1927.
   The inspector. Transl. by J. L. Seymour and G. R. Noyes. (*In:*
      G. R. Noyes, *Masterpieces of the Russian drama,* 1933.)
   The mantle, and other stories. Transl. by C. Field. Ld. Laurie,
      1915. [Contains: 'The mantle'; 'The nose'; 'A may-night'.]
   Marriage. (*In:* E. L. Voynich, *Humour of Russia,* 1909.)
   —— Same. Transl. by A. Berkman. N.Y. Macaulay, 1927.

Taras Bulba. Transl. by B. C. Badkerville. 295 pp. Ld. Scott, 1907.

Taras Bulba, and other tales. With an introduction by J. Cournos. Ld. Dent, 1918. (Everyman's Library.) Repr. 1930. [Contains: 'Taras Bulba'; 'St. John's eve'; 'Old-fashioned farmers'; 'How Ivan Ivanovitch quarrelled'; 'The portrait'; 'The cloak'; 'The king of the gnomes'; 'The calash'.]

Biography, criticism, etc.:

OSBOURNE (E. A.): Early transl. from the Russian: 4. *N. V. Gogol.* (*Bookman.* Ld. Oct. 1932.)

BARING (M.): *Gogol and the cheerfulness of the Russian people.* (*In his: Landmarks in Russian literature,* 1910.)

LAVRIN (J.): *Gogol.* 264 pp. Ld. Routledge, 1925; N.Y. Dutton, 1926. [Contains a bibliography.]

NABOKOV (V. V.): *Nikolay Gogol.* Connecticut. New Directions, 1942.

GOMBERG (Vladimir Germanovich). *See:* LIDIN (Vladimir) [pseud. of Vladimir Germanovich Gomberg.]

GONCHAROV (Ivan Aleksandrovich), 1812–91.

Oblomov. Transl. by C. J. Hogarth. 317 pp. [Abridged.] Ld. Allen & Unwin; N.Y. Macmillan, 1915.

—— Same. Transl. by N. Duddington. Ld. Allen & Unwin, 1929.

—— Re-issued. 517 pp. Ld. Dent, 1932. (Everyman's Libary.)

The precipice. Anon. transl. 319 pp. Ld. Hodder & Stoughton; N.Y. Knopf, 1915.

Biography, criticism, etc.:

DOBROLYUBOV (N. A.): *What is Oblomovism?* (*In:* L. Wiener, *Russian anthology,* vol. 2, 1903.)

GORBATOV (Boris).

After death. (*In:* I. Montagu and H. Marshall, *Soviet short stories,* 1944.)

Alexei Kulikov—Red armyman. (*In: Soviet war stories,* 1943.)

The trial of a comrade. (*In:* E. Fen, *Soviet stories of the last decade,* 1945.)

Zero hour. (*In:* I. Montagu and H. Marshall, *Soviet short stories,* 1943.)

GORENKO (Anna Andreevna). *See:* AKHMATOVA (Anna), pseud. of Anna Andreevna Gorenko.

GORKY (Maksim) [pseud. of Aleksey Maksimovich Peshkov], 1869–1936.

A book of short stories. Ed. by A. Yarmolinsky and M. Budberg. Foreword by A. Huxley. 403 pp. Ld. Cape, 1939.
A boy. Transl. by M. Budberg. (*In:* J. Rodker, *Soviet anthology,* 1943.)
Bystander. Transl. by B. G. Guerney. 729 pp. Ld. Cape, 1930. [The first pt. of the tetralogy, *The life of Klim Samghin.*]
Chelkash, and other stories. Transl. by E. Jakowleff and D. B. Montefiore. N.Y. Knopf, 1902.
—— Same. With title: *Twenty-six men and a girl.* Ld. Duckworth, 1902.
A confession. Transl. from the German by W. F. Harvey. Ld. Everett, 1910.
—— Same. Transl. by R. Strunsky. Ld. Stokes, 1916.
Creatures that once were men. Transl. by D. B. Montefiore and E. Jakowleff. (*In:* S. Graham, *Great Russian short stories,* 1929.)
—— Same. Transl. by J. K. M. Shirazi. With an introduction by G. K. Chesterton. Ld. Rivers; N.Y. Boni & Liveright, 1905.
Culture and the people. 224 pp. Ld. Lawrence & Wishart, 1939.
Days with Lenin. 64 pp. Ld. Lawrence, 1932.
Decadence. Transl. by V. Scott-Gatty. 324 pp. Ld. Cassell; N.Y. McBride, 1927.
Foma Gordyeeff. Transl. by I. F. Hapgood. Ld. Fisher Unwin; N.Y. Scribner, 1901.
—— Same. Transl. by H. Bernstein. N.Y. Ogilvie, 1901.
—— Same. With title: *Foma.* N.Y. Dimondstein, c. 1943.
—— Same. With title: *The man who was afraid.* Ld. Fisher Unwin, 1905. Repr. Ld. Benn, 1929.
Fragments from my diary. 320 pp. Ld. Allen, 1924.
—— Same. Repr. Ld. 1940 and 1942. (Penguin Books.)
—— Same. Transl. by M. Budberg. N.Y. McBride, 1924.
Heartache, and *The old woman Izerofel.* Transl. by A. S. Rappoport. Ld. Maclaren, 1905.
The individualists; Cain and Arteme; Strange companion. Transl. by A. S. Rappoport. Ld. Maclaren, 1906.
In the world. Transl. by G. M. Foakes. 464 pp. Ld. Laurie, 1917.
The judge. Transl. by M. Zakrevsky and B. H. Clark. N.Y. McBride, 1924.
Last plays. Transl. and adapted by Gibson-Cowan. 74 pp. N.Y. International Publishers, 1937; Ld. Lawrence & Wishart. [Contains: 'Yegot Bulichoff'; 'Dostigaeff and the others'.]

The life of Klim Samghin; or, *Forty years, the life of Klim Samghin.* A tetralogy. *See:* the separate pts., *Bystander*; *Magnet*; *Other fires*; *Specter.*

The lower depths. Transl. by L. Irving. Ld. Fisher Unwin, 1910.
—— Same. Transl. by J. Coran. (*In:* O. M. Sayler, *Moscow Art Theatre series of Russian plays,* 1st series, 1923.)
—— Same. With title: *Submerged.* Transl. by E. Hopkins. Boston. Four Seasons, 1915.
—— Same. With title: *At the bottom.* A new transl. by W. L. Laurence. 133 pp. N.Y. French, 1930.
—— Same. With title: *Down and out.* Transl. by G. R. Noyes and A. Kaun. (*In:* G. R. Noyes, *Masterpieces of the Russian drama,* 1933.)

Magnet. Transl. by A. Bakshy. Ld. Cape, 1931. [The second pt. of the tetralogy, *The life of Klim Samghin.*]

The mother. N.Y. Appleton, 1907; Ld. Hodder & Stoughton, 1907. Repr. 1921.

My childhood. Transl. by G. M. Foakes. 308 pp. Ld. Laurie, 1915.

A naughty girl. Transl. by A. S. Rappoport. Ld. Maclaren, 1905.

On guard for the Soviet Union. Introduction by R. Rolland. 173 pp. Ld. Lawrence, 1933.

Orloff and his wife. Transl. by I. F. Hapgood. N.Y. Scribner, 1902.

Orloff and his wife: tales of the barefoot brigade. Transl. by I. F. Hapgood. N.Y. Scribner, 1901. [Contains: 'Orloff and his wife'; 'Konovaloff'; 'The khan and his son'; 'The exorcism'; 'Men with pasts'; 'The insolent man'; 'Varenka Olesoff'; 'Comrades'.]

The Orloff couple. Transl. by E. Yakovlev and D. B. Montefiore. Ld. Heinemann, 1901.

Other fires. Transl. by A. Bakshy. 507 pp. N.Y. Appleton, 1933. [The third pt. of the tetralogy, *The life of Klim Samghin.*]

The outcasts, and other stories. Ld. Fisher Unwin, 1902. [Contains: 'The outcasts'; 'Waiting for the ferry', both transl. by D. B. Montefiore. 'The affair of the clasps', transl. by V. Volkhovsky.] 2nd ed. 1910.

Reminiscences of Leonid Andreev. Transl. by K. Mansfield and S. S. Koteliansky. 118 pp. N.Y. Random House; Ld. Dulau, 1928; Ld. Heinemann, 1931.

Reminiscences of my youth. Transl. by V. Dewey. 344 pp. Ld. Heinemann, 1924,

—— Same. With title: *My university days.* 327 pp. N.Y. Boni & Liveright, 1924.

Reminiscences of Tolstoy. Transl. by S. S. Koteliansky and L. Woolf. 71 pp. Ld. Hogarth Pr., 1920; 115 pp. Hogarth Pr., 1921.

Reminiscences of Tolstoy, Chekhov and Andreev. Transl. by K. Mansfield, S. S. Koteliansky and L. Woolf. 191 pp. Ld. Hogarth Pr., 1934.

The specter. Transl. by A. Bakshy. 680 pp. N.Y. and Ld. Appleton, 1938. [The fourth pt. of the tetralogy, *The life of Klim Samghin.*]

The spy: The story of a superfluous man. Transl. by T. Seltzer. Ld. Duckworth; N.Y. Huebsch, 1908.

Stories of the Steppe. Transl. by H. T. Schnittkind and I. Goldberg. Boston. Stratford Co., 1918. [Contains: 'Makar Chudra'; 'Because of monotony'.]

The story of a novel, and other stories. Transl. by M. Zahrkrevsky. 273 pp. N.Y. Dial Pr.; Ld. Jarrolds, 1925. [Contains: 'The story of a novel'; 'The sky blue life'; 'An incident'; 'The rehearsal'; 'The hermit'.]

Tales. N.Y. Brentano's, 1923. [Contains: 'Twenty-six and one'; 'Tchelkach'; 'Malva'.]

Tales from Gorky. Transl. by R. N. Bain. Ld. Jarrolds; N.Y. Brentano's, 1902. [Contains: 'Chelkash'; 'A rolling stone'; 'In steppe'; 'One autumn night'; 'The green kitten'; 'Comrades'; 'Her lover'; 'Chums'; 'Twenty-six of us'.] Another issue by Funk & Wagnalls, 1902.]

—— Same. With title: *Chelkash, and other stories.* Transl. by R. N. Bain. Ld. Knopf, 1917.

Tales of two countries. [America and Italy]. Ld. Laurie; N.Y. Huebsch, 1914.

Three men. Transl. by C. Horne. Ld. Isbister, 1902.

—— Same. With title: *Three of them.* Transl. by A. Linden. Ld. Fisher Unwin, 1902; N.Y. Knopf, 1922.

Through Russia: a book of stories. Transl. by C. J. Hogarth. [Contains: 'Gubin'; 'A woman'; 'Kalinin'; 'The birth of a man'; 'The ice-breaker'; 'Nilushka'; 'The cemetery'; 'On a river steamer'; 'In a mountain defile'; 'The dead man'.]

To American intellectuals. 31 pp. U.S.A. 1932. (International pamphlets, 28.)

Twenty-six and one, and other stories. Transl. by I. Stranik. N.Y. Taylor, 1902. [Contains: 'Twenty-six and one'; 'Tchelkash'; 'Malva'.]

Twenty-six men and a girl. Transl. by E. Yakovlev and D. B. Montefiore. Ld. Duckworth, 1902. [Contains: 'Twenty-six men and a girl'; 'Chelkash'; 'On a raft'; 'My fellow-travellers'.]

—— Same. Ed. by A. Yarmolinsky and M. Budberg. N.Y. Holt, 1939.

Yegor Bulichov and others: a play in three acts. Transl. by A. Wixley. (*In:* B. Blake, *Four Soviet plays,* 1937.)

Biography, criticism, etc.:

DILLON (E. J.): *Maxim Gorky: his life and writings.* 390 pp. Ld. Isbister, 1902.

KAUN (A. S.): *Maxim Gorky and his Russia.* 620 pp. Ld. Cape, 1932. [Contains a bibliography.]

OLGIN (M. J.): *Maxim Gorky; writer and revolutionist.* 64 pp. Ld. Lawrence, 1933.

OSTWALD (H.): *Maxim Gorky.* Transl. by F. A. Welby. Ld. Heinemann, 1905.

GORODETSKY (Sergey), 1884–.

Poems. (*In:* B. Deutsch and A. Yarmolinsky, *Russian poetry,* 1929.)

Poems. (*In:* P. Selver, *Anthology of modern Slavonic literature,* 1919.)

GREBENSHCHIKOV (Georgiy Dmitrievich), 1882–.

The turbulent giant; an epic novel on Russian peasantry. 392 pp. Southbury, Conn. Alatas Publishing Co., 1940.

GRIBOEDOV (Aleksandr Sergeevich), 1795–1829.

The mischief of being clever. Transl. by B. Pares. With introduction by D. S. Mirsky. Published by The School of Slavonic Studies. Ld. Eyre & Spottiswoode, n.d. 68 pp. (Masterpieces of the Slavonic Literature.)

—— Same. With title: *The misfortune of being clever.* Transl. by S. W. Pring. Ld. Nutt, 1914.

—— Same. With title: *Wit works woe.* Transl. by B. Pares. (*In:* G. R. Noyes, *Masterpieces of the Russian drama,* 1933.)

Biography, criticism, etc.:

TYNYANOV (Y. N.): *Death and diplomacy in Persia.* Transl. by A. Brown. Ld. Boriswood, 1938. [Historical novel on Griboedov.]

GRIGOROVICH (Dmitri Vasilevich), 1822–1900.

The fisherman. Transl. by A. S. Rappoport. Philadelphia. McKay, 1916.

GRINBERG (I.), *See:* BRAMM (M.) and GRINBERG (I.)

GROSSMAN (Vassili).

> *In the town of Berdichev.* (*In*: J. Rodker, *Soviet anthology*, 1943.)
> *The people immortal; a novel of the Red Army in action.* 120 pp. Ld. Hutchinson, 1943.

GUL (Roman Borisovich).

> *Provocateur; a historical novel of the Russian terror.* Authorised transl. by L. Zarine. Ed. by S. Graham. 332 pp. N.Y. Harcourt, 1931.
> —— Same. With title: *General B. O.* Transl. by L. Zarine. 332 pp. Ld. Benn, 1932.

GUMILEV (Nikolay Stefanovich), 1886–1921.

> Poems. (*In*: C. M. Bowra, *A book of Russian verse*, 1943.)
> Poems. (*In*: C. F. Coxwell, *Russian poems*, 1929.)
> Poems. (*In*: G. Reavey and M. Slonim, *Soviet Literature*, 1933.)

GUSEV-ORENBURGSKI (Sergey Ivanovich), 1867–.

> *The land of the children.* Transl. by N. N. Selivanova. 421 pp. N.Y. Longmans, 1928.
> —— Same. Cheap ed. 1931.
> *The land of the fathers.* Transl. by N. N. Selivanova. 298 pp. Ld. Cape, 1925.

HERMAN (Yuri Pavlovich). *See:* GERMAN (Yuri Pavlovich).

HERTSEN (Aleksandr Ivanovich), 1812–70.

> *Memoirs*, pts. 1–2. Transl. by J. D. Duff. Ld. Oxf. Univ. Pr., 1923.
> *My past and thoughts: the memoirs of Alexander Herzen.* Transl. by C. Garnett. 6 vols. Ld. Chatto & Windus, 1924–27.

> Biography, criticism, etc.:
> > CARR (E. H.): *The romantic exiles.* 391 pp. Ld. Gollancz, 1933. [Deals with the life of Hertsen, Bakunin and their circle.]

HIPPIUS (Zinaida Nikolaevna) [Mme Merezhkovsky], 1867–.

> *The green ring;* a play. Transl. by S. S. Koteliansky. Ld. Daniel, 1920.
> Poems. (*In*: C. F. Coxwell, *Russian poems*, 1929.)
> Poems. (*In*: B. Deutsch and A. Yarmolinsky, *Russian poetry*, 1929.)
> Poems. (*In*: P. Selver, *Modern Russian poetry*, 1917.)

HODASEVICH (Vladislav). *See:* KHODASEVICH (Vladislav).

ILENKOV (Vasiliy Pavlovich).

> *Driving axle; a novel of socialist construction.* 455 pp. Ld. Lawrence, 1934.
> *White mittens.* (*In*: I. Montagu and H. Marshall, *Soviet short stories*, 1944.)

ILF (Ilya Arnoldovich), 1897–1937, and PETROV (Evgeny), –1942.
Diamonds to sit on: a Russian comedy of errors. Transl. by E. Hill and D. Mudie. 280 pp. Ld. Methuen, 1930.
Little golden America; two famous Soviet humorists survey these U.S. 387 pp. Ill. N.Y. Farrar, 1937.
Little golden calf; a satiric novel. Transl. by C. Malamuth. With an introduction by A. V. Lunacharsky. 402 pp. Ld. Grayson, 1932.
—— Same. Cheap ed. 384 pp. 1933.
ILIN (Mikhail Andreevich) [pseud. Mikhail Ossorgin], 1878–.
My sister's story. 235 pp. N.Y. Dial Pr., 1931.
—— Same. Transl. by N. Helstein and G. Harris. 238 pp. Ld. Secker, 1932.
Quiet Street. Transl. by N. Helstein. 344 pp. Ld. Secker; N.Y. Dial Pr., 1930.
ISBACH (Aleksandr), 1904–.
Duty. (*In:* I. Montagu and H. Marshall, *Soviet short stories*, 1943.)
The parcel. (*In:* I. Montagu and H. Marshall, *Soviet short stories*, 1942.)
IVANOV (Vsevelod Vyacheslavovich), 1895–.
Adventures of a fakhir. Abbreviated transl. 300 pp. N.Y. Vanguard Pr., 1935.
—— Same. With title: *Patched breeches.* Toronto. Macmillan.
—— Same. With title: *I live a queer life: an extraordinary autobiography.* 317 pp. Ld. Dickson, 1936.
—— Same. Extract, with title: *When I was a fakhir.* (*In:* J. Cournos, *Short stories out of Soviet Russia*, 1929.)
Armoured train 14–69; a play in eight scenes. Transl. by Gibson-Cowan and A. T. K. Grant. 59 pp. Ld. Lawrence, 1933.
The baby. (*In:* J. J. Robbins and J. Kunitz, *Azure cities*, 1929.)
The child. (*In:* J. Cournos, *Short stories out of Soviet Russia*, 1929.)
The desert of Tubskoy. (*Extract in :* G. Reavey and M. Slonim, *Soviet literature*, 1933.)
Unfrozen water. (*In:* S. Konovalov, *Bonfire*, 1932.)
IVANOV (Vyacheslav), 1866–.
Poems. (*In:* C. M. Bowra, *A book of Russian verse*, 1943.)
Poems. (*In:* C. F. Coxwell, *Russian poems*, 1929.)
Poems. (*In:* B. Deutsch and A. Yarmolinsky, *Russian poetry*, 1929.)
Poems. (*In:* P. Selver, *Anthology of modern Slavonic literature*, 1919.)

KALLINIKOV (Josif), 1890–.
Land of bondage. Transl. by P. Kirwin. 128 pp. Ld. Grayson, 1931.
Women and monks. Transl. by P. Kirwin. 873 pp. Ld. Secker; N.Y. Harcourt, 1930.
KASSIL (Lev Abramovich), 1905–.
Land of Shvanbrania: a novel with maps, a coat of arms and a flag. Transl. by S. Glass and N. Guterman. 289 pp. N.Y. Viking Pr., 1935.
One quarter of an hour. (*In:* I. Montagu and H. Marshall, *Soviet short stories,* 1943.)
On the captain's bridge. (*In:* Mayakovsky and his poetry, 1942.)
The story of Alesha Ryazan and Uncle White Sea. 46 pp. N.Y. Co-operative Publ. Society, 1935. [Story for children.]
KATAEV (Valentin Petrovich), 1897–.
The embezzlers. Transl. by L. Zarine. With introduction by S. Graham. 300 pp. N.Y. Dial Pr., 1929; 254 pp. Ld. Black, 1929; Ld. Benn, 1930.
Fellow countrymen. Transl. by J. Cournos. (*In:* J. Cournos, *Short stories out of Soviet Russia,* 1929.)
—— Same. Repr. in: *Russian short stories,* 1943.
The golden pen. (*In:* G. Reavey and M. Slonim, *Soviet literature,* 1933.)
How he stood the test. (*In:* S. Konovalov, *Bonfire,* 1932.)
The infant. Transl. by S. Garry. (*In:* J. Rodker, *Soviet anthology,* 1943.)
Knives. Transl. by A. Brown. (Ibid.)
Peace is where the tempests blow. Transl. by C. Malamuth. 341 pp. Toronto. Farrar, 1937.
—— Same. With title: *Lonely white sail; or Peace is where the tempests blow.* 341 pp. Ld. Allen, 1937.
Squaring the circle. Transl. by N. Goold-Verschoyle and adapted for Engl. performance. 111 pp. Ld. Wishart, 1934.
—— Same. Mercury Theatre version: a farce in three acts. Rev. by A. Dukes. N.Y. Baker, 1935.
—— Same. A play in three acts. Transl. and adapted by E. Lyons and C. Malamuth. (*In:* E. Lyons, *Six Soviet plays,* 1935.)
Things. Transl. by L. Zarine. (*In:* S. Graham, *Great Russian short stories,* 1929.)
Time, forward! Authorised transl. by C. Malamuth. 345 pp. Toronto. Farrar, 1933.

—— Same. With title: *Forward, oh Time!* 432 pp. Ld. Gollancz, 1935.

—— Same. (*Extract in:* G. Reavey and M. Slonim, *Soviet literature*, 1933.)

KAVERIN (Veniamin Aleksandrovich), 1902–.

The anonymous artist. (*Extract in:* G. Reavey and M. Slonim, *Soviet literature*, 1933.)

The larger view. Transl. by E. L. Swan. 484 pp. N.Y. Stackpole; Ld. Cassell, 1938. Repr. Cheap ed. Ld. Cassell, 1940.

The last night. (*In:* I. Montagu and H. Marshall, *Soviet short stories*, 1944.)

The return of the Kirghiz. (*From the prologue in:* G. Reavey and M. Slonim, *Soviet literature*, 1933.)

A simple lad. (*In:* I. Montagu and H. Marshall, *Soviet short stories*, 1944.)

Thomas the ostrich. Transl. by S. Garry. (*In:* J. Rodker, *Soviet anthology*, 1943.)

Three meetings. (*In:* I. Montagu and H. Marshall, *Soviet short stories*, 1944.)

Two captains. Transl. by E. L. Swan. 484 pp. Ld. Cassell, 1938; 442 pp. N.Y. Modern Age, 1942.

KAZIN (Vasiliy), 1898–.

The heavenly factory. (*In:* G. Z. Patrick, *Popular poetry in Soviet Russia*, 1929.)

Poems. (*In:* C. M. Bowra, *A book of Russian verse*, 1943.)

Poems. (*In:* B. Deutsch and A. Yarmolinsky, *Russian poetry*, 1929.)

KERASH (Tembot).

Trial by elders. (*In:* I. Montagu and H. Marshall, *Soviet short stories*, 1942.)

KHLEBNIKOV (Velemir), 1885–.

The image of rebellion. (From LEF, in: G. Reavey and M. Slonim, *Soviet literature*, 1933.)

KHODASEVICH (Vladislav), 1886–1938.

Poems. (*In:* C. M. Bowra, *A book of Russian verse*, 1943.)

Poems. (*In: New Directions in prose and poetry*, pp. 535, 1941.)

KHOMYAKOV (Aleksey Stepanovich), 1804–60.

Poem. (*In:* C. M. Bowra, *A book of Russian verse*, 1943.)

Poem. (*In:* C. F. Coxwell, *Russian poems*, 1929.)

KIRSANOV (Semjen), 1906

Poems. (*In: New Directions*, 1941.)

KIRSHON (Vladimir Mikhailovich), 1902–.
> Bread; a play in five acts and nine scenes. Transl. by S. Volochova. (*In :* E. Lyons, *Six Soviet plays*, 1935.)

KIRSHON (V. M.) and USPENSKIY (Andrey Vasilevich).
> Red rust. Transl. by V. and F. Vernon. 182 pp. N.Y. Brentano's, 1930.

KLUCHANSKY (Anna M.).
> Commissar Krilenko. N.Y. Liveright, 1939.

KLUYEV (Nikolay), 1889–.
> Poems. (*In :* B. Deutsch and A. Yarmolinsky, *Modern Russian poetry*, 1923.)
> Poems. (*In :* G. Z. Patrick, *Popular poetry in Soviet Russia*, 1929.)
> Poems. (*In :* G. Shelley, *Modern poems from Russia*, 1942.)

KNORRE (Fedor).
> In the dark. (*In :* I. Montagu and H. Marshall, *Soviet short stories*, 1944.)

KOCHERGA (Ivan).
> Masters of Time ; a play in four acts. Transl. by A. Wixley. (*In :* B. Blake, *Four Soviet plays*, 1937.) [Russian title : *The watchmaker and the hen.*]

KOCHKUROV (Nikolay Ivanovich). *See :* VESELY (Artem), pseud.

KOLLONTAI (Aleksandra Mikhailovna), 1872–.
> Free love. Transl. by C. J. Hogarth. 279 pp. Ld. Dent, 1934. (Dent's Popular Modern Fiction.)
> —— Same. With title : *Great love*. Transl. by L. Lore. 243 pp. N.Y. Vanguard Pr., 1929.
> —— Same. With title : *Red love*. 286 pp. N.Y. Seven Arts Publishing Co., 1927.

KOLTSOV (Aleksey Vasilevich), 1808–42.
> Poems. (*In :* C. M. Bowra, *A book of Russian verse*, 1943.)
> Poems. (*In :* F. Cornford and E. P. Salaman, *Poems from the Russian*, 1943.)
> Poems. (*In :* C. F. Coxwell, *Russian poems*, 1929.)
> Poems. (*In :* B. Deutsch and A. Yarmolinsky, *Russian poetry*, 1929.)
> Poems. (*In :* P. E. Matheson, *Holy Russia*, 1917.)

KORNEICHUK (Aleksandr), 1910–.
> The front. (*In :* Four Soviet war plays, 1943.)
> Guerillas of the Ukrainian steppes. (Ibid.)

KOROLENKO (Vladimir Galaktionovich), 1853–1921.
> Birds of heaven, and other stories. Transl. by C. A. Manning. N.Y. Duffield, 1919.
> The blind musician. Transl. by J. W. Luce. N.Y. 1915.

In a strange land. Transl. by G. Zilboorg. 214 pp. N.Y. Richards, 1925.

Makar's dream. Transl. by M. Fell. N.Y. Duffield, 1916.

—— Same. (*In:* S. Graham, *Great Russian short stories,* 1929.)

The murmuring forest, and other stories. Transl. by M. Fell. Ld. Duckworth; N.Y. Duffield, 1916. [Contains: 'The murmuring forests'; 'Makar's dream'; 'In bad company'; 'The day of atonement'.]

Kossatch (Larissa Petrovna). *See:* Ukrainka (Lesya) [pseud.]

Kozhevnikov (Vadim).

The girl who led the way. (*In:* I. Montagu and H. Marshall, *Soviet short stories,* 1944.)

March–April. (*In:* E. Fen, *Soviet stories of the last decade,* 1945.)

The scout. (*In:* I. Montagu and H. Marshall, *Soviet short stories,* 1944.)

Kravchinsky (Sergey M.). *See:* Stepniak (Sergey) [pseud. of Sergey M. Kravchinsky.]

Kropotkin (Prince Petr Alekseevich), 1842–1921.

Memoirs of a revolutionist. 502 pp. N.Y. Houghton, 1930. (Riverside Library Series.)

Selections from his writings. Ed. with an introduction by H. Read. 150 pp. N.Y. Universal Distributors, 1942; Ld. Freedom Pr., 1943.

Krylov (Ivan Andreevich), 1768–1844.

Fables. Transl. into Engl. verse, with a preface, by B. Pares. Ld. Cape, 1926; 271 pp. N.Y. Harcourt, 1927.

—— Same. *Selections, with Russian text.* 88 pp. Ld. Penguin Books, 1942.

—— Same. With title: *Fables from the Russian.* Adapted by S. Mead. 16 pp. Oxf. 1943. (Chameleon series, No. 23.)

Poems. (*In:* F. Cornford and E. P. Salaman, *Poems from the Russian,* 1943.)

Poems. (*In:* C. F. Coxwell, *Russian poems,* 1929.)

Kunina (Irina) pseud. *See:* Aleksander (Irina).

Kuprin (Aleksandr Ivanovich), 1870–1938.

The bracelet of garnets, and other stories. Transl. by L. Pasvolsky. Ld. Duckworth; N.Y. Scribner, 1919. [Contains: 'The bracelet of garnets'; 'The horse thieves'; 'The Jewess'; 'Anathema'; 'The Laestrygonians'.]

The duel. Anon. transl. Ld. Allen & Unwin; N.Y. Macmillan, 1916.

Gambrinus, and other stories. Transl. by B. G. Guerney. N.Y. Adelphi, 1926. [Contains: 'Gambrinus'; 'Monte Carlo'; 'Roach hole'.]

In honour's name. Transl. by W. F. Harvey. Ld. Everett, 1907.

Olessia; a novel. Transl. by A. E. Harrison. Ld. Sisley, 1909.

The river of life, and other stories. Transl. by S. S. Koteliansky and J. M. Murry. Ld. Maunsell; Boston. Luce, 1916. [Contains: 'The river of life'; 'Captain Ribnikov'; 'The outrage'; 'The witch'.]

—— Same. New ed. 248 pp. Ld. Allen & Unwin, 1943.

Sasha, and other stories. Transl. by D. Ashby. Ld. Stanley Paul, 1920; Philadelphia. McKay, 1928.

Shulamite. N.Y. Luce, 1915.

Sulamith. Transl. by B. G. Guerney. N.Y. Adelphi, 1926.

A Slav soul, and other stories. Transl. by S. Graham. Ld. Constable, 1916. [Contains: 'A Slav soul'; 'Captain Ribnikov'; 'Mechanical justice'; 'The song and the dance'; 'Tempting providence'.]

Yama. A novel in three pts. Transl. by B. G. Guerney. 447 pp. N.Y. B. G. Guerney, 1929; 340 pp. Ld. Hamilton, 1935.

KUZMIN (Mikhail A.), 1877–.

Poems. (*In:* C. F. Coxwell, *Russian poems*, 1929.)

Poems. (*In:* B. Deutsch and A. Yarmolinsky, *Russian poetry*, 1929.)

LANDAU (Mark Aleksandrovich). *See:* ALDANOV (Mark) pseud.

LAVRENOV (Boris), 1894–.

The old woman. (*In:* I. Montagu and H. Marshall, *Soviet short stories*, 1944.)

LENCH (Leonid).

Russian hospitality. Transl. by A. Brown. (*In:* J. Rodker, *Soviet anthology*, 1943.)

LEONOV (Leonid Maksimovich), 1899–.

By the bonfire. (*In:* S. Konovalov, *Bonfire*, 1932.)

The invasion. (*In: Four Soviet war plays*, 1943.)

Ivan's misadventure. Transl. by J. Cournos. (*In:* J. Cournos, *Short stories out of Soviet Russia*, 1929.) (*Repr. in: Russian short stories*, 1943.)

Road to the ocean. Transl. by N. Guterman. 510 pp. N.Y L. B. Fischer, 1944.

Skutarevsky. Transl. by A. Brown. 444 pp. N.Y. Harcourt; Ld. Dickson, 1936.

—— Same. (*Extract in:* G. Reavey and M. Slonim, *Soviet literature*, 1933.)

Sot. Transl. by I. Montagu and S. S. Nolbandov. With a preface by M. Gorky. 387 pp. Ld. Putnam, 1931.
—— Same. With title: *Soviet river.* 382 pp. N.Y. Dial Pr., 1932.
The thief. Authorised transl. by H. Butler. 566 pp. Ld. Secker, 1931.
Three tales. (*In:* E. Fen, *Modern Russian stories,* 1943.)
The town of Gogulev. (*In:* S. Konovalov, *Bonfire,* 1932.)
Tuatamur. Transl. by I. Montagu and S. S. Nolbandov. 50 pp. Ld. Collet's Bookshop, 1935.

LERMONTOV (Mikhail Yurevich), 1814–41.
Ashib Kerib. (*In:* A. E. Chamot, *Selected Russian short stories,* 1925. World's Classics.)
The demon. Transl. by E. Richter. A literal transl. in the metre of the original. 52 pp. Ld. Nutt, 1910.
—— Same. Transl. by R. Burness. 50 pp. Edinburgh. Douglas & Foulis, 1918.
—— Same. Transl. by G. Shelley, with an introduction by D. S. Mirsky. 56 pp. Ld. Richards Pr., 1930.
Elegy on the death of Pushkin. Transl. by R. Hillyer. (*In:* S. H. Cross and E. J. Simmons, *Centennial essays for Pushkin,* 1937.)
A hero of our time. Transl. by R. Merton, with a foreword by D. S. Mirsky. 247 pp. Ld. Allan, 1928.
—— Same. 265 pp. N.Y. Knopf, 1924. (Borzoi Pocket Books.)
—— Same. With title: *The heart of a Russian.* Transl. by J. H. Wisdom and M. Murray. Ld. Herbert & Daniel, 1912. [Erroneously described in the preface as the first Engl. transl.]
—— Same. With title: *A hero of our own times.* Transl. by E. and C. Paul, for the Lermontoff centenary. 283 pp. Ld. Allen & Unwin, 1940.
—— Same. With title: *A hero of nowadays.* Transl. by J. S. Phillimore. Ld. Nelson, 1924.
—— Same. With title: *Modern hero.* With Engl. transl. and biographical sketch by I. Nestor-Schnurmann. N.Y. Macmillan, n.d.
Poems. (*In:* C. M. Bowra, *A book of Russian verse,* 1943.)
Poems. (*In:* F. Cornford and E. P. Salaman, *Poems from the Russian,* 1943.)
Poems. (*In:* C. F. Coxwell, *Russian poems,* 1929.)
Poems. (*In:* J. Krup, *Six poems from the Russian.* 317 pp. N.Y. The Translator, 1936.)

Poems of Michael Lermontoff. The Russian text with Engl. verse transl., introduction, notes, biography and glossary by E. N. Steinhart. 36 pp. Ld. Paul, Trench, Trubner, 1917.

A sheaf from Lermontov. Transl. by J. J. Robbins. N.Y. Lieber & Lewis, 1923.

Six lyrics from the Ruthenian of Taras Shevchenko; also *The song of the merchant Kalashnikov, from the Russian of Lermontov,* rendered into Engl. verse by E. L. Voynich. 63 pp. Ld. E. Matthews, 1911.

A song about Tsar Ivan Vasilevich, his young bodyguard and the valiant merchant Kalashnikov. Transl. by J. Cournos, with decorations by P. Nash. Ld. Aquila Pr., 1929.

The testament. Transl. by M. Baring. (*In: The Oxford Book of Russian verse,* 1924.)

—— Same. (*Repr. in:* M. Baring, *Have you anything to declare?* Ld. Heinemann, 1936.)

Biography, criticism, etc.:

HEIFETZ (A.): *Lermontov in English; a list of works by and about the poet.* 18 pp. (*Bulletin of the N.Y. Public Library,* Sept. 1942.)

OSBOURNE (E. A.): *Early translations from the Russian,* 3: *Lermontov.* (*Bookman.* Ld., 1932.)

LESKOV (Nikolay Semenovich), 1831–95.

Cathedral folk. Transl. by I. F. Hapgood. N.Y. Knopf; Ld. Lane (U.S.A. printed), 1924. [The second pt. of a trilogy.]

The enchanted wanderer. Transl. by A. G. Pashkoff. Ld. Jarrolds, 1926.

The musk-ox, and other tales. Transl. by R. Norman. 208 pp. Ld. Routledge, 1944. [Contains: 'Kotin and Platonida'; 'The spirit of Mme Genlis'; 'The stinger'; 'A flaming patriot'; 'The clothes-mender'; 'The devilchase'; 'The Alexandrite'.]

The sentry, and other stories. Transl. by A. E. Chamot. Ld. Lane; N.Y. Knopf, 1922.

Steel flea. Adapted from the Russian by B. Deutsch and A. Yarmolinsky. 64 pp. N.Y. Harper, 1943.

LIBEDINSKY (Yury), 1898–.

A letter. (*In:* S. Konovalov, *Bonfire,* 1932.)

A week. Transl. by A. Ransome. 160 pp. Ld. Allen & Unwin, 1923.

LIDIN (Vladimir) [pseud. of Vladimir Germanovich Gomberg), 1894–.

The apostate. Transl. by H. C. Matheson. 336 pp. Ld. Cape, 1931.

—— Same. With title: *The price of life.* [The Russian title.] N.Y. Harper, 1932.

Glaciers. (*In:* J. Cournos, *Short stories out of Soviet Russia,* 1929.)

Hamlet. (*In:* I. Montagu and H. Marshall, *Soviet short stories,* 1942.)

Harps. (*In:* S. Konovalov, *Bonfire,* 1932.)

The master cook. (*In:* E. Fen, *Soviet stories of the last decade,* 1945.)

Youth. (*In:* J. J. Robbins and J. Kunitz, *Azure cities,* 1929.)

LUGOVSKOY (Vladimir Aleksandrovich), 1901–.

Poems. (*In: New Directions in prose and poetry,* 1941, pp. 543.)

LUKASH (Ivan Sozontovich).

The flames of Moscow. Transl. by N. Duddington. 475 pp. N.Y. Macmillan, 1930.

LUNACHARSKY (Anatoly Vasilevich), 1876–1933.

The bear's wedding. Transl. by L. Zamkovsky and N. Borudin. Ld. 1926.

Three plays. Transl. by L. A. Magnus and K. Walter. 299 pp. Ld. Routledge, 1923. (Broadway Translations.) [Contains: 'Faust and the city'; 'Vasilisa the wise'; 'The magi'.]

LUNTS (Lev Nataovich), 1901–24.

The city of truth; a play in three acts. Transl. by J. Silver. 52 pp. Ld. 1929.

MAKARENKO (Anton Semenovich), 1888–.

The road to life. [Autobiography.] Transl. by S. Garry. 287 pp. Ld. Drummond, 1936.

The road to life: the story of the Gorky colony. Transl. by S. Garry. 287 pp. Ld. Drummond, 1938.

MALYSHKIN (Aleksandr Georgievich), 1890–.

South-bound. (*In:* E. Fen, *Soviet stories of the last decade,* 1945.)

MANDELSTAM (Osip E.), 1892–.

Poem. (*In:* C. F. Coxwell, *Russian poems,* 1929.)

Poems. (*In:* C. M. Bowra, *A book of Russian verse,* 1943.)

MATVEEV (Vladimir).

Bitter draught. Transl. by D. Flower. 297 pp. Ld. Cassell, 1935.

Commissar of the Gold Express; an episode in the Civil War. 212 pp. Ld. Lawrence, 1933; N.Y. International Publishers Co., 1933.

MAYAKOVSKY (Vladimir Vladimirovich), 1894–1930.

'I'; 'Listen'; 'The cloud in trousers'; 'Brother writers'; 'Command no. 1'; 'Hands off China'. (*In:* G. Reavey and M. Slonim, *Soviet literature,* 1933.)

Mayakovsky and his poetry. Compiled by H. Marshall. Ld. Pilot Pr., 1942. (Life and Literature in the Soviet Union, 3.) [Contains: Report of Mayakovsky's twentieth anniversary exhibition, and other material concerning Mayakovsky.]

Mystery-Bouffe. Transl. by G. R. Noyes and A. S. Kaun. (*In:* G. R. Noyes, *Masterpieces of the Russian drama*, 1933.)

Our march. Transl. by J. Freeman. (*In:* J. Freeman and others, *Voices of October*, 1930.)

Poems. (*In:* C. M. Bowra, *A book of Russian verse*, 1943.)

Poems. (*In:* C. F. Coxwell, *Russian poems*, 1929.)

Poems. (*In:* B. Deutsch and A. Yarmolinsky, *Modern Russian poetry*, 1923, and in their: *Russian poetry*, 1929.)

Poems. (*In: New Directions, anthology in prose and poetry*, 1941, pp. 605–18.)

Biography, criticism, etc.:

DRAKE (W. A.): *Contemporary European writers.* 408 pp. Ld. Harrap. (U.S.A. printed), 1929. [Contains: a chapter on Mayakovsky.]

MAYKOV (Apollon Nikolaevich), 1821–98.

Poems. (*In:* C. M. Bowra, *A book of Russian verse*, 1943.)

Poems. (*In:* F. Cornford and E. P. Salaman, *Poems from the Russian*, 1943.)

Poems. (*In* C. F. Coxwell, *Russian poems*, 1929.)

MEREZHKOVSKY (Dmitri Sergeevich), 1865–1941.

Akhnaton, king of Egypt. Transl. by N. A. Duddington. 372 pp. N.Y. Dutton, 1927.

Birth of the gods. Transl. by N. A. Duddington. 233 pp. Ld. Dent, 1926.

Death of the gods. Transl. by H. Trench. N.Y. Putnam, n.d.

December the fourteenth; a novel. Transl. by N. A. Duddington. 319 pp. Ld. Cape, 1925.

Jesus the unknown. Transl. by E. N. Matheson. N.Y. Scribner, 1934.

—— Same. With title: *Jesus manifest.* Transl. by E. Gellibrand. N.Y. Scribner, 1936.

Julian Apostate. Transl. by B. G. Guerney. N.Y. Modern Library Co., 1929.

The life work of Calderon, etc. Transl. by G. A. Mounsey. 1908–12.

Menace of the mob. Transl. by B. G. Guerney. N.Y. Frank Maurice, 1926.

Michael Angelo, and other sketches. Transl. by N. A. Duddington. 184 pp. Ld. Dent, 1930. [Contains: 'Michael Angelo'; 'Love is stronger than death'; 'Science of love'.]

My life. (*In:* P. Selver, *Anthology of modern Slavonic literature,* 1919.)

Peter and Alexis, the romance of Peter the Great. N.Y. Putnam, n.d.

Poems. (*In:* P. Selver, *Anthology of modern Slavonic literature,* 1919.)

The romance of Leonardo da Vinci. Transl. by H. Trench. N.Y. Putnam, 1924.

—— Same. Transl. by B. G. Guerney. N.Y. Modern Library Co., 1928.

—— Same. With 100 reproductions of the work of Leonardo da Vinci. 580 pp. Ld. Faber, 1938.

—— Same. With title: *Forerunner: the romance of Leonardo da Vinci.* Ld. Constable, 1938.

The secret of the West. Done into Engl. by J. Cournos. 449 pp. Ld. Cape, 1936.

Tolstoy as man and artist, with an essay on Dostoevsky. Ld. Constable, 1902. [Abr. transl. of Tolstoy and Dostoevsky.]

MEREZHKOVSKY (Mme). *See:* HIPPIUS (Zinaida Nikolaevna) [Mme Merezhkovsky.]

MINSKY (N. M.) [pseud. of Nikolay Vilenkin], 1855–.
Poems. (*In:* C. F. Coxwell, *Russian poems,* 1929.)
Poems. (*In:* B. Deutsch and A. Yarmolinsky, *Russian poetry,* 1929.)
Poems. (*In:* P. Selver, *Anthology of modern Slavonic literature,* 1919.)

NABOKOV (Vladimir Vladimirovich) [pseud. Serin], 1899–.
Despair. Transl. by the author. 286 pp. Ld. Long, 1937.

NADSON (Semen Yakovlevich), 1862–87.
Poems. (*In:* C. F. Coxwell, *Russian poems,* 1929.)
Poems. (*In:* P. E. Matheson, *Holy Russia,* 1917.)

NAZAROV (Pavel Szepanovich).
Moved on! from Kashgar to Kashmir. Rendered into Engl. by M. Burr. 317 pp. Ill. Ld. Allen, 1935.

NAZHIVIN (Ivan Fedorovich), 1874–.
According to Thomas; an historical novel of the first century. Transl. by E. Burns. 397 pp. N.Y. Harper, 1931.
The dogs. 336 pp. N.Y. Lippincott, 1931; Ld. Allen & Unwin.
Rasputin. Transl. by C. J. Hogarth. 2 vols. N.Y. Knopf, 1929.

E

NEKRASOV (Nikolay Alekseevich), 1821–77.

Poems. Transl. by J. M. Soskice. With an introduction by Lascelles Abercrombie. Ld. Oxf. Univ. Pr., 1929. (World's Classics.)

Poems. (*In*: C. M. Bowra, *A book of Russian verse*, 1943.)

Poems. (*In*: F. Cornford and E. P. Salaman, *Poems from the Russian*, 1943.)

Poems. (*In*: C. F. Coxwell, *Russian poems*, 1929.)

Poems. (*In*: B. Deutsch and A. Yarmolinsky, *Russian poetry*, 1929.)

Poems. (*In*: O. Elton, *Verse from Pushkin and others*, 1935.)

Poems. (*In*: N. Jarintsov, *Russian poets and poems*, 1917.)

Poems. (*In*: P. E. Matheson, *Holy Russia*, 1917.)

NEMIROVICH-DANCHENKO (Vasiliy Ivanovich), 1848–.

My life in the Russian theatre. Transl. by J. Cournos. 358 pp. Ld. Bles, 1936.

Peasant tales of Russia. Transl. by C. Field. Ld. Scott, 1917.

The princes of the stock exchange. Transl. by A. S. Rappoport. Ld. Holden & Hardingham, 1914.

With a diploma and *The whirlwind.* Transl. by W. J. S. Pyper. N.Y. Luce, 1915.

NEVEROV (Aleksandr) [pseud. of Aleksandr Sergeevich Skobolov], 1886–1923.

Andron the good-for-nothing. (*In*: E. Fen, *Modern Russian stories*, 1943.)

Marya, the Bolshevik. (*In*: J. J. Robbins and J. Kunitz, *Azure cities*, 1929.)

Tashkent. Transl. by R. Merton and W. G. Walton. 224 pp. Ld. Gollancz, 1930.

——Same. With title: *City of Bread.* Anon. transl. N.Y. Doubleday, 1927.

——Same. (*Extract in*: S. Konovalov, *Bonfire*, 1932).

NIKITIN (Ivan Savich), 1824–61.

Poems. (*In*: C. F. Coxwell, *Russian poems*, 1929.)

Poems. (*In*: P. E. Matheson, *Holy Russia*, 1917.)

NOVIKOV-PRIBOY (Aleksey Silich), 1877–.

Tsushima. Trans. by E. and C. Paul. 425 pp. Ld. Allen & Unwin, 1936.

ODOEVTSEVA (Irina).

Out of childhood. Transl. and ill. by D. Nachshen. 252 pp. N.Y. Smith, 1930; Ld. Constable, 1934.

OGAREV (Nikolay Platonovich), 1813–79.

Poems. (*In*: C. F. Coxwell, *Russian poems*, 1929.)

Poems. (*In*: P. E. Matheson, *Holy Russia*, 1917.)

OGNEV (N.) [pseud. of Mikhail Grigorevich Rozanov], 1890–.
Diary of a communist schoolboy. Transl. by A. Werth. 288 pp.
Ld. Gollancz, 1928.
Diary of a communist undergraduate. Transl. by A. Werth.
288 pp. Ld. Gollancz, 1929.
Sour grapes and sweet. (*In:* Penguin New Writing, 1. Ld.
Penguin Books, 1940.)

OKULEV (A.).
The unexpected meeting. (*In:* S. Graham, *Great Russian short
stories*, 1929.)

OLESHA (Yuri Karlovich), 1899–.
The cherry stone. (*In:* G. Reavey and M. Slonim, *Soviet literature*,
1933.)
—— Same. Another transl. (*In:* I. Montagu and H. Marshall,
Soviet short stories, 1942.)
The conspiracy of feelings. (*In:* S. Konovalov, *Bonfire*, 1932.)
Envy. Transl. by A. Wolfe. 275 pp. Ld. Hogarth Pr., 1936.
—— Same. (*Extract in:* S. Konovalov, *Bonfire*, 1932.)
Love. Transl. by A. Wolfe. (*In:* Penguin New Writing, 9. Ld.
Lane, 1942.)

ORENBURGSKI (Sergey Gusev-) [pseud.]. *See:* GUSEV-ORENBURGSKI
(Sergey Ivanovich.)

ORESHIN (Piotr V.), 1887–.
Poems. (*In:* B. Deutsch and A. Yarmolinsky, *Modern Russian
poetry*, 1923.)

OSSORGIN (Mikhail) [pseud.]. *See:* ILIN (Mikhail Andreevich)
[Mikhail Ossorgin, pseud.].

OSTROVSKY (Aleksandr Nikolaevich), 1823–86.
A domestic picture. (*In:* E. L. Voynich, *Humour of Russia*, 1911.)
Easy money, and two other plays. Ld. Allen, c. 1944.
Enough stupidity in every wise man. (*In:* O. M. Sayler, *Moscow
Art Theatre of Russian plays*, second series, 1923.)
The forest. Transl. by C. V. Winslow and G. R. Noyes. 126 pp.
N.Y. French, 1926. (World's Best Plays by European
Authors.)
Incompatibility of temper. (*In:* E. L. Voynich, *Humour of Russia*,
1911.)
King of comedy [play]. Transl. by J. M. Petrie. 96 pp. Ld.
Stockwell, 1937.
Plays. Transl. and ed. by G. R. Noyes. N.Y. Scribner, 1917.
[Contains: 'A protégé of the mistress'; 'Poverty is no crime';
'Sin and sorrow are common to all'; 'It's a family affair,
we'll settle it ourselves'.]

The poor bride. Transl. by J. L. Seymour and G. R. Noyes. (*In:* G. R. Noyes, *Masterpieces of the Russian drama*, 1933.)

The storm. Transl. by C. Garnett. 120 pp. Chicago. Sergel, 1899 and 1911; Boston. Luce, 1907; Ld. Duckworth, 1899 and 1930.

—— Same; a play in three acts. Engl. version by G. F. Holland and M. Morley. 112 pp. Ld. Allen, 1930. (Plays of Everyman Theatre Guild, no. 1.)

—— Same. With title: *Thunderstorm*; a drama in five acts. Transl. by F. Whyte and G. R. Noyes. 83 pp. N.Y. French, 1927. (World's Best Plays by European Authors.)

We won't brook interference; a farce in two acts. Transl. by J. L. Seymour and G. R. Noyes. 39 pp. San Francisco. Banner, 1938.

OSTROVSKY (Nikolay Alekseevich), 1904–1937.

Born of the storm. Transl. by L. L. Hiler. 251 pp. N.Y. Critics Group, 1939.

Making of a hero. Transl. by A. Brown. 440 pp. Ld. Secker & Warburg, 1938.

OUTKIN (Iosif): Poems. (*In:* New Directions in prose and poetry, 1941.)

PANFEROV (Fedor Ivanovich), 1896–.

And then the harvest. Transl. by S. Garry. 457 pp. Ld. Putnam, 1939.

Brusski; a story of peasant life in Soviet Russia. Transl. by Z. Mitrov and J. Tabrisky. 300 pp. Ld. Lawrence, 1931.

PASTERNAK (Boris Leonidovich), 1890–.

Childhood. Transl. by R. Tayne. Singapore. Straits Times Pr., 1941.

The death of a poet. From: *The safe conduct*. (*In:* G. Reavey and M. Slonim, *Soviet literature*, 1933.)

Poems. (*In:* C. M. Bowra, *A book of Russian verse*, 1943.)

Poems. (*In:* C. F. Coxwell, *Russian poems*, 1929.)

Poems. (*In:* G. Reavey and M. Slonim, *Soviet literature*, 1933.)

Poems. (*In:* New Directions in prose and poetry, 1941.)

PAVLENKO (Petr Andreevich), 1899–.

Nightpiece. Transl. by S. Garry. (*In:* J. Rodker, *Soviet anthology*, 1943.)

Red 'planes fly east. Transl. by S. Garry. 523 pp. Ld. Routledge, 1938.

PAVLOVA (Caroline), 1820–98.

Poems. (*In:* C. F. Coxwell, *Russian poems*, 1929.)

PAVSTOVSKY (Konstantin).
The copper plates. (*In:* J. Rodker, *Soviet anthology*, 1943.)
The razor. (*In:* I. Montagu and H. Marshall, *Soviet short stories*, 1943.)
The sailmaker. (*In:* I. Montagu and H. Marshall, *Soviet short stories*, 1942.)
PERELMAN (O. I.). *See:* DYMOV (Osip) [pseud. of O. I. Perelman].
PERETZ (Isaac Loeb), 1851–1915.
Bontshe, the silent. Transl. from the Yiddish with preface and glossary by A. S. Rappoport. 259 pp. McKay, n.d.
One-act plays from the Yiddish, by I. L. Peretz and others. Transl. by E. Block. 123 pp. N.Y., 1929.
Stories and pictures. Transl. from the Yiddish by H. Frank. Philadelphia. Jewish Publ., 1906.
Biography, criticism, etc.:
ROBACK (A. A.): *I. L. Peretz, psychologist of literature.* N.Y. Science and Art Publ., 1935.
PERVENTSEV (Arkady).
Cossack commander. Transl. by S. Garry. 313 pp. Ld. Routledge, 1939.
PESHKOV (Aleksey Maksimovich). *See:* GORKY (Maksim) [pseud. of Aleksey Maksimovich Peshkov.].
PETROV (Evgeny),-1942. *See also:* ILF (Ilya Arnoldovich) and PETROV (Evgeny).
The professor of music. (*In:* I. Montagu and H. Marshall, *Soviet short stories*, 1943.)
PETROV (Stepan Gavrilovieh). *See:* Skitalets, [pseud. of Stepan Gavrilovich Petrov].
PILNYAK (Boris) [pseud. of Boris Andreevich Vogau], 1894–.
His majesty Kneeb Piter Komondor. (*In:* S. Graham, *Great Russian short stories*, 1929.)
The human mind. (*In:* J. Cournos, *Short stories out of Soviet Russia*, 1932.)
Ivan Moscow. Transl. by A. S. Schwartzmann. 92 pp. N.Y. Christopher, 1935.
The law of the wolf [short story]. (*In:* J. J. Robbins and J. Kunitz, *Azure cities*, 1929.)
The naked year. Transl. by A. Brown. 305 pp. N.Y. Brewer, 1928. [The Russian title: *A bare year.*]
—— Same. (*Extract in:* S. Konovalov, *Bonfire*, 1932.)
—— Same. (*Extract in:* G. Reavey and M. Slonim, *Soviet literature*, 1933.)
—— Same. (*Extract in:* J. Rodker, *Soviet anthology*, 1943.)

Tales of the wilderness. Transl. by F. O. Dempsey. With an introduction by D. S. Mirsky. 223 pp. Ld. Routledge, 1924.

The volga falls to the Caspian sea. Transl. by C. Malamuth. 322 pp. Ld. Davies, 1932.

—— Same. Cheap ed. 1935.

A year of their life. (In: E. Fen, *Modern Russian stories,* 1943.)

PISEMSKY (Aleksey Teofilaktovich), 1820–81.

A bitter fate. Transl. by A. Kagan and G. R. Noyes. *(In:* G. R. Noyes, *Masterpieces of the Russian drama,* 1933.)

PLATONOV (A.).

The third son. (In: I. Montagu and H. Marshall, *Soviet short stories,* 1942.)

POGODIN (Nikolay Fedorovich), 1900–.

Aristocrats; a comedy in four acts. Transl. by A. Wixley and R. S. Carr. *(In:* B. Blake, *Four Soviet plays,* 1937.)

—— Same. Acting ed. Ld. Lawrence, 1937.

Tempo; a play in four acts. Transl. by I. D. W. Talmadge. *(In:* E. Lyons, *Six Soviet plays,* 1935.)

POLONSKY (Yakov Petrovich), 1819–98.

Poems. *(In:* C. M. Bowra, *A book of Russian verse,* 1943.)

Poems. *(In:* C. F. Coxwell, *Russian poems,* 1929.)

Poems. *(In:* B. Deutsch and A. Yarmolinsky, *Russian poetry,* 1929.)

POPOV (Aleksandr Serafimovich). *See:* SERAFIMOVICH (Aleksandr) [pseud. of Aleksandr Serafimovich Popov].

PRIDVOROV (Yefim Alekseevich). *See:* BEDNY (Demyan) [pseud. of Yefim Alekseevich Pridvorov].

PRISHVIN (Mikhail Mikhailovich), 1873–.

Jen Sheng, the root of life. Engl. version by G. Walton and P. Gibbons. Foreword by J. S. Huxley. 177 pp. Ld. Melrose, 1936.

A werewolf of the steppe. (In: J. Cournos, *Short stories out of Soviet Russia,* 1929.)

—— Same. *(Repr. in: Russian short stories,* 1943.)

PUSHKIN (Aleksandr Sergeevich), 1799–1837.

The works of Alexander Pushkin: lyrics, narrative poems, folk tales, plays, prose. Selected and ed. with an introduction by A. Yarmolinsky. 893 pp. N.Y. Random House; Ld. Nonesuch Pr. (Faber), 1936. Contains:

46 lyrical poems and ballads. Transl. by M. Baring, T. B. Shaw, M. Eastman, C. Garnett and B. Deutsch.

Narrative poems: 'Poltava' (from canto 3), transl. by B.

Deutsch; 'The Bronze Horseman', transl. by O. Elton; 'Eugene Onegin', transl. by B. Deutsch.

Folk tales: 'The tale of the Pope and of his workman Balda', transl. by O. Elton; 'The tale of the golden cockerel', transl. by B. Deutsch.

Plays: 'Boris Godunov', transl. by A. Hayes; 'The covetous knight'; 'Mozart and Salieri', and 'The stone guest', transl. by A. F. B. Clark.

Prose: 'The shot'; 'The snowstorm'; 'The undertaker'; 'The postmaster'; 'The Queen of Spades'; 'Mistress into maid'; 'Kirdjali.' Transl. by T. Keane. 'The captain's daughter', transl. by N. Duddington. 'The negro of Peter the Great'; 'Dubrowsky'; 'Egyptian nights', transl. by T. Keane.

The avaricious knight. Transl. by E. J. Simmons. (Harvard studies and notes in philology and literature. Cambridge, Mass., vol. 15, 1933.)

Boris Godunov. Rendered into Engl. verse by A. Hayes. 117 pp. Ld. Kegan Paul; N.Y. Dutton, 1918.

The captain's daughter, and other stories. Ld. Hodder & Stoughton, 1915.

The captain's daughter, and other tales. Transl. by N. Duddington. Ld. Dent, 1923; N.Y. Dutton, 1935. (Everyman's Library.) [Contains: 'The captain's daughter'; 'The Queen of Spades'; 'Dubrowsky'; 'Peter the Great's negro'; 'The stationmaster'.]

The captain's daughter. Transl. by N. Duddington, with an introduction by E. Garnett. 212 pp. Ld. Dent, 1928.

Eugene Onegin: a novel in verse. Transl. by D. Prall Radin and G. Z. Patrick. 226 pp. Berkeley. Univ. of California Pr., 1937.

—— Same. Transl. by O. Elton. Ill. With a foreword by D. MacCarthy. Ld. Pushkin Pr., 1937.

—— Same. Ordinary ed. 1939.

The fountain of Bakchesarai. (*Extract in:* L. Wiener, *Anthology of Russian literature*, vol. 2. 1903.)

Gabriel: a poem in one song. Transl. by M. Eastman. Ill. N.Y. Covici, Friede, 1929.

The golden cockerel, from the original Russian fairy tale, by E. Pogany. Ill. 48 pp. U.S.A. 1938; Ld. Nelson, 1939.

—— Same. Rendered into Engl. verse by N. Katkoff. Ld. Beaumont, 1918.

—— Same. With title: *The tale of the golden cockerel.* Transl. by H. Waller. Ill. 22 pp. Ld. Golden Cockerel Pr., 1937, Ltd. ed.

Mozart and Salieri. [Play.]   Transl. by A. Werth.   (*In: The Glasgow book of prose and verse.* Glasgow. Hodge, 1923.]

Poems.   Transl. by M. Baring.   Ld.   Privately printed, 1931.

Poems.   (*In: Bechhofer, A Russian anthology in English,* 1917.)

Poems.   (*In: Bowra, A book of Russian verse,* 1943.)

Poems.   (*In:* Cornford and Salaman, *Poems from the Russian,* 1943.)

Poems.   (*In: Coxwell, Russian poems,* 1929.)

Poems.   (*In:* Deutsch and Yarmolinsky, *Modern Russian poetry,* 1923, and: *Russian poetry, 1927 and 1929.*)

Poems.   (*In: Elton, Verse from Pushkin and others,* 1935.)

Poems.   (*In: Jarintsov, Russian poets and poems,* 1917.)

Poems.   (*In: Krup, Six poems from the Russian,* 1936.)

Poems.   (*In: Matheson, Holy Russia,* 1918.)

Poems.   (*In: Pollen, Russian songs and lyrics,* 1917.)

Poems.   (*In: Wiener, Anthology of Russian literature,* vol. 2, 1903.)

Poems.   (*In: Zeitlin, Skazki: tales and legends of old Russia,* 1926.)

The Queen of Spades. Transl. by R. S. Townsend.   (*In his: Short stories by Russian authors,* 1924.)

—— Same.   Transl. by A. E. Chamot.   (*In his: Selected Russian short stories,* 1925.)

—— Same.   Transl. by J. E. Pouterman and C. Bruerton. Introductory essay by D. S. Mirsky. Ill. 110 pp. Ld. Blackamore Pr., 1929.

The Russian wonderland: a metrical translation by B. L. Brasol. 62 pp. Ld. Williams & Norgate, 1936.

Three tales: The snowstorm; The postmaster; The undertaker. Transl. by R. T. Currall. With Russian text. Ld. Harrap, 1919. (Harrap's bilingual series.)

The Zigany. Transl. by G. Borrow.   (*In:* Borrow, *Works,* vol. 16. Ld. Constable, 1924.)

Biography, criticism, etc.:

OSBOURNE (E. A.): *Early translation from the Russian: 2, Pushkin and his contemporaries.* (*Bookman,* vol. 82. Ld. 1932.)

Pushkin in English. A list of works by and about Pushkin. Compiled by the Slavonic division of the New York Public Library. (*Bulletin of the New York Public Library,* July, 1932.)

BARING (M.): *Lost lectures; or the fruits of experience.* Ld. Heinemann, 1932. [Contains: pp. 178–99, essay on Pushkin and transl. of some lyrics.]

BATES (A.): *Russian drama.* Ld. Historical Publishing Co., 1906. [Contains: a short biography of Pushkin and a critical analysis of Boris Godunov and the miniature dramas and fragments.]

BECKWITH (M. W.) and others: *Pushkin the man and artist.* By various authors. 245 pp. Ld. Williams & Norgate; N.Y. Paisley Pr., 1937.

BRASOL (B. L.): *Poushkin, the Shakespeare of Russia.* [Address delivered before the Brooklyn Institute of Arts and Sciences, 1931.] N.Y. Privately printed, 1931.

CLEUGH (J.): *Prelude to Parnassus: scenes from the life of A. S. Pushkin.* 342 pp. Ld. Barker, 1936.

CROSS (S. H.) and SIMMONS (E. J.): *A. Pushkin; his life and literary heritage.* 79 pp. N.Y. American-Russian Institute for Cultural Relations with the Soviet Union, 1937.

CROSS (S. H.) and SIMMONS (E. J.) ed.: *Centennial essays for Pushkin.* 226 pp. Cambridge, Mass. Harvard Univ. Pr., 1937.

ELTON (O.): *Alexander Pushkin.* (*In his: Essays and addresses,* 1939.) [Contains: transl. of several poems by Elton, Baring, R. M. Hewitt, B. Pares.]

HERFORD (C. H.): *A Russian Shakespearean: a centenary study.* 30 pp. Skemp Memorial Lecture in the University of Bristol, 1925.

—— Same. Enlarged version in his: *The post-war mind of Germany, and other European studies.* 248 pp. Oxf. Clarendon Pr., 1927.

MIRSKY (D. S.): *Pushkin.* 266 pp. Ld. Routledge, 1926. (Republic of letters.)

Pushkin: a collection of articles and essays. Ed. by M. P. Sokolnikov. 188 pp. Moscow. VOKS, 1939.

TALMADGE (I. D. W.): *Pushkin; homage by Marxist critics.* Transl. by B. G. Guerney. 104 pp. N.Y. Critics' Group, 1937. [Contains: essays by Gorky, Zeitlin, Lunacharsky, Vinogradov.]

WILSON (E.): *In honour of Pushkin.* (*In his: The triple thinkers,* Oxf., 1938.)

RABINOWITZ (Shalom). *See:* ALEICHEM (Shalom) [pseud. of Shalom Rabinowitz].

RASKIN (A.) and SLOBODSKY (M.).
My birthday. Transl. by A. Brown. (*In:* J. Rodker, *Soviet anthology,* 1943.)

REMIZOV (Aleksey Mikhailovich), 1877–.
The clock and *Three prose lyrics from Shumy Goroda.* Transl. by J. Cournos. 222 pp. Ld. Chatto & Windus, 1924.
Fifth pestilence, together with *The history of the tinkling cymbal and sounding brass, Ivan Semyonovich Stratilatov.* Transl.

with a preface by A. Brown. 235 pp. N.Y. Payson & Clarke, 1928.

ROMANOV (Panteleimon Sergeevich), 1884–1936.

Black fritters. (*In*: J. J. Robbins and J. Kunitz, *Azure cities*, 1929.)

Diary of a Soviet marriage: a study of a woman, her husband and the friend. Transl. by J. P. Furnivall and R. Parmenter. Introduction by J. Lavrin. 143 pp. Ld. Nott, 1936.

The new commandment. Transl. by V. Snow. 288 pp. N.Y. Scribner, 1933; 341 pp. Ld. Benn, 1933.

—— Same. Cheap ed. Ld. Benn, 1935.

On the Volga, and other stories. Transl. by A. Gretton. 286 pp. Ld. Benn, 1934.

—— Same. Cheap ed. 1936.

The rye cakes. (*In*: S. Konovalov, *Bonfire*, 1932.)

Sex problems. Transl. by E. Fen. (*In her: Modern Russian stories*, 1943.)

Three pairs of silk stockings: a novel of the life of the educated classes under the Soviet. Transl. by L. Zarine. Ed. by S. Graham. 344 pp. Ld. Benn, 1931.

—— Same. Cheap ed. 352 pp. 1932.

White flowers. (*In*: S. Konovalov, *Bonfire*, 1932.)

Without cherry blossom. Transl. by L. Zarine. Ed. by S. Graham. 287 pp. Ld. Benn, 1930.

—— Same. Cheap ed. 1931.

ROONOVA (Olga).

The thief. (*In*: E. Fen, *Soviet stories of the last decade*, 1945.)

ROPSHIN (pseud). *See*: SAVINKOV (Boris Viktorovich).

ROZANOV (Mikhail Grigorevich). *See*: OGNEV (N.) [pseud. of Mikhail Grigorevich Rozanov].

ROZANOV (Vasiliy Vasilevich), 1856–1919.

Fallen leaves. Transl. by S. S. Koteliansky. 166 pp. Ld. Mandrake Pr., 1929.

Solitaria. Transl. by S. S. Koteliansky. With a sketch of the author's life by E. Gollerbach. 188 pp. Ld. Wishart, 1927.

"RUSSIAN BOY".

Russian boy. Fragment of an autobiography from 1916–24. With a glossary. 139 pp. Ld. King & Staples, 1942.

SALTYKOV (Mikhail Evgrafovich) [pseud. Shchedrin], 1826–89.

Fables. Transl. by V. Volkhovsky. 257 pp. Ld. Chatto & Windus, 1931. (Phoenix Library.)

The Golovlyov family. Transl. by A. Ridgeway. Ld. 1916.

—— Same. Transl. by N. Duddington. 336 pp. Ld. Allen & Unwin, 1931.

—— Reissued with an introduction by E. Garnett. 324 pp. Ld. Dent, 1934. (Everyman's Library.)

Biography, criticism, etc. :

STRELSKY (N.) : *Saltykov and the Russian Squire.* 176 pp. Oxf., 1940.

SAVINKOV (Boris Viktorovich) [pseud. Ropshin], 1879–1925.
The black horse. Ld. Williams & Norgate, 1924.
Memoirs of a terrorist. Transl. by J. Shaplen. With a foreword and epilogue. 364 pp. N.Y. Boni, 1931.
The pale horse. Transl. by Z. Vengerova. Dublin. Maunsel; Ld. Allen & Unwin, 1917. (Modern Russian Library.)
What never happened. Transl. by T. Seltzer. Ld. Allen & Unwin, 1917.

SCHWARZMAN (Lev Isaakovich). *See :* SHESTOV (Lev) [pseud.].

SEIFULLINA (Lydia Nikolaevna), 1899–.
The law-breakers. (*In :* G. Reavey and M. Slonim, *Soviet literature*, 1933.)
The old woman. (*In :* J. J. Robbins and J. Kunitz, *Azure cities*, 1929.)

SELVINSKY (Ilya Lvovich), 1899–.
The golden melody, from 'Pao-Pao'. (*In :* G. Reavey and M. Slonim, *Soviet literature*, 1933.)
Poems. (*In : New directions in prose and poetry*, 1941, pp. 558–664.)

SEMENOV (Sergey), 1893–.
The birth of a slave. (*In :* S. Konovalov, *Bonfire*, 1932.)
Natalia Tarpova. (*Extract in :* G. Reavey and M. Slonim, *Soviet literature*, 1933.)

SERAFIMOVICH (Aleksandr) [pseud. of Aleksandr Serafimovich Popov), 1863–.
The iron flood. Anon. transl. 246 pp. Ld. Lawrence, 1935.

SERGEEV–TSENSKY (Sergey Nikolaevich), 1876–.
The demigod. (*In :* P. Selver, *Anthology of modern Slavonic literature*, 1919.)
The man you couldn't kill. (*In :* J. Cournos, *Short stories out of Soviet Russia*, 1929.)
—— Same. Repr. in: *Russian short stories*, 1943.
Transfiguration. Transl. by M. Budberg. Ed. with an introduction by M. Gorky. 300 pp. N.Y. MacBride, 1926.

SHAGINYAN (Marietta Sergeevna), 1888–.
Three looms. (*In :* J. J. Robbins and J. Kunitz, *Azure cities*, 1929.)

SHCHEDRIN [pseud.]. *See :* SALTYKOV (Mikhail Evgrafovich).

SHENSHIN. *See :* FET (Afanasy Afanasevich), afterwards Shenshin.

SHESTOV (Lev) [pseud. of Lev Isaakovich Schwarzman), 1866–1938.
All things are possible. Transl. by S. S. Koteliansky. Ld. Secker & Warburg, 1921.
Anton Chekhov, and other essays. Transl. by S. S. Koteliansky and J. M. Murry. Ld. 1916. (Modern Russian Library.)
—— Same. With title: *Penultimate words, and other essays.* 205 pp. N.Y. Luce, 1917.
In Job's balances; on the sources of the eternal truths. Transl. from the German by C. Coventry and C. A. Macartney. 413 pp. Ld. Dent, 1932.
SHEVCHENKO (Taras Grigorevich), 1814–61.
Autobiography. (*In:* P. Selver, *Anthology of modern Slavonic literature,* 1919.)
Poems. (*In:* P. Selver, *Anthology of modern Slavonic literature,* 1919.)
Six lyrics from the Ruthenian of Taras Shevchenko. Also: *The song of the Merchant Kalashnikov from Lermontov,* rendered into Engl. verse, with a biographical sketch, by E. L. Voynich. 63 pp. Ld. Elkin Matthews, 1911.
SHIRYAEV (Petr Alekseevich), 1888–1935.
Flattery's foal. Transl. by A. Fremantle. 295 pp. N.Y. Knopf, 1938. (Borzoi Books.)
—— Same. With title: *Taglioni's grandson; the story of a Russian horse.* 291 pp. Ld. Putnam, 1939.
—— Cheap ed. 1941.
SHISHKOV (Vyacheslav Yakovlevich), 1873–.
Children of darkness. 288 pp. Ld. Gollancz, 1931.
Cranes. [Short story.] (*In:* J. J. Robbins and J. Kunitz, *Azure cities,* 1929).
SHKLOVSKY (Viktor).
St. Petersburg in 1920. (*In:* S. Konovalov, *Bonfire,* 1932.)
SHMELEV (Ivan Sergeevich), 1875–.
The inexhaustible cup. Transl. by T. D. France. 147 pp. N.Y. Dutton, 1928.
Story of a love. Transl. by N. Tsytovich. 323 pp. N.Y. Dutton, 1931.
Sun of the dead. Transl. by C. J. Hogarth. 297 pp. Ld. Dent, 1927.
That which happened. Transl. by C. J. Hogarth. Ld. 1924.
SHOLOKHOV (Mikhail Aleksandrovich), 1905–
And quiet flows the Don. Transl. by S. Garry. 755 pp. Ld. Putnam, 1934.

The Don flows home to the sea (*Silent Don*, pt. 1), with *And quiet flows the Don* (*Silent Don*, pt. 2). Transl. by S. Garry. 868 pp. Ld. Putnam, 1940.

Down south. (*In :* I. Montagu and H. Marshall, *Soviet short stories,* 1943.)

The science of hatred. (*In :* Soviet war stories, 1944.)

Seeds of tomorrow. Transl. by S. Garry. 404 pp. N.Y. Knopf, 1935.

—— Same. 404 pp. N.Y. Knopf, 1942. (Alblabooks.)

—— Same. With title: *Virgin soil upturned.* Transl. by S. Garry. 488 pp. Ld. Putnam, 1935.

—— Same. (*Extract in :* G. Reavey and M. Slonim, *Soviet literature,* 1933.)

SHOSHIN (M.).
  A rendezvous. (*In :* E. Fen, *Soviet stories of the last decade,* 1945.)

SHPANOV (Nikolay).
  The musician. (*In :* I. Montagu and H. Marshall, *Soviet short stories,* 1943.)

SIMONOV (Konstantin).
  The cossack. (*In :* I. Montagu and H. Marshall, *Soviet short stories,* 1944.)
  'Moscow'; 'On the Petsamo Road'; 'His only son'; 'The cossack song'; 'The bridge under the water'; 'Three days'; 'Paramon Samsovovich'; 'Maturity'. (*In :* Soviet war stories, 1943.)
  No quarter. 231 pp. N.Y. Fischer, 1943.
  The only son. (*In :* E. Fen, *Soviet stories of the last decade,* 1945.)
  On the cliffs of Norway. (*In :* I. Montagu and H. Marshall, *Soviet short stories,* 1943.)
  The Russians. (*In :* Four Soviet war plays, 1943.)
  The third adjutant. (*In :* I. Montagu and H. Marshall, *Soviet short stories,* 1943.)

SIRIN [pseud.]. *See :* NABOKOV (Vladimir Vladimirovich).

SKITALETS [pseud. of Stepan Gavrilovich Petrov], 1868–.
  The Czar's charter. Transl. by P. L. Ld. Henderson's, 1907.
  Publican and serf. Transl. by J. K. M. Shirazi. Ld. Alston Rivers, 1905.

SKOBOLOV (Aleksandr Sergeevich). *See :* NEVEROV (Aleksandr) [pseud.].

SLOBODSKY (M.). *See :* RASKIN (A.) and SLOBODSKY (M.).

SMIDOVICH (Vikenty Vikentevich). *See :* VERESAEV (Vikenty) [pseud.].

SMIRNOVA (N.).
  Marfa; a Siberian novel. Transl. by M. Burr. 246 pp. Ld. Boriswood, 1932.

SOBOL (Andrey Mikhailovich), 1888–1926.
   Freak show. Transl. by J. Covan. 416 pp. N.Y. Kendall, 1930.
SOBOLEV (Leonid).
   The blue scarf. (*In:* I. Montagu and H. Marhsall, *Soviet short stories,* 1943.)
   Romanoff. Abridged version by N. M. Gubsky. Transl. by A. Fremantle. 311 pp. Ld. Longmans, 1935.
   —— Same. With title: *Storm warning.* 320 pp. Ld. Dickson, 1935.
   The sniper. (*In:* I. Montagu and H. Marshall, *Soviet short stories,* 1943.)
SOKOLOV (Boris Fedorovich), 1893–.
   The crime of Doctor Garine. Anon. transl. With an introduction by T. Dreiser. 144 pp. N.Y. Covici, 1928. [Short stories. Contains: 'The crime of Doctor Garine'; 'Strategy'; 'In Stantzia'.]
SOKOLOV-NIKITOV (I.).
   The sea breeze. (*In:* E. Fen, *Soviet stories of the last decade,* 1945.)
SOLOGUB [pseud. of Fedor Kuzmich Teternikov], 1863–1927.
   The created legend. Transl. by J. Cournos. Ld. Secker, 1916. [This is only the first pt. of the work of the same name. The Russian title of this pt. is *Drops of blood.*]
   The little demon. Transl. by J. Cournos and R. Aldington. Ld. Secker, 1916.
   Little tales. Transl. by J. Cournos. Ld. 1917.
   The old house, and other stories. Transl. by J. Cournos. Ld. Secker, 1915. [Contains: 'The old house'; 'The unitor of souls'; 'The invoker of the beast'; 'The white dog'; 'The glimmer of hunger'.]
   Poems. (*In:* C. M. Bowra, *A book of Russian verse,* 1943.]
   Poems. (*In:* C. F. Coxwell, *Russian poems,* 1929.)
   Poems. (*In:* B. Deutsch and A. Yarmolinsky, *Russian poetry,* 1929.)
   Poems. (*In:* P. Selver, *Anthology of modern Slavonic literature,* 1919.)
   The sweet-scented name, and other fairy tales, fables and stories. Transl. by R. Graham, with an introduction by S. Graham. Ld. Constable, 1915. (Constable's Russian Library.) [Contains: 'The sweet-scented name'; 'Wings'; 'Turandina'; 'Lohengrin'; 'The herald of the beast'; 'Equality'; 'Adventures of a cobblestone'.]
   The tiny man. (*In:* P. Selver, *Anthology of modern Slavonic literature,* 1919.)

'Turandina'; 'The herald of the beast'; 'Equality', and 'Adventures of a cobblestone', repr. in: S. Graham, *Great Russian short stories*, 1929.

SOLOVYOV (Vladimir Sergeevich), 1853–1900.

God, man and the church; the spiritual foundations of life. Transl. by D. Attwater. 192 pp. Milwaukee, Bruce Publ., 1938.

The justification of the good. Transl. by N. Duddington. Ld. Constable, 1918. (Constable's Russian Library.)

Poems. (*In:* C. M. Bowra, *A book of Russian verse*, 1943.)

Poems. (*In:* C. F. Coxwell, *Russian poems*, 1929.)

The two hermits. (*In:* S. Graham, *Great Russian short stories*, 1929.)

War and Christianity. N.Y. Putnam, 1915.

War, progress and the end of history, including a short history of Anti-Christ. Transl. by A. Bakshy. Ld. Univ. Pr., 1915.

Biography, criticism, etc.:

BAKSHY (A.): *The philosophy of Vladimir Solovyov.* Aberdeen. Univ. Pr., 1916.

D'HERBIGNY (M.): *Vladimir Solovyov: a Russian Newman.* Transl. by A. M. Buchanan. Ld. Washbourne, 1918.

STEPNIAK (Sergey) [pseud. of Sergey M. Kravchinsky], 1852–95.

The career of a nihilist: a novel. Ld. Scott, 1890; N.Y. Harper, 1907. [Written in English.]

The new convert. Transl. by T. B. Eyges. Boston. Stratford, 1917.

SURGUCHEV (Ilya Dmitrievich).

Autumn: a play in four acts. Transl. by D. A. Modell. 86 pp. N.Y. and Ld. Appleton, 1924. [Appleton's Modern Plays.)

SURIKOV (I. Z.), 1841–80.

Poems. (*In:* C. M. Bowra, *A book of Russian verse*, 1943.)

SVETLOV (Mikhail Arcadevich), 1903–.

Poems. (*In:* *New Directions in prose and poetry*, 1941.)

TARASOV–RODIONOV (Aleksandr Ignatevich), 1885–.

Chocolate. Transl. by C. Malamuth. 311 pp. Ld. Heinemann, 1933.

—— Same. Cheap ed. 1934.

February 1917. Transl. by W. A. Drake. 378 pp. N.Y. Covici, 1931.

TETERNIKOV (Fedor Kuzmich). *See:* SOLOGUB [pseud. of Fedor Kuzmich Teternikov.]

TIKHONOV (Nikolay Semyonovich), 1896–.

A child is born. (*In:* I. Montagu and H. Marshall, *Soviet short stories*, 1943.)

The family. (*In:* same.)

Fritz. Transl. by A. Brown. (*In:* J. Rodker, *Soviet anthology,* 1943.)

The mother. (*In:* I. Montagu and H. Marshall, *Soviet short stories,* 1943.)

The old soldier. (*In:* same.)

Poem. (*In: New Directions in prose and poetry,* p. 650, 1941.)

The Soviet writer. (*In:* I. Montagu and H. Marshall, *Soviet short stories,* 1944.)

Story with a footnote. Transl. by S. Garry. (Penguin New Writing, 5. Ld. 1941.)

Yorgyy, and two poems from 'The horde'. (*In:* G. Reavey and M. Slonim, *Soviet literature,* 1933.)

TIKHONOV (Valentin).

Mountains and the stars: a novel. 426 pp. Ld. Heinemann, 1939.

TOLSTOY (Aleksey Konstantinovich, Count), 1817–75.

Czar Feodor Ivanovich. Transl. by A. Hayes. Ld. Kegan Paul, 1924. [Pt. 2 of a trilogy.]

—— Same. Transl. by J. Covan. (*In:* O. M. Sayler, *Moscow Art Theatre series of Russian plays,* first series, 1923.)

The death of Ivan the Terrible. Transl. by A. Hayes. Ld. Kegan Paul, 1926. [Pt. 1 of a trilogy.]

—— Same. Transl. by G. R. Noyes. (*In his: Masterpieces of the Russian drama,* 1933.)

Poems. (*In:* C. M. Bowra, *A book of Russian verse,* 1943.)

Poems. (*In:* F. Cornford and E. P. Salaman, *Poems from the Russian,* 1943.)

Poems. (*In:* C. F. Coxwell, *Russian poems,* 1929.)

A prince of outlaws. Transl. by C. A. Manning. N.Y. Knopf, 1927. [Transl. before under the title: *The terrible Czar,* 1892; and *Prince Serbryani, a historical novel,* 1892.]

TOLSTOY (Aleksey Nikolaevich), 1882–1945.

The affair on the Basseynaya street. (*In:* J. Cournos, *Short stories out of Soviet Russia,* 1929.)

Azure cities. (*In:* J. J. Robbins and J. Kunitz, *Azure cities,* 1929.)

Bread: a novel. Transl. by S. Garry. 447 pp. Ld. Gollancz, 1938.

Darkness and dawn. Transl. by E. Bone and E. Burns. 570 pp. Ld. Gollancz, 1936.

Death box. Transl. by B. G. Guerney. 357 pp. Ld. Methuen, 1937.

Imperial Majesty. Transl. by H. C. Matheson. 444 pp. Ld. Matthews & Marrot, 1932. [Vol. 1 of *Peter the Great.*]

My country; articles and stories of the Great Patriotic War of the Soviet Union. Transl. by D. L. Fromberg. 117 pp. Ld. Hutchinson, 1943.

Peter the Great. Transl. by E. Bone and E. Burns. 463 pp. Ld. Gollancz, 1936.

The road to Calvary. Transl. by R. S. Townsend. N.Y. Boni, 1923.

Smashnose. (*In:* S. Konovalov, *Bonfire,* 1932.)

Vasily Suchkov. (*Extract in:* S. Konovalov, *Bonfire,* 1932.)

The Viper. Transl. by E. Fen. (*In her: Modern Russian stories,* 1943.)

A white night. (*In:* J. Cournos, *Short stories out of Soviet Russia,* 1929.)

TOLSTOY (Ilya Lvovich).

Reminiscences of Tolstoy by his son. Transl. by G. Calderon. N.Y. Century, 1914.

TOLSTOY (Lev Nikolaevich, Count), 1828–1910.

Collected works:

The novels and other works of Lyof N. Tolstoi. Edited by N. H. Dole, translated by I. F. Hapgood, N. H. Dole and others. N.Y. Scribner, 1902. 22 vols.

Also known as the International Edition. Reprinted in 1923 in 24 vols.

(Works) by Count Lev N. Tolstoy; translated from the original Russian and edited by Prof. Leo Wiener. Boston. Colonial Press Co., 1904–12. 14 vols. (Vols. 13 and 14 not numbered by the publisher, contain posthumous works, edited by Hagberg Wright. Vol. 14 contains 'Hadji Murad', translated by Aylmer Maude.) This edition appeared in England under the imprint of Dent.

Tolstoy Centenary edition. Edited by Aylmer Maude. Ld. For the Tolstoy Society, Oxf. Univ. Pr. (Humphrey Milford), 1928–37. 21 vols. (Translation by Louise and Aylmer Maude.)

Contents:

Vols. 1–2. *Maude: Life of Tolstoy.*

Vol. 3. *Childhood, Boyhood and Youth.*

Vol. 4. *Tales of army life:* 'Sevastopol in Dec. 1884, Sevastopol in May 1855, Sevastopol in August 1855'; 'The Cossacks'; 'The raid'; 'The wood-felling'; 'Meeting a Moscow acquaintance in the detachment'.

F

Vol. 5. *Nine stories:* 'Two Hussars'; 'A Landlord's morning'; 'Polikushka'; 'A billiard-marker's notes'; "The snow-storm'; 'Lucerne'; 'Albert'; 'Three deaths'; 'Strider, the story of a horse'.

Vols. 6–8. *War and Peace.*

Vol. 9. *Anna Karenina.*

Vol. 11. *Confession,* and *The Gospel in brief:* 'What I believe'; 'Conclusion of "A criticism of dogmatic theology"'; 'Introduction to "An examination of the Gospels"'; 'Prefaces to editions of "The four Gospels".'

Vol. 12. *On life,* and *Essays on religion:* 'What is religion?'; 'The teaching of Jesus'; 'Religion and morality'; 'Reason and religion'; 'How to read the Gospels'; 'Preface to *The Christian teaching*'; 'An appeal to the clergy'; 'A reply to the Synod's Edict of excommunication'; 'The restoration of Hell'; 'Church and state'.

Vol. 13. *Twenty-three tales:* 'God sees the truth but waits'; 'A prisoner in the Caucasus'; 'The bear hunt'; 'What men live by'; 'A spark neglected burns the house'; 'Two old men'; 'Where love is, God is'; 'Ivan the fool'; 'Evil allures but good endures'; 'Little girls wiser than men'; 'Elias'; 'The three hermits'; 'The imp and the crust'; 'How much land does a man need?'; 'A grain as big as a hen's egg'; 'The godson'; 'The repentant sinner'; 'The empty drum'; 'The coffee-house of Surat'; 'Too dear!'; 'Esarhaddon, King of Assyria'; 'Work, death and sickness'; 'Three questions'.

Vol. 14. *What then must we do?:* 'Letter to Engelhardt'.

Vol. 15. *Ivan Ilych,* and *Hadji Murad:* 'Master and man'; 'Fedor Kuzmich'; 'Memoirs of a madman'; 'Walk in the light while there is light'; 'A talk among leisured people'.

Vol. 16. *The Devil and cognate tales:* 'Family happiness'; 'The Kreutzer sonata'; 'The porcelain doll'; 'Francoise'; 'Father Sergius'.

Vol. 17. *Plays:* 'The first distiller'; 'The power of darkness'; 'The fruits of enlightenment'; 'The light shines in darkness'; 'The live corpse'; 'The cause of it all'.

Vol. 18. *What is art?* and *Essays on art:* 'On truth in art'; Introduction to 'Amiel's journal', to 'Semenov's Peasant stories', to Guy de Maupassant. Preface to 'Der Buttnerbauer'; An afterword to Chekhov's 'Darling'; 'On art'.

Vol. 19. *Resurrection.*

Vol. 20. *The kingdom of God is within you,* and *Peace essays.*

Vol. 21. *Recollections, and Essays:* 'Why do men stupefy themselves?'; 'The first step'; 'Non-acting'; 'An afterword to Famine articles'; 'Modern science'; 'An introduction to Ruskin's works'; 'Letters on Henry George'; 'Thou shalt not kill'; 'Bethink yourselves'; 'A great iniquity'; 'Shakespeare and the drama'; 'What's to be done?'; 'I cannot be silent'; 'A letter to a Hindu'; 'Gandhi letters'; 'Letter to a Japanese'; 'The wisdom of children'; 'Thoughts from private letters'.

This ed. is also issued by the Oxf. Univ. Pr. in the World's Classics Series.

Anna Karenina. Transl. by C. Garnett. 2 vols. Ld. Heinemann, 1901.

—— Same. Transl. by R. S. Townsend. 2 vols. Ld. Dent, 1912. (Everyman's Library.)

The death of Ivan Ilyitch, and other stories. A new transl. by C. Garnett. Ld. Heinemann, 1902. [Contains: 'The death of Ivan Ilyitch'; 'Family happiness'; 'Polikushka'; 'Two hussars'; 'The snowstorm'; 'Three deaths'.]

The dominion of darkness. Transl. by L. and A. Maude. Ld. 1905.

—— Same. With title: *The power of darkness.* Transl. by G. R. Noyes and G. Z. Patrick. (*In:* G. R. Noyes, *Masterpieces of the Russian drama,* 1933.)

Living thoughts of Tolstoy. Presented by S. Zweig. 154 pp. N.Y. Longmans, 1939; Ld. Cassell, n.d.

Resurrection. Transl. by L. Maude. Ld. 1900.

—— Same. Rev. ed. Ld. 1902.

—— Same. Transl. by L. Wiener. 2 vols. Boston. Dana Estes, 1904.

—— Same. Transl. by A. J. Wolfe. 2 vols. N.Y. International Publishing Co., 1920.

Sevastopol; Two hussars, etc. Transl. by L. and A. Maude. 325 pp. Ld. Constable, 1905.

War and peace. Transl. by C. Garnett. 3 vols. Ld. Heinemann, 1904.

—— Same. Popular ed. 1911.

—— Same. Anon. transl. 3 vols. Ld. Dent, 1911. (Everyman's Library.)

—— Same. Transl. by L. and A. Maude. With an introduction. 1,352 pp. Ld. Macmillan; Oxf. Univ. Pr., 1942. [Repr. from the Centenary ed.]

—— Same. Rev. Ill. by Verestchagin and F. Eichenberg. 2 vols. N.Y. Heritage, 1943.

Diaries: youth, 1847–1852. Transl. by C. J. Hogarth and A. Sirnis. With a preface by C. H. Wright. Ld. Dent, 1917.

The private diary of Leo Tolstoy, 1853–1857. 256 pp. N.Y. Doubleday, 1927.

The letters of Tolstoy and his cousin Countess Alexandra Tolstoy, 1857–1903. 232 pp. Ld. Methuen, 1929.

The journal of L. Tolstoy, 1895–1899. 427 pp, N.Y. Knopf, 1917.

Tolstoy. Literary fragments, letters and reminiscences. 330 pp. N.Y. Dial Pr., 1931.

Tolstoy's love-letters. Transl. by V. Woolf and S. S. Koteliansky. With a study of the autobiographical element in Tolstoy's work by P. Biryukov. 134 pp. Ld. Hogarth Pr., 1923.

Biography, criticism, etc.:

WIENER (L.): *Bibliography of works and articles on Tolstoy in Engl., German and French. (In: Complete works of Tolstoy.* Transl. and ed. by L. Wiener. Vol. of 1905.)

YASSUKOVICH (A.): *Tolstoy in English, 1878–1929 ; a list of works by and about Tolstoy available in the New York Public Library. (Bulletin of the New York Public Library,* vol. 33, no. 7, July 1929.)

ABRAHAM (G.): *Tolstoy.* 144 pp. Ld. Duckworth, 1935.

BARING (M.): *Tolstoy and Turgenev. (In his: Landmarks in Russian literature,* 1910.)

BAUDOUIN (C.): *Tolstoi: the teacher.* 218 pp. N.Y. Dutton, 1923.

BIRYUKOV (P.): *L. Tolstoy; his life and work; autobiographical memoirs, letters and biographical material.* 2 vols. N.Y. 1906.

—— Same. *The life of Tolstoy.* Transl. from the Russian. 168 pp. Ld. 1911.

CHESTERTON (G. K.) and PERRIS (G. H.) and GARNETT (E.): *Leo Tolstoy.* 40 pp. Ill. Ld. 1903. (Bookman Biographies.)

DAVIS (H. E.): *Tolstoy and Nietzsche: a problem in biographical ethics.* 271 pp. N.Y. New Republic, 1929.

DILLON (E. J.): *Count L. Tolstoy: a new portrait.* 286 pp. Ld. Hutchinson, 1934.

FAUSSET (H. l'A.): *Tolstoy, the inner drama.* 320 pp. Ld. Cape, 1927.

GARNETT (E.): *Tolstoy: his life and writings.* Ld. Constable, 1914.

GARROD (H. W.) : *Tolstoi's theory of art.* 25 pp. Oxf. Clarendon Pr., 1935. (Taylorian Lecture.)
GOLDENVEIZER (A. B.) : *Talks with Tolstoi.* 182 pp. Richmond. L. & V. Woolf, 1923.
GORKY (M.) : *Reminiscences of Leo Nikolaevich Tolstoi.* Transl. by S. S. Koteliansky and V. Woolf. 70 pp. Richmond. L. & V. Woolf, 1920.
GUTHRIE (A. L.) : *Wordsworth and Tolstoi, and other papers.* 124 pp. Edinburgh. Constable, 1922.
KNIGHT (G. W.) : *Shakespeare and Tolstoy.* 27 pp. Ld. Oxf. Univ. Pr., 1934.
KNOWLSON (T. S.) : *Leo Tolstoy: a biographical and critical study.* 190 pp. Ld. and N.Y. Warner, 1904.
KVITKO (D.) : *A philosophical study of Tolstoy.* 119 pp. N.Y. 1927.
LAVRIN (J.) : *Tolstoy: a psycho-critical study.* 223 pp. Ld. Collins, 1924.
LLOYD (J. A. T.) : *Two Russian reformers: Ivan Turgenev, Leo Tolstoy.* 325 pp. N.Y. Lane, 1911.
MANN (T.) : *Past masters, and other essays.* 275 pp. N.Y. Knopf, 1933. [Contains essay on Tolstoy.]
—— Same. *Three essays.* 261 pp. N.Y. Knopf, 1929. [Contains essay on : Goethe and Tolstoy.]
MAUDE (A.) : *Family views on Tolstoy.* Ed. by A. Maude. Transl. by L. and A. Maude. 220 pp. Ld. Allen & Unwin, 1926.
—— Same. *The life of Tolstoy: first fifty years.* 464 pp. Ld. Constable, 1908. And: *Later years.* 688 pp. Ld. Constable, 1910.
MEREZHKOVSKY (D. S.) : *Tolstoi as man and artist, with an essay on Dostoevsky.* 310 pp. N.Y. and Ld. Putnam, 1902.
NAZAROFF (A. J.) : *Tolstoy, the inconstant genius: a biography.* 332 pp. N.Y. Stokes, 1930.
NOYES (G. R.) : *Tolstoy.* 395 pp. N.Y. Duffield, 1918; Ld. 1919.
ROLLAND (R.) : *Tolstoy.* Transl. from the French by B. Miall. 321 pp. Ld. 1911.
TOLSTOY (A., Countess) : *The tragedy of Tolstoy.* 294 pp. New Haven. Yale Univ. Pr., 1933.
TOLSTOY (I. L.) : *Reminiscences of Tolstoy by his son.* Transl. by G. Calderon. N.Y. Century, 1914.
—— Same. *The truth about my father.* 229 pp. N.Y. Appleton, 1927.

TOLSTOY (S. A.). *See:* under her own works: TOLSTOY (Sophie Andreevna).

ZWEIG (S.): *Adepts in self-portraiture: Casanova, Stendhal, 'Tolstoy.* 357 pp. N.Y. Viking Pr., 1928.

TOLSTOY (Sophie Andreevna, Countess):

Autobiography of the Countess Sophie Tolstoy. With a preface and notes by V. Spiridonov. Transl. by S. S. Koteliansky and L. Woolf. Ld. Hogarth Pr., 1922.

The diary of Tolstoy's wife: 1860–1891. Transl. by A. Werth. 272 pp. Ld. Gollancz, 1928.

The final struggle: being Countess Tolstoy's diary for 1910, with extracts from Tolstoy's diaries. Transl. by A. Maude. 407 pp. Ld. Allen, 1936.

The later diary: 1891–1897. Transl. by A. Werth. Ld. Gollancz, 1929.

TRENYEV (Konstantin).

The birthday. (*In:* I. Montagu and H. Marshall, *Soviet short stories,* 1944.)

TRETYAKOV (Sergey Mikhailovich), 1892–.

Chinese testament. The autobiography of Tan Shih-hua as told to Tretyakov. 383 pp. Ld. Gollancz, 1934.

Roar China! an episode in nine scenes. Transl. by F. Polianovska and B. Nixon. 87 pp. Ld. Lawrence, 1931.

TSVETAEVA (Marina), 1892–.

The separation. (*In:* G. Reavey and M. Slonim, *Soviet literature,* 1933.)

TUPIKOV (Pavel Georgevich), 1882–.

Ocean. Transl. by J. Cournos. 421 pp. Ld. Hamilton, 1936.

TURGENEV (Ivan Sergeevich), 1818–83.

The novels and tales. Transl. by Constance Garnett. Ld. Heinemann, 1894–99. 15 vols.

—— Library ed., 1919–1923. 17 vols.

Contents:

Vol. 1. *Rudin.*

Vol. 2. *A house of gentlefolk.*

Vol. 3. *On the eve.*

Vol. 4. *Fathers and children.*

Vol. 5. *Smoke.*

Vols. 6–7. *Virgin soil.*

Vols. 8–9. *Sportsman's sketches.*

Vol. 10. *Dream tales and prose poems:* 'Clara Militch'; 'Phantoms'; 'The song of triumphant love'; 'The dream'; 'Poems in prose'.

Vol. 11. 'Torrents of Spring'; 'First Love'; 'Mumu'.

Vol. 12. *A Lear of the Steppes*, etc.

Vol. 13. 'Diary of a superfluous man'; 'A tour in the forest'; 'Yakov Pasinkov'; 'Andrei Kolosov'; 'A correspondence'.

Vol. 14. 'A desperate character'; 'A strange story'; 'Punin and Baburin'; 'Old portraits'; 'The brigadier'; 'Pyetushkov'.

Vol. 15. 'The Jew'; 'An unhappy girl'; 'The duellist'; 'Three portraits'; 'Enough'.

Vol. 16. *The two friends, and other stories.*

Vol. 17. *Knock, knock, knock, etc.*

Novels and tales. Translated by I. F. Hapgood. N.Y. Scribner, 1903. 13 vols.

The plays of Ivan S. Turgenev. Transl. by M. S. Mandell. N.Y. Macmillan; Ld. Heinemann, 1924.

    Contents: 'Carelessness'; 'Broke'; 'Where it is thin, there it breaks'; 'The family charge'; 'The bachelor'; 'An amicable settlement'; 'A month in the country'; 'The country woman'; 'A conversation on the highway'; 'An evening in Sorrento'.

Three plays. Transl. by Constance Garnett. Ld. Cassell, 1934. [*Contains:* 'A month in the country'; 'A provincial lady'; 'A poor gentleman'.]

Asya. [Formerly transl. under the title: *Annouchka*.] Transl. by A. E. Chamot. (*In his: Selected Russian short stories*, 1925.)

Fathers and sons. Transl. by C. J. Hogarth. 276 pp. Ld. Dent, 1921. (Everyman's Library.)

Hamlet and Don Quixote. Transl. by R. Nichols. 88 pp. Ld. Henderson's, 1930.

A house of gentlefolk. [Formerly transl. under the title: *Liza*.] Transl. by I. F. Hapgood. N.Y. 1903.

—— Same. With title: *A nest of hereditary legislators.* Done into Engl. by F. Davies. Ld. Simkin & Marshall, 1914.

A month in the country. Transl. by G. R. Noyes. (*In his: Masterpieces of the Russian drama*, 1933.)

—— Same. *A comedy.* Adapted into Engl. by E. Williams 93 pp. Ld. Heinemann, 1943.

Poems. (*In:* C. F. Coxwell, *Russian poems*, 1929.)

Biography, criticism, etc.:

OSBOURNE (E. A.): *Russian literature and translation. 6. Ivan S. Turgenev.* (*Bookman*, vol. 83. Ld. 1932.)

BARING (M.): *The place of Turgenev*, and: *Tolstoy and Turgenev.* (*In his: Landmarks in Russian literature*, 1910.)

GARNETT (E. W.) : *Turgenev: a study.* Ld. Collins, 1917.

GETTMANN (R. A.) : *Turgenev in England and America.* 196 pp. Urbana, 1941. (*Illinois studies in language and literature,* Vol. 27, No. 2.)

HERSHKOWITZ (H.) : *Democratic ideas in Turgenev's works.* Columbia, 1932.

LLOYD (J. A. T.) : *Ivan Turgenev : a literary biography.* Ld. Hale, 1943.

—— Same. *Two Russian reformers: I. Turgenev, L. Tolstoy.* 325 pp. N.Y. Lane, 1911.

YARMOLINSKY (A.) : *Turgenev: the man, his art and his age.* 386 pp. N.Y. Century, 1926; Ld. Hodder & Stoughton, 1927.

TYNYANOV (Yuri Nikolaevich), 1894–.
Death and diplomacy in Persia. Transl. by A. Brown. 357 pp. Ld. Boriswood, 1938. [Historical novel on the life of the author A. S. Griboedov.]
Second Lieutenant Also. (*In :* I. Montagu and H. Marshall, *Soviet short stories,* 1942.)

TYUCHEV (Fedor Ivanovich), 1803–73.
Poem. (*In :* O. Elton, *Verse from Pushkin and others,* 1935.)
Poems. (*In :* C. M. Bowra, *A book of Russian verse,* 1943.)
Poems. (*In :* F. Cornford and E. P. Salaman, *Poems from the Russian,* 1943.)
Poems. (*In :* C. F. Coxwell, *Russian poems,* 1929.)
Poems. (*In :* N. Jarintzov, *Russian poets and poems,* 1917.)

UKRAINKA (Lesya) [pseud. of Larissa Petrovna Kossatch], 1872– 1913.
The Babylonian captivity. (*In :* C. E. Bechhofer, *Five Russian plays,* 1916.)

USHAKOV (Nikolay), 1899–.
Karabash. (*In :* G. Reavey and M. Slonim, *Soviet literature,* 1933.)

USPENSKIY (Andrey Vasilevich). *See :* KIRSHON (V. M.) and USPENSKIY (A. V.).

VERESAEV (Vikenty) [pseud. of Vikenty Vikentevich Smidovich], 1867–.
The confessions of a physician. Transl. by A. S. Linden. Ld. Grant Richards, 1904.
The deadlock. Transl. by N. Vissotsky and C. Coventry. 352 pp. Ld. Faber, 1927.
The sisters. Transl. by J. Soskice. 288 pp. Ld. Hutchinson, 1934.

VESELY (Artem) [pseud. of Nikolay Kochkurov], 1899–.
Russia drenched in blood. (*In :* S. Konovalov, *Bonfire,* 1932.)

VILENKIN (Nikolay). *See:* MINSKY (N. M.) [pseud. of Nikolay Vilenkin.].

VINOGRADOV (Anatoly Kornelevich), 1888–.
The black consul. Transl. by E. Burns. 438 pp. Ld. Gollancz, 1935.

VIRTA (Nikolay).
The root of life. Transl. by S. Garry. (*In:* J. Rodker, *Soviet anthology*, 1943.)

VISHNEVSKY (Vsevelod Vitalevich), 1900–.
An optimistic tragedy: a play in three acts. Transl. by H. G. Scott and R. S. Carr. [*In:* B. Blake, *Four Soviet plays*, 1937.)

VOGAU (Boris Andreevich). *See:* PILNYAK (Boris) [pseud. of Boris Andreevich Vogau].

VOINOVA (Aleksandra Ivanovna).
Semi-precious stones. Transl. by V. Snow. 604 pp. Ld. Cape, 1931.
—— Same. 531 pp. Ld. Heinemann, 1934.

VOITEKHOV (Boris Ilich), 1913–.
Last days of Sevastopol. Transl. by R. Parker and V. M. Genne. 224 pp. N.Y. Knopf, 1943; 150 pp. Ld. Cassell, 1943.

VOLKOV (Mikhail), 1886–.
The miracle. [Short story.] (*In:* J. J. Robbins and J. Kunitz, *Azure cities*, 1929.)

VOLOSHIN (Maksimilian Aleksandrovich), 1877–.
Poems. (*In:* C. F. Coxwell, *Russian poems*, 1929.)
Poems. (*In:* B. Deutsch and A. Yarmolinsky, *Russian poetry*, 1929.)
Poems of Russia. (*In:* G. Reavey and M. Slonim, *Soviet literature*, 1933.)

VOLOSOV (Mark).
Six rats. Transl. by A .Brown. (*In:* J. Rodker, *Soviet anthology*, 1943.)

VORONSKY (Aleksandr Konstantinovich), 1884–.
Waters of life and death. Transl. by L. Zarine. 343 pp. Ld. Allen & Unwin, 1936.

WASSILEWSKA (Wanda), 1905–.
'The commonwealth of nations'; 'Children'; 'The iron cross'. (*In: Soviet war stories*, 1943.)
Inside the hut. (*In:* I. Montagu and H. Marshall, *Soviet short stories*, 1943.)
The party cards. (*In:* I. Montagu and H. Marshall, *Soviet short stories*, 1943.)

Rainbow; the story of a Ukrainian village under German occupation.
Transl. by E. Bone. 184 pp. Ld. Hutchinson, 1943;
American ed. transl. by S. Bleeker. 230 pp. N.Y. Simon &
Schuster, 1944. [Stalin prize novel, 1943.]
WEISSENBERG (Leo).
The alarm clock. (*In:* J. Rodker, *Soviet anthology*, 1943.)
YAKOVLEV (Aleksandr).
The Chinese vase. (*In:* S. Konovalov, *Bonfire*, 1932.)
YAZYKOV (Nikolay Mikhailovich), 1803–46.
Poems. (*In:* C. F. Coxwell, *Russian poems*, 1929.)
Poems. (*In:* P. E. Matheson, *Holy Russia*, 1918.)
Poems. (*In:* L. Wiener, *Anthology of Russian literature*, 1902.)
ZAITSEV (Boris Konstantinovich), 1881–.
Anna. Transl. by N. Duddington. 156 pp. Ld. Allen, 1937.
ZAMYATIN (Evgeny Ivanovich), 1884–1937.
Mamai. (*In:* G. Reavey and M. Slonim, *Soviet literature*, 1933.)
We. Transl. by G. Zilboorg. 286 pp. N.Y. Dutton, 1924.
ZAYAITSKY (S.).
The forgotten night. (*In:* S. Konovalov, *Bonfire*, 1932.)
ZHABOTINSKY (Vladimir Evgenevich), 1880–1940.
Judge and fool. Transl. from the German by C. Brooks. 348 pp.
N.Y. Liveright, 1930.
Samson the Nazarite. Transl. by C. Brooks. 314 pp. Ld.
Secker, 1930.
ZHAROV (Aleksandr Alekseevich), 1904–.
Poems. (*In: New Directions in prose and poetry*, 1941.)
ZHUKOVSKY (Vasily Andreevich), 1783–1852.
Poem. (*In:* P. E. Matheson, *Holy Russia*, 1918.)
Poems. (*In:* C. F. Coxwell, *Russian poems*, 1929.)
The three girdles. Transl. by L. Zarine. (*In:* S. Graham, *Great Russian short stories*, 1929.)
ZOSHCHENKO (Mikhail Mikhailovich), 1895–.
A damp business. (*In:* S. Konovalov, *Bonfire*, 1932.)
Dawn of a new day. (*In:* I. Montagu and H. Marshall, *Soviet short stories*, 1942.)
For children. Transl. by M. Budberg. (*In:* J. Rodker, *Soviet anthology*, 1943.)
Gold teeth. [*Short story.*] (*In:* J. J. Robbins and J. Kunitz, *Azure cities*, 1929.)
A great king's love. Transl. by A. Fremantle. (*In:* J. Rodker, *Soviet anthology*, 1943.)
A hasty affair. (*In:* S. Konovalov, *Bonfire*, 1932.)
The illiterate woman. (*In:* J. Rodker, *Soviet anthology*, 1943.)

A mistake. (*In:* G. Reavey and M. Slonim, *Soviet literature,* 1933.)

Nero and his mother. (*In:* J. Rodker, *Soviet anthology,* 1943.)

The night of horror. (*In:* S. Konovalov, *Bonfire,* 1932.)

The old rat. (*In:* S. Graham, *Great Russian short stories,* 1929.)

Russia laughs. [Short stories.] Transl. by H. Clayton. 352 pp. Toronto. Longmans, 1935.

A story of adventure. (*In:* S. Konovalov, *Bonfire,* 1932.)

What the nightingale sang of. (*In:* E. Fen, *Modern Russian stories,* 1943.)

The woman who could not read, and other tales. Transl. by E. Fen. 153 pp. Ld. Methuen, 1940.

The wonderful dog, and other tales. Transl. by E. Fen. 180 pp. Ld. Methuen, 1942.

ZOZULYA (Efim), 1891–.

The mother, and *A tale about Ak and humanity.* (*In:* J. Cournos, *Short stories out of Soviet Russia,* 1929.)

V. LINGUISTIC APPENDIX

I. DICTIONARIES

ALEXANDROV (A.): *Complete English-Russian, Russian-English dictionary.* 5th ed. 2 vols. St. Petersburg and Ld. 1915; Milwaukee. Caspar, 1918.

BOYANUS (S. K.) and MÜLLER (V. K.): *Russian-English dictionary.* Moscow. 1932; New ed. 800 pp. N.Y. Four Continent Book Corp. 1937. (New orthography.)

—— *English-Russian dictionary.* 1,466 pp. N.Y. Bookniga, 1935.

CURRALL (R. T.): *Russian pronouncing vocabulary.* 160 pp. Ld. Harrap. 1942.

FREESE (J. H.): *Russian-English, English-Russian dictionary.* 2 vols. N.Y. Stechert, 1917.

GOLOVINSKY (M.): *The new English-Russian and Russian-English dictionary.* Milwaukee. Caspar, 1920.

Hossfeld's new pocket dictionary of the English and Russian languages. 464, 396 pp. Ld. 1906.

MILLER (A. D.) and MIRSKY (D. S.): *English-Russian dictionary.* 552 pp. N.Y. Bookniga, 1936.

MUELLER (V. K.): *English-Russian dictionary, with the addition of short grammatical rules. With Russian-English dictionary.* New ed. 776 pp. N.Y. Dutton, 1944. [Based on Boyanus and Müller, see above.]

—— *Russian-English dictionary.* 3rd ed. 822 pp. Ld. Lawrence, 1943. With English-Russian dictionary.

—— —— Same. 3rd ed. rev. 822 pp. N.Y. Dutton, 1944.

O'BRIEN (M. A.): *New English-Russian, Russian-English dictionary.* 2 vols. 363, 344 pp. Ld. Allen, 1942.

—— —— Same. In 1 vol. Ld. Allen, 1942; new ed. N.Y. Dove Publ., 1944.

ROTHSTEIN (N. F.): *New Russian-English dictionary.* 346 pp. Ld. 1944.

SCHAPIRO (W.): *Russian-English, English-Russian pocket dictionary.* 384 pp. Ld. Harrap, 1939.

SEGAL (L.): *New complete Russian-English dictionary.* 2nd ed. 965 pp. Ld. Lund Humphries, 1944.

ZAIMOVSKIY (S. G.): *English-Russian dictionary.* 1,086 pp. Milwaukee. Caspar, c. 1932.

2. GRAMMARS, ETC.

BIRKETT (G. A.): *A modern Russian course.* 330 pp. Ld. Methuen, 1937.

BISKE (R.): *Russian handwriting.* Ld. Jaschke, 1919.

BONDAR (D.): *Bondar's simplified Russian method, conversational and commercial.* 6th ed. rev. by L. Segal. 325 pp. Ld. Pitman, 1942.

BOTELHO (F. M.): *What you want to say and how to say it in Russian.* 128 pp. Philadelphia. Macrae Smith, c. 1943.

BOYANUS (S. K.): *A manual of Russian pronunciation.* 123 pp. Ld. Sidgwick & Jackson, 1935.

BOYANUS (S. K.) and JOPSON (N. B.): *Spoken Russian; a practical course.* Written and spoken colloquial Russian with pronunciation, intonation, grammar, English translation and vocabulary. (Illustrated by 12 H.M.V. records.) 366 pp. Ld. Sidgwick & Jackson, 1939.

DAVIS (I.): *The motherland; a book for the study of the Russian language.* 2 vols. Riga, 1915–16.

DUFF (C.) and KROUGLIAKOFF (A. M.): *The basis and essentials of Russian.* Published for the Orthological Institute. 215 pp. N.Y. Nelson, 1936.

FORBES (N.): *Elementary Russian grammar, with exercises.* 184 pp. Oxf. Clarendon Pr., 1919.

—— *Russian grammar.* 2nd ed. 276 pp. Oxf. Clarendon Pr., 1916.

—— *First Russian book: a practical manual of Russian declensions.* 2nd ed. 224 pp. Oxf. Clarendon Pr., 1919.

—— *Second Russian book: a practical manual of Russian verbs.* 2nd ed. 336 pp. Oxf. Clarendon Pr., 1917.

—— *Third Russian book. See under:* BILINGUAL PUBLICATIONS AND READERS.

—— *Fourth Russian book: Exercises on first and second books.* 122 pp. Oxf. Clarendon Pr., 1918.

FOURMAN (M.): *Teach yourself Russian.* 276 pp. Ld. Hodder & Stoughton, 1943. (E.U.P. Teach yourself books.)

JARINTZOV (N.): *The Russians and their language, with an introduction discussing the problems of pronunciation and transliteration.* 2nd ed. 230 pp. Oxf. Blackwell, 1916.

KANY (C. E.) and KAUN (A. S.) : *Elementary Russian conversation.* 76 pp. Boston. Heath, c. 1943.

—— *Intermediate Russian conversation.* 103 pp. N.Y. Heath, 1944. (Heath modern language series.)

KOLNI-BALOZKY (J.) : *A progressive Russian grammar.* Complete ed. 477 pp. Ld. Pitman, 1938.

PATRICK (G. Z.) : *One thousand commonly used Russian words, with illustrative sentences.* 107 pp. Institute of Pacific Relations, 1935.

—— *Roots of the Russian language; an elementary guide to Russian word-building.* 239 pp. Ld. Pitman, 1938.

SEGAL (L.) : *Russian grammar and self-educator.* 8th ed. 223 pp. N.Y. Stechert; Ld. Lund, 1943.

—— *Russian idioms and phrases.* 4th ed. 52 pp. Ld. Pitman, 1943.

—— *Say it in Russian : English-Russian word and phrase book with pronunciation.* 100 pp. Southport. Zeltser, 1942; Transatlantic, 1943.

SEMEONOFF (A. H.) : *Brush up your Russian.* (Forty up-to-date conversations in everyday Russian, with a supplement of useful information and practical vocabularies.) 161 pp. Ld. Dent, 1933.

—— *A new Russian grammar.* 4th ed. 322 pp. Ld. Dent, 1933.

SIEFF (M.) : *Colloquial Russian.* 323 pp. Ld. Routledge, 1943. (Trubner's colloquial manuals.)

—— *Practical guide to the Russian accent.* 214 pp. Ld. Jaschke, 1918.

SMIRNITSKII (A. I.) : and others : *Russian for English-speaking workers ; first year course.* Ed. by L. I. Basilevich. 332 pp. N.Y. Amkniga, 1933.

SMIRNITSKII (A. I.) and SVESHNIKOV (P. P.) : *Russian textbook : elementary course.* Ill. 363 pp. Ld. Lawrence, 1935. [2nd ed. of above.]

SOMMER (F. E.) : *Essentials of modern Russian.* 64 pp. N.Y. Ungar, c. 1943.

TROFIMOV (M. V.) and JONES (D.) : *The pronunciation of Russian.* Ld. Cambridge Univ. Pr., 1923. (Cambridge Primers of Pronunciation.)

UNDERWOOD (E. G.) : *Russian accentuation.* 71 pp. Edinburgh. Blackie, 1918.

WHITFIELD (F. J.) : *Russian reference grammar.* 222 pp. Cambr. Mass. Harvard Univ. Pr., 1944.

WILLIAMS (A. M.) : *Russian made easy : a practical introduction to the language.* 40 pp. Ld. Muller, 1943 ; N.Y. Transatlantic, 1944.

3. BILINGUAL PUBLICATIONS AND READERS

AKSAKOV (S. T.) *in* : FORBES (N.), *Third Russian book.* 1925.

BOYER (P.) and SPERANSKII (N.) : *Russian reader. Accented texts. grammatical and explanatory notes, vocabulary.* Adapted for English-speaking students by S. V. Harper. 386 pp. Chicago. Univ. of Chicago Pr., 1915.

CHEKHOV (A. P.) : *The album, and five other tales.* Ed. with introduction, notes and vocabulary by L. Segal. 2nd ed. 60 pp. Ld. Pitman, 1938.

—— *Selections of humorous stories.* Ed. by D. Bondar. 82 pp. Ld. Pitman, 1943. (Bondar's Russian Reader, 2.)

—— *Stories.* Ed. by A. S. Kaun and O. Maslenikov. 59 pp. Univ. of California, 1943. (Advanced Russian Reader, 1.)

DUDDINGTON (N. A.) : *First Russian reader.* 160 pp. Ld. Harrap, 1943.

FEN (E.) : *A beginner's Russian reader.* 35 pp. Ld. Methuen, 1942.

FORBES (N.) : *Third Russian book ; extracts from Aksakov, Grigorovich, Hertsen, Saltykov.* Accented and ed. with full notes. 204 pp. Oxf. Clarendon Pr., 1917. [Repr. 1925.]

—— *Word-for-word Russian story book.* With interlinear phonetic transcription. 55 pp. Oxf. Blackwell, 1916.

GOGOL (N. V.) : *The greatcoat.* With Engl. transl. by Z. Shoenberg and J. Domb. 56 pp. Ld. Harrap, 1944. (Harrap's bilingual series.)

GRIGOROVICH (D. V.) *in* : FORBES (N.), *Third Russian book.* 1925.

HERTSEN (A. I.) *in* : FORBES (N.), *Third Russian book.* 1925.

PATRICK (G. Z.) : *Elementary Russian reader.* 159 pp. Ld. Pitman, 1938.

—— *Advanced Russian reader.* 262 pp. Ld. Pitman, 1938.

PUSHKIN (A. S.) : *The captain's daughter.* Russian reader ed. with notes, by A. H. Semeonoff. 188 pp. Ld. Dent, 1937 ; N.Y. Dutton, 1938.

PUSHKIN (A. S.) : *The Queen of Spades.* Ed. by D. Bondar. 2nd ed. 82 pp. Ld. Pitman, 1938. (Bondar's Russian reader, 1.)

—— —— 3rd ed. 77 pp. 1943.

—— *Three tales;* 'The snowstorm'; 'The postmaster'; 'The undertaker'. Transl. by R. T. Currall. Russian text accented by A. H. Semeonoff. 56 pp. Ld. Harrap, 1919, 1929 and 1942. (Harrap's bilingual series.)

SALTYKOV (M. E.) *in*: FORBES (N.), *Third Russian book*. 1925.

SEGAL (L.): *Russian reader*. 94 pp. Ld. Lund, 1943. (Humphreys' modern language readers.)

—— *A second Russian reader*. Ed. with vocabularies. New series. Ld. 1939.

SEMEONOFF (A. H.): *First Russian reader, with notes and vocabulary*. 118 pp. Ld. Dent, 1935.

TILLYARD (H. J. W.) and HOPFEN (B.): *Nelson's simplified Russian reader*. 140 pp. Ld. and Edinburgh. Nelson, 1917.

TILLYARD (H. J. W.) and SEMEONOFF (A. H.): *Russian poetry reader*. Ed. with introduction, notes and vocabulary. Ld. 1917. (Kegan Paul's Russian texts.)

TOLSTOY (L. N.): *A first Russian reader from L. N. Tolstoy*. With English notes and a vocabulary by P. Dearmer and V. A. Tananevich. 80 pp. Oxf. Clarendon Pr., 1917.

—— *First Russian reader, tales from L. N. Tolstoy*. Ed. with transl. of text by L. Segal. Ld. British Russian Gazette and Trade Outlook. n.d.

—— *Two tales;* 'What men live by'; 'Put out the fire before it spreads'. Transl. by R. T. Currall. Russian text accented by A. H. Semeonoff. 63 pp. Ld. Harrap, 1920, 1935 and 1942. (Harrap's bilingual series.)